*Rememb'ring*

*McIntyre Faries, Presiding Judge of the*
*Los Angeles Superior Court, retired*

# PEPPERDINE UNIVERSITY
## SCHOOL OF LAW
### JUDGE MCINTYRE FARIES SCHOLARSHIP

≈≈≈≈≈≈≈≈≈≈≈≈≈≈≈

Pepperdine University is an independent university enrolling approximately 6,800 students in four colleges and schools. The School of Law, located on the Malibu campus, provides an excellent legal education within a value-centered context. Approved by the American Bar Association and holding membership in the Association of American Law Schools, the School of Law attracts students from throughout the nation.

John C. Herklotz, originally from the Middle West, a graduate of De Paul University, was financial officer for seventeen years with the Chicago Tribune/WGN Broadcasting. Moving to the West Coast, his business interests in broadcasting and communications as president of Herklotz Enterprises, Inc., led him to the entertainment field and especially family entertainment in films, which he is now producing.

John has established a legacy of helping promote numerous worthy causes. His contributions have been wide in scope, from support of Alzheimer's research; to the restoration of The Santuario de Guadalupe, an historic church in Santa Fe; to construction grants and scholarship funds to his favorite institutions of higher learning including De Paul University, Greenville College, John Brown University and Pepperdine University.

He early became aware of the value of his education and the need to encourage others. Expanding his gifts, he has made donations to Pepperdine University for the specific purpose of publishing and distributing the memoirs of Judge McIntyre Faries. Mr. Herklotz has pledged, as a challenge grant, the amount of $50,000 on a one-to-one basis to establish a scholarship in the name of Judge Faries.

It is the hope of Mr. Herklotz and of Pepperdine University that *Rememb'ring* will be of interest to you and may encourage you to make a gift to support a worthy student at the School of Law. With your help, the Judge McIntyre Faries scholarship will provide support to many students who will benefit for years to come.

*Rememb'ring*
*Memoirs of*
*Judge McIntyre Faries*

is being sent to you through a generous gift from John C. Herklotz to Pepperdine University.

*Contributions to the Judge McIntyre Faries Scholarship Fund may be made to the Chancellor's Office, Pepperdine University, Malibu, California 90263.*
*For information call (310) 456-4546.*

# Rememb'ring

*by*
*McIntyre Faries*

GRIFFIN PUBLISHING
Glendale,California

ISBN: 1-882180-11-9


Griffin Publishing
544 West Colorado Street
Glendale, California

Co-Publisher with Pepperdine University Press

Manufactured in the United States of America

This book is dedicated to my family: the
adult children, grandchildren and great
grandchildren. Also, to my chosen country,
the United States of America. I have tried to
"stand beside her and guide her…with a
light from above."

# Contents

# Foreword

My friends said, "You have to introduce yourself. If you aren't an interesting person in about a page and a half, they will read Danielle Steel or Henry Kissinger—yes, or Richard Nixon."

So, I looked up the word "Introduction" in my *Webster's New World Dictionary*, and its definition said, "In strict usage [introduction] refers to the preliminary section of a book, etc., that explains or leads into the subject proper."

Well, my life is the subject proper, and I have to lead you into it.

The title of the book is supposed to be "catchy." I decided on "Rememb'ring" when I was writing about school days. That part was nostalgia, as is much of the book. You will find mention of the Duncan sisters, Rosetta and Vivian, whom I knew both as neighbors and in school, though not well. They were, even then, writing the book and music for their "Topsy and Eva" musical which became quite a hit. One of the songs was "Rememb'ring," apostrophized as is my title: "Rememb'ring the times we've had, dear...Rememb'ring our love so true...So try to remember, too, dear...Rememb'ring is all I do."

First, my story is about Chinese Boxers in 1900—10,000 to 100,000! Thousands were at the back door when I was helped over the back wall of our mission compound into a "Shenza," and escaped because a missionary reverend held off crowds of Chinese Boxers with his handgun.

Second, I take you to the 1900-1917 period in southern California, to Orange, where we start a ranch in Coachella Valley, living in Los Angeles when it was one fiftieth of the present population, and you could ride the yellow streetcars about 50 miles for a nickel.

Third, I talk about people. Politically speaking, you'll read facts about people such as Wendell Willkie (I was his California campaign chairman when he ran against Roosevelt in 1940); Earl Warren (whom I feel I personally understood, though several of his biographers apparently did not); Dwight D. Eisenhower (under whom I was a member of the Republican National Campaign Executive Committee); Senators Knowland (campaign chairman three terms), Kuchel, Nixon, Murphy, etc.; and also friends and co-workers.

Fourth, commencing with 1922 (when I was admitted to the Bar), legal stories abound. For example, I tell the reasons I wouldn't become active in Los Angeles politics. Also, the reasons I was a deputy public defender and the deputy county counsel for Los Angeles County. And I tell about some interesting people I legally represented, how I admired my brother David R. Faries, and my judicial peers.

"Well, my life is and was different," I thought. So, I wrote. It is my wish in writing that I have expressed my life well—its events, its interests, its people—and that you, the reader, will enjoy sharing it all with me.

*Many kind friends assisted me in the preparation of my memoirs, and I would like to thank them, including Dorathi Bock Pierre, John Herklotz, John Capshaw (deceased), and my friends at Pepperdine University in Malibu.*

# Introduction

No, I did not start out to write an autobiography. After some twenty years in California and national politics, when I was fifty-six, we Republicans elected Eisenhower to the presidency. Nixon was our vice president; Senator William Knowland had been re-elected by a grand majority; Kuchel was an active U.S. senator; and I was Republican national committeeman for California. I had vowed to keep at politics until we had elected a Republican president, and now we had accomplished it. During all this period, I had refused to take politically-tinged law business. However, one cannot devote seventy percent of one's time to politics and still get a great deal of law business. I needed at least enough to put away something for old age, and to do justice to the needs and standing of my family. Thus, after Eisenhower's election, I told Bill Knowland that I intended to divorce myself from politics in order to give the necessary time to my law business. Bill asked, "Would you like to be a federal judge?" I said, "My practice has been largely confined to the state courts. I never have aspired to the federal bench, or for that matter, any other. In fact, I've been too busy to think of it. I can build my law position back; meantime you should appoint a well-known state judge to the federal opening. That's good politics and good for the country. Later on I might be interested in a judgeship." I could do a good job there, I could turn the firm over to associates. Five days later, Governor Warren phoned me saying that a judgeship in the Superior Court of Los Angeles County was mine if I wanted it. I went on the bench in 1953.

I had started some writings for the purpose of helping inexperienced Republican campaigners with their work, so when I went on the bench, my notes went on the shelf. A judge must not write on politics; he is out of politics.

I have had some interesting cases, and many that were not, but I have remembered best those in which I was not too sure I was right. Some of those have found their way into these memoirs.

After I retired I did need something to do. I'd retired after three uncontested election periods of six years each, and further years of serving by appointment. So, off and on I would write.

One day I was thinking about my philosophy. Every man should have a philosophy. But, am I a philosopher? That word "philosopher" covers a great deal of territory. In Webster's definition of "philosophy" he says, "The science which investigates, the most general facts and principles of reality and of human nature and conduct; specifically, and now usually, the science which comprises logic, ethics, aesthetics, metaphysics and the theory of knowledge."

I hesitate to call myself a philosopher, but I love to know something about everything: poetry, politics, psychiatry, psychology, palindromes, and phthisic. I love to find or figure out what makes people "tick," the possibility and probability of things to come, the laws of cause and effect, the past and present growth of religion. I love humanity—I even love people!

As a child, with my father's insistence as my powerful motive, I learned the entire Westminster Shorter Catechism. I recall hearing about the old Westminster Church, just at the edge of London. The Protestants were in convention, at the instance of the king, and were working on the catechism. They were wrestling with the definition of God. Not arriving at a satisfactory answer, someone suggested that they call upon a younger member of the assembly to lead them in a prayer for guidance. His prayer began, "O, God, Thou spirit, infinite, eternal, unchangeable in Thy being, wisdom, power, holiness, justice and truth..." The wise men at the convention felt that they had received divine guidance in this prayer, and thereupon adopted this as a definition of God, and who can say that it was not inspired?

Another instance of significance, the great men who drafted our American Constitution, were well acquainted with the "rights of Englishmen" which had been won over the centuries and were embodied in English Common Law. They took it as a matter of course that these rights were the birthright of the people of the Colonies and therefore saw no need to spell them out in the

Constitution. But we may be very thankful that wider assemblies agreed that these specific rights should be spelled out and voted upon for adoption with the rest of the Constitution. Thus we have the first ten amendments which together make up the Bill of Rights. With these amendments, the Constitution passed, and we have the American Union of States.

One of the nicest things about philosophizing is that everything is grist for the mill of our minds. Long ago, when I was young enough to be doing those things, I made a resolve: "I will give to my country more than I take from it." Many will recognize this as a paraphrase of that most interesting president, Theodore Roosevelt. But while I devoutly believe in God, I have not the same ardency that my parents had. To refer to a work I repeatedly quote, I would be inclined to say to the angel, as did Abou-ben-Adhem, "Write me as one who loves his fellow men."

I am indebted to our attorney general and Supreme Court justice, Tom Clark, for sending me this thought found in old St. Paul's Church in 1692: "Go placidly amid the noise and haste, and remember what peace there may be in silence. As far as possible without surrender, be on good terms with all persons. Speak your truth quietly and clearly; and listen to others, even the dull and ignorant; they too have their story. Avoid loud and aggressive persons, they are vexations to the spirit. If you compare yourself with others, you may become vain and bitter; for always there will be greater and lesser persons than yourself. Enjoy your achievements as well as your plans. Keep interested in your own career, however humble; it is a real possession in the changing fortunes of time. Exercise caution in your business affairs; for the world is full of trickery. But let this not blind you to what virtue there is; many persons strive for high ideals, and everywhere, life is full of heroism. Be yourself. Especially, do not feign affection. Neither be cynical about love, for in the face of aridity and disenchantment it is as perennial as the grass. Take kindly to the counsel of the years, gracefully surrendering the things of youth. Nurture strength of spirit to shield you in sudden misfortune. But do not destroy yourself with imaginings. Many fears are born of fatigue and loneliness. Beyond a wholesome discipline, be gentle with yourself. You are a child of the universe, no less than the trees and the stars; you have a right to be here. And whether or not it is clear to you, no doubt the universe is unfolding as it should. Therefore, be at peace with God, whatever you conceive Him to be, and whatever your labors and aspirations, in the noisy confusion of life keep peace with your soul. With all its sham, drudgery and broken dreams, it is still a beautiful world. Be careful. Strive to be happy."

And then there is the philosophy of action. So, with my age, and my father's Scottish background, let me quote from an immortal fighting poem, the Scottish version of which, I think, is called "The Ballad of St. Andrews."

> *I am hurt, but I am not slain;*
> *I'll lay me down and bleed awhile,*
> *Then rise and fight with you again.*

# Chapter 1
# China

China, in the last years of the nineteenth century, was a land in ferment. This proud nation, then as now, the most populous in the world, had been largely enslaved to opium through the Calvinistic greed of English merchants, backed by the might of the British military establishment. Her ports, much of her territory, and many of her people were under the direct military and economic control of European nations. Both military and politico-economic representatives of these exploiting nations considered, and treated, the Chinese as lower orders, fit only to be exploited.

In counterpoise to these exploiters were such organizations as the Christian missions, and such men as my father, Dr. William Reid Faries.

In the reign of the Great Empress Dowager, Tzu-hsi of Cathay (also called the Dowager Empress), in the brick hospital of the Presbyterian Mission Compound, I was born on April 17, 1896, the third son of this much-loved and greatly admired man. The compound that was our home, and the base for my father's wide-ranging medical service, was located near the town of Wei Hsien. I note that on the modern map it is also known as Wei Jing. This Wei Hsien is in the province of Shantung, some one hundred li (34 miles) south of the Gulf of Pechili, on which lies the city of Tien Tsien. This, in turn, is the gateway city to the great capital of China, the city of Peking.

So, as an ordinary curly-haired, blond Caucasian, mainly Scots plus English, Irish, Dutch and French, I began my life as a distinct minority-group member in a great nation which then numbered some 400 million people. Now it is more than double that, over one

*The Missionaries return to China. Dr. William Reid Faries, center*

billion Chinese. There were, perhaps, twenty-five to thirty Caucasians in that particular compound, situated outside the city of Wei Hsien. A compound in China usually had dirt or unburned brick walls, the houses inside being ordinarily of burned brick. Our house and the compound wall were of burned brick. Ours was one of the largest houses in the compound, owing to the financial contribution by my grandfather. Because of his generosity, we lived in a two-story house.

Father was commonly addressed as Fa-Shan-Sung. This, I think, meant "the eminent and respected Doctor Fa." Fa stood for Faries. Of course his good wife, Aa-Sa Nong, was the person most responsible for my being there. I, as the third son, was respectfully known as San-Shan-Shung. Doubtless, behind my back I was also known as a "gwai-lo"—a foreign devil. We were all foreign devils to most of the Chinese. Nevertheless, few people, if any, were more greatly respected than my father, the medical doctor. He was a member of a foreign group in good standing in China. As for me, I was not always accepted, a fact which caused me several fights as a boy. Strange as it may seem, I was left-handed and mirror-visioned; I saw things backward. This was not recognized until I started writing. I wrote backward from the blocks my brothers gave me. Thus their ploy to keep me occupied and out of their hair disclosed what might have become a serious problem. But the problem, once discovered, was quickly corrected, and by age four I was writing letters of four pages—four small pages—to relatives in the great country of America.

Henry Luce (we called him Harry) was born in Peking after my own birth and went to school with my brothers, David and Culbert. They attended the China Inland Mission School in Chi Foo. This was also in Shantung Province, and about 100 li from Wei Hsien. Also in this province, in the hills not far from us, was the home, centuries earlier, of the great Confucius. It is still the home of his descendants and followers.

Our compound was about a hound dog's howl from Wei Hsien, which is to say one could hear the howling of the dogs when the wind was right, or was absent. Father had, in addition to the hospital, dispensaries in the compound in the city. He enlarged the original hospital which had been started by a Dr. Wells. Dr. Wells left for Japan about the time my father arrived. Beyond his work at the hospital and the dispensaries in the compound Wei Hsien, Father often went on medical trips to other villages or cities. I don't recall the size of Wei Hsien at that time, but I understand it is now close to a hundred thousand population, so it is no longer a village. In addition to the hospital and dispensary, the compound held a church, a boys' and a girls' high school. There were the homes of the missionaries, places for their Chinese servants and religious assistants, an orchard of fruit trees and some vegetable gardens. A small gate in the wall opened into the dispensary. This enabled the Chinese to be served without need for opening the large gate. This large gate, called the North Gate, faced toward the city of Wei Hsien. I recall that two large geese used to sit nightly on the arch over this gate, and they were better than watchdogs. They honked loudly at any movement.

There was no Chinese pharmacist, as I remember my father filled all the prescriptions. However, he did train and have some assistants.

We used to routinely take, after each meal, a capsule of quinine. There would be a dish of quinine on the table with gelatin capsules along side it, open. We would fill a capsule with the quinine and swallow it, because all of us had malaria. In spite of the quinine, bitter-tasting even in capsule form, we would each get the malarial "shakes" about every three months.

The practice of medicine has changed so much since those days! My father once told me that he treated or prescribed for some ten thousand persons yearly. This was a lot for one M.D. and a small staff. Every so often a large box, or boxes, of medicinal supplies would come from Germany from a factory I believe was known as Merck. We enjoyed opening those boxes, just as we enjoyed opening other boxes of food and clothing which came from the United States or from Great Britain. We didn't actually have much coffee; the missionaries used to crush wheat with a rolling pin and put it in the oven until it was really browned, and it tasted like Postum.

Mother, who was dearly loved by everyone, taught high school and also piano, so we had help in the house. I remember Jong Da Jeh, our amah or nurse, who took care of both my brothers and me. Then there was a houseboy, Jong Shi Dai, to whom my brothers taught mathematics and English. He left us and went to Tsin Sin where he became a prosperous banker with several banks. Then there was the cook, Wong Chong Loa. I should mention that these spellings are my own, and may not be correct, either to what they were or what they are now.

We were somewhat better off financially than most of the missionary families. Grandfather Faries paid for the building of our two-story brick house. I think, too, that his brother-in-law, Judge Vanderburg of Minnesota, helped with money for the Mission hospital.

A watchman would make his way around the inside of the compound about once each hour. He carried a covered wooden box with a handle. The box held a ball inside. He also carried a walking stick. The ball could be shaken, or the stick pounded on it, so one would know he was in the neighborhood. It was presumably a comfort to know that this sturdy little Chinese was around. The whole thing seemed a little foolish to me, since the noise he made let prospective burglars know exactly where he was.

Back of the houses, but still inside the compound, were fruit trees and vegetable gardens. I remember chard, and the long white radishes which I relished, although they were very hot. I recall, too, that we had only one dog in the compound, a black German dog. I think perhaps it was part, or perhaps a full-blooded, Weimaraner. We loved this dog. He could take on, and defeat, any two Chinese dogs. It was a friend to us at all times, and a great comfort.

I often visited the dispensaries at the compound and in Wei Hsien, and, in addition, Father took me with him on medical trips to other villages. I was his only son there, my brothers being in Chi Foo in the China Inland Mission Boys' School. Then there were "mission meetings," conferences of missionaries at various places in the area. I remember the rutted dirt roads and the wooden wheelbarrows which were sometimes pulled by donkeys, sometimes fitted with a sail. The men walked at the rear and steered, sometimes pushing, too. Some of these had both a sail and a donkey, though these were very hard to keep steady. The big wheel rose up in the center, and merchandise was piled on each side.

A traveler, coming to an inn at night, would find groups sitting around the courtyard. There would be a community kettle or wok, and families would take turns cooking. The fuel was the dry, hard stalks of corn we called Gowliong. Elsewhere it is called sorghum or kaffircorn, and I have heard it called Milo Maize. The Shantung area was bare, had very few trees and thus very little firewood. I can recall, too, fields of millet, a staple commodity, and I remember the millet gruel, or porridge, which we had for breakfast. And in my mind's eye I can see the gravestones, and the people in white attending funerals at the cemeteries near the compound.

Poverty was rife, and sanitation as we know it almost nonexistent. I can remember seeing children in the streets fighting with a dog or a pig over some sort of crust. Sewage ran down the edges of the street and sometimes even in the middle. I saw a grown man lying, apparently dying, in the gutter; people simply stepped over him, paying no attention, and went on. It is no wonder that so dedicated a Christian missionary doctor as my father desired to stay in China after the first two years. He had expected to stay a couple of years and then return to be an eye specialist in the United States. He had exceptional use of his hands; I remember him telling me the most important of the digits was the thumb. He wanted me to be a doctor, but I did not take to it. Also, I was left-handed. In any event, I wound up in the legal profession, spending my life in service to the law of man as he had devoted his to serving the law of God. When China was closed down by the Boxer outbreak, Father offered to go to India to continue his work there.

Father had a riding mule which he said was good because its gait was smoother than that of a horse. Considering Father's hunchback and terribly twisted body, this was no doubt his best choice. He had had spinal tuberculosis as a boy. It had cut his stature to about five feet. Had this terrible misfortune not occurred, he would have been over six feet.

I confess I was somewhat annoyed as a youngster when asked by people, when they learned I was born in China, to "say something in Chinese," because languages, when no longer used, slip away. Mother had a Chinese scholar who taught her the Chinese language. He was from Nanking, hence his dialect or the tonals in his Mandarin had about nine tonals. Some Chinese dialects have more, a few have less.

In 1900 the Boxer outbreak occurred, which so dramatically affected our lives.

The Chinese have always considered themselves the greatest nation in the world. This was particularly true of the people in the North and the Manchus, who were originally invited in by the Chinese. The Hans, after centuries, were ruled by the Mongols, and before that by the Khans, like Kubla, Agha and their associates from the Mongolian area–fierce tribes. Then the Manchus ruled China for hundreds of years. They considered themselves Chinese, and the ruling class. And, though there was constant trouble between the Manchus and the people of the South who were ninety percent Hans, they all considered themselves Chinese. In the late 1800's the world-wide expansion of the European powers was still taking place. The British were the leaders. At that time, opium was raised in Burma and parts of India. British trading companies of the time, much of whose stock was owned by the royalty and nobility, saw the great market possibilities of China, and by means of a war, forced many Chinese into the opium habit. There are still those who deny this, but it is not really in dispute. An attempt was made in South China to put a puppet king on the throne of China, to rally around him and fight back the "foreign devils" who were exploiting the people and taking over the nation's ports—"treaty ports" they were called. Portugal had several; the Germans took Tlen Tsien and Kao Cho; the British took by "lease" Hong Kong. France took Indo-China, now called Vietnam. So the Chinese began to wonder—perhaps they were

*Gate where Boxer mob entered the Mission Compound*

no longer the greatest nation in the world. Hence came the unrest that culminated in the Boxer outbreaks. Younger Chinese became activists, and the mob feeling grew. These Boxer activists began to believe that they were immune to the white man's bullets and could overthrow his forces. Mobs in seacoast cities began to rise against the foreign devils. Some say the Dowager Empress and her wily generals, particularly Yuan Shi-Kai, Governor of Shantung Province, stirred up the mobs against the missionaries, the traders, and the foreign military garrisons in these treaty ports because they feared the mobs might attack the Dowager Empress and the Manchus. These mobs gathered in various cities, including Wei Hsien, and ranted and screamed, "Drive out the foreign devils."

Father and David at that time were in Shanghai. At home in the compound were my mother; my older brother, Culbert; myself, aged four; and brother Van, Charles Vanderberg Faries, then a baby of four months.

Along with other missionaries and their families, there were in the compound numerous Chinese Christians. Many people refer to these as "rice Christians," but they were, in fact, sound, fundamentally believing Christians who never faltered.

The rebellion had now spilled over into Shantung Province,

*A Chinese Shenza*

whether or not it was encouraged by the Empress and her General Yuan Shi-Kai. I am sure they did not encourage killing, but I suspect they cleverly turned the Boxers' rage from themselves to hatred of the foreigners. I do remember the growing unrest about the town, and that our gates were barred. The Christian Chinese tried to quiet the mobs, as did some of the missionaries, but without much success.

It was decided that we must leave on a night late in June 1900. The American Consulate in Chi Foo had chartered an old Japanese steamer to meet us near the town of Wei Hi Wei, on the muddy Yalu River near the Gulf of Pechili. There were too many of us, so a small Russian cargo ship was added. I remember the Chinese helping my mother, my older brother, the baby and me over the back wall of the compound into shenzas. A shenza is, as far as I know, a creation of the Chinese. It is "powered" by two mules, one in front and one in the rear. Long poles are fitted, one on each side, into sockets in the saddles worn by the mules. Mats are attached to the poles between the two mules in such a way that the weight will not break through. Over this is stretched a half-circular cover, also of matting, like the top of a covered wagon. Inside this ride the people, or other load, as the case may be. Usually the mules wear bells, but on this night the bells were removed, and the feet of the mules were muffled. These shenzas are comfortable; one can sit or lie quite peacefully. The mule-teers were apprehensive and impatient, and we got away as fast and as quietly as we possibly could. I remember seeing from the shenza as we passed outside the walls, the fires in the city of Wei Hsien and in adjoining villages where Boxers were setting fire to buildings—not only those of foreigners, but also of Chinese. Apparently, the pillaging and burning had no special objective, just to destroy.

I cannot vouch for all the details of the story, but it seems that in Wei Hsien, in order to prevent the Boxers from breaking down the gates and getting into our compound before we could get away, one of the missionaries or someone in the missionary group, took his pistol and threatened the men attacking the gate. At last he shot one, much to the surprise and confusion of the Chinese who, up to this time, believed they were impervious to the white man's bullets and that his firearms could not harm them. On discovering that this was not the case, they quieted down. His action had made it possible for us to escape, and he was able later to follow us on foot to the ship, a distance of some forty miles. Subsequently, the Chinese did break in and looted and sacked and burned every building, but all of the missionaries of the compound did get away, one way or another.

We arrived in the early morning at the village of Wei Hi Wei, on the Gulf of Pechili. There on the shallow, muddy stream was a decrepit old Japanese steamer, certainly a no-account-looking vessel. The coolies carried us on their shoulders out to the bumboats, or sampans, which took us to the gangway of the steamer. Our assigned area was down at the very bottom of the boat, right on the hull. We spread our blankets and sat, ate and slept there. Our food was Captain's biscuits, or sea biscuit. I remember sleeping on, and under, blankets and quilts. During the night there was a great fight of rats on our bed, which I watched into the morning. Perhaps it was over our crumbs. Our bedding bore patches of blood where the rats had fought. A typhoon blew while we moved through the China (or was it the Japanese) Sea, and the old ship had a difficult time. However, we survived to reach Shanghai, over twenty-four hours late, where we were joined by my father and brother. Later, we got to Nagasaki and there we were given the right to live in a British mission school. It was vacation time, and we lived in the classrooms, sheets on wires providing partitions between families. My grandfather Faries sent us money on which to live.

At this time Father feared that this was the end of his Chinese medical missionary work, and decided that he wanted to go to India to continue his calling. However, before this could take place, he received clearance and safe conduct from the old Dowager Empress and, in turn, from General Yuan Shi Kai, to return to China, particularly, Shantung Province. It was also at this time that the Americans landed troops or marines in Nanking, the gateway to Peking. There were a great many foreigners interned there, holding out against the Chinese. A young Quaker engineer took over the organizing of the available food supply and the feeding of the Americans, other foreigners, and some Chinese interned there. He made a great name for himself with this beginning of his career in public service. His name was Herbert Hoover.

It is odd, on reflection, that the very capitalists, both in government and in private business, who carved up China for their profit were, in the end, directly responsible for the takeover of China by Communism. China's original type of civilization had, at least apparently, failed them, and they did not choose to accept the civilization of the people who were responsible for the treaty ports, opium, economic exploitation and their defeat in the Boxer outbreak. Nor would they accept the civilization of their ancient enemy, Japan. One must remember the Russo-Japanese War, and the early struggles with Japan, as contributing factors to the unrest in China, to the realization that their country was being carved up so that it was no longer as great as they thought it to be. The Russians put their railroad across Manchuria and took over not only Port Arthur and Vladivostok, but great areas of Manchuria and Mongolia. Then Korea was taken over and made a colony of the Japanese. And, when the Japanese fought the Chinese in the early 1900s, and Russians fought with the Chinese, China was always the loser. This prepared the way thirty years later, when the Japanese invaded and took over large parts of China, forcing the Chinese back inland. They were a proud people, and they were humiliated. So, after World War II, China was ready for something new, and Communism took over from the American-sponsored Chiang Kai Shek, reaping great amounts of military supplies that the U.S. had provided, many supplies left by the losing Japanese and great masses of Russian supplies. The Communists supported Mao Tse Tung and Lin Pao, the smart boys of the revolution.

In any event, when the Communists had moved in under Mao Tse

Tung and the war was over, China again became united under Chinese, and its people began to feel that Communism was the answer. Their national spirit and identity had been restored, and they were convinced that Communism had done this. Thus followed the rejection of the governmental theories of the United States and the great Western European countries. China was again the great nation of the universe, as they had thought themselves, and they had still a great passion to rid themselves of the "foreign devils."

I think it may be properly said that much of the success during the second World War, especially as to the southern part of China and the South Sea Islands, was because of the friendly attitude of many of the coastal common people. This, in turn, was largely to the credit of the missionaries and missionary doctors who had done much for these people, and whose kindness was remembered. Another thing that undoubtedly helped was the refusal on the part of the United States to accept, or use for ourselves, the reparations which had been required of China at the end of the Boxer outbreak. We gave back our portion of the Boxer Rebellion indemnity to educate young Chinese in the United States. They went back to China and were thoroughly dissatisfied with it on their return. Many became interested in the Russian experiment just beginning, and many of them became Communists. There were exceptions; Chiang Kai Shek was largely educated in Russia, but did not agree with the Russian theory of what was best for China.

The Dowager Empress' favorite General Yuan Shi Kai, governor of Shanghi, who was responsible for Father's return to China, was the transitional president. We speak of Sun Yat-Sen as the first president, but the transitional period between rule by the Dowager Empress and Sun Yat-Sen's accession found Yuan Shi Kai in that position.

It is not much wonder that the wily old Dowager Empress, and in turn, the old diplomat, General Yuan Shi Kai, wanted Father back. No doubt he wanted a doctor for himself and his officers. He gave us safekeeping until the Chinese army left the general area of Shantung Province. The missionary board agreed, so Father returned as an American-trained doctor to take care of the general's group and to rebuild, or at least plan, the rebuilding of the mission.

My mother's mother was ill, and Mother went back to New York to take care of her, taking baby Van with her. David and Culbert went to the China Inland Mission School in Che Foo, and I stayed with

*Our house in China, restored after the Rebellion*

Father. This was smart, because he needed some protection. The Chinese love children, and there would be less danger if I went along. I had some danger, though, because of a ram, given me as a lamb, by General Yuan Shi Kai. He used to butt me when I came out the door, because he was so fond of me. He did this so much that he finally lost his life.

Father was busy planning the rebuilding, and for a semester I attended Miss Jewel's school in Shanghai. I enjoyed the time there in the kindergarten. There was a party at Christmas time, and I was called upon to make the opening speech. I was making my speech when the tree behind, or beside me, caught fire. I had to be pulled away while they put the fire out, but it didn't bother me. I had my speech to make—"We will try to do and say what will please you all today," and I put the emphasis on the "all."

When I went back to Wei Hsien, bricks were being burned for the rebuilding of the mission. They were formed in wooden forms and, when dry, were dumped from the frames, dried a little more, and then put in the kiln and burned. Also, the men were sawing trees into rough boards, using a two-man saw.

The houses in the compound were duly rebuilt, although I seem to recall they were not complete at the time we left. Father had gone in with the idea of serving in the rebuilding of the Protestant missions, but he turned the job over to a missionary minister named Henry Luce, then serving in Peking. He was the father of the publisher,

Henry, whom we called Harry. The Luces remained our friends over the years.

Summer in Wei Hsien was very hot, and the air quite humid; the rainy season started around July. During this period we had to wipe off our books every few weeks, because they became covered with mold. We all had malaria; it ruined my father's health. In spite of the quinine we took, we all had the "shakes." Mine continued for years.

Father's health had failed, and he felt he should return to the United States to recuperate. Where could be a better place to bake malaria out of one's system than California? Mother was still in New York with her mother.

When we left Wei Hsien, we were given a tremendous send-off in Father's honor. We were each carried in a Mandarin sedan chair to the city's great hall where there was a big banquet with many speeches, and Chinese silk scrolls with Chinese characters in gold thread from top to bottom. They hung from ceiling to floor, all extolling Father and his work. They were presented to Father. Tragically, they were lost some years later in a fire. We boys had to stand in a line during some of the speeches, but my brother, Culbert, told me that we were made members of an organization known as the "Sons of the Dragon," an honor from the Dowager Empress of China.

I remember very well our 1903 trip, via Japan to Seattle, on the Japanese steamer, Aki Maru, then considered a fine passenger ship. There were a number of children on board, and we had a children's table. I was very fond of the curry they served—lamb curry, chicken curry and other forms, generally on rice. I would have eaten curry three times a day if given a chance.

I was seven when we returned, Culbert was nearly ten, and David was twelve.

It is unfortunate, but true, that upon our return to the United States we stopped speaking Chinese in the home. To most of us now, the Chinese language is gone.

Some forty-five years or so after we had left Wei Hsien, about 1948, my wife, Lois, and I were driving north on the road from Escondido and San Diego toward Riverside. It was a very hot day in midsummer and, standing at a country intersection, hoping someone would pick him up, was a Marine top sergeant. As was customary in those days, we stopped to pick him up. He said that he was going to

Beaumont where he was to meet friends or relatives. He had come from Camp Pendleton, the Marine base, and was hitchhiking home to be discharged. This was later than most wartime servicemen had stayed in, and he explained that he had been in charge of dismantling what had been a Japanese internment camp in North China. My wife said, "Oh, you should talk with my husband. He was born in North China." He laughed and said, "Well, you never heard of the place I was in, I'm sure. It was just a little place out in the middle of North China, a mission compound which the Japanese used as an internment camp. It was in Shantung Province in a little place called Wei Hsien." Lois told him I had been born there, so we talked, and it developed that he had been in charge of the final dismantling of the Presbyterian Mission compound camp, and of sending to their homes the people the Japanese had interned there. These had included missionaries of all denominations and other white foreigners. He spoke of how fine these missionary people had been to our troops, and how they had each written letters which the Marines wanted to take home as souvenirs. He showed me one. It was a lovely, grateful letter from an old lady whose name I have forgotten.

When I got home, I got in touch with my mother and asked her about the lady. Mother said, "Oh she was my very dear friend. I stayed at her home in Peking (now Beijing) for a week." Did I say it's, perhaps, not so big a world?

# Chapter 2
# Becoming
# Californians

When we returned to the United States, we took the train down from Seattle to San Francisco, where we were to meet my mother, grandmother, and little brother, Van. I recall the train stopped at Grant's Pass, Oregon, a beautiful green, wooded area, far different from the area in China in which we had lived. Alongside the train were women and boys with big trays filled with boxes of strawberries. We bought a number of boxes. I don't believe I had ever eaten a strawberry before.

Later, it must have been in Sausalito, California, we went into what I thought was a big waiting room and sat on long benches. Wondering why nothing was happening, I looked out and discovered we were not in a waiting room at all, but on a big ferry crossing San Francisco Bay. We were met by Mother, Grandmother, Van, a cousin, and Father's sister, Ann, who had rented a house for us in Saratoga, down the peninsula from San Francisco. The house was up a hill on the main street. It was rather a large house, rented for a short time while the owners were away. I remember the front porch, with its rocking chairs, and the calla lilies on both sides of the front steps. My older brothers found jobs on the King Ranch picking prunes. I got a job along with the others, and was paid ten cents a box. The prunes are shaken to the ground and then packed into the lug or field boxes which weigh about forty pounds when filled. I didn't make much money, though it seemed quite a bit to me. The older brothers did much better than I. Right after the prune-picking the apricot season started. These had to be split, pitted and dried, as did the peaches.

Poor Father, with his compulsive anxiety to get well and back to work, had to sit around while we were out picking fruit. He did a great deal of reading. He soon tired of doing nothing but read and walk to the store. Also, the chill and damp of Saratoga did nothing to further his recovery, so he decided to try southern California, and my beautiful Aunt Ann went back to her home in Minneapolis.

Our next move, therefore, was south to Tustin, where we rented a house. Tustin lies alongside Santa Ana, in Orange County. Our house was very imposing for that time, situated on a corner of the main street. Tustin was then an orange grove area. There wasn't a great deal to do in Tustin. I used to lie out on the lawn and watch the teams go by as they hauled the big loads of field-boxed oranges to the packing plants. It seemed to be a custom for the drivers to keep boxes of oranges beside them on their seats. The drivers would toss down an orange or two to the boys, and naturally, we would eat them on the spot.

Tustin was beautiful, but there was nothing for Father to do. He did some hunting on the Irvine Ranch, having a letter of permission from James Irvine II, but he spent most of his time looking for a small ranch. Finally he settled on a twenty-one acre place near the city of Orange. This I remember very well. At seven, I was the right age to appreciate it. When, years later, we moved to Los Angeles, I remained unhappy for a long time because I had loved Orange, and our Los Angeles home did not compare with the ranch.

Orange was about three and a half miles from Santa Ana, the county seat of Orange County. There was a little train which ran between Santa Ana and Orange that we called "the peanut." With its one car and little engine, it made two or three round trips every day.

Turning into our driveway, one passed between long rows of Italian cypress trees. It was a pretty drive, about three hundred feet long, culminating in a circle drive around the house. The house was surrounded by pepper trees.

I don't recall whether our twenty-acre ranch was planted when we arrived, or if Father planted it immediately. Along one side lay a very young navel orange grove of about five acres. Father got a Chinaman to plant peas in this grove. This crop grew in the winter. The peas were harvested and put into jute grain sacks. We would haul the peas to the Santa Fe Railroad station about two and a half miles away, and ship them to a produce house in Los Angeles.

At one side of the house was an apricot orchard of about five acres. We kept in the kitchen, near the stove, a wooden box with dried apricots which we boys would eat when we came home from school. The quality of the apricots was only fair, and the time came when we pulled them out and planted alfalfa, which we needed for the cows and horses. Maude and Dave were our regular team, and used to pull the surrey and do the ordinary work around the ranch.

In those days people with ranches, mostly small ranches in those areas, were practically self-supporting. If there was a failure in the orange or the apricot crop, or some other tragedy, people could go on living on the ranch. They could feed themselves from their vegetable gardens and chickens and turkeys they raised, and they could sell oranges or other produce at the roadside.

I'm not sure whether I was seven or eight when I entered school. I was a year older than I should have been, and was entered in the second grade. I already could read and write, and had more education than most of the second-graders. Then I was skipped from third into fourth grade. I could spell better than most of them, but I remember we had a spelling bee, attended by the principal, the superintendent of schools and others. I was leader of the team, and I was quite flustered. The first word given me was "village," and in front of all those people I spelled it v-i-l-l-i-a-g-e, and went down immediately. I was very red-faced and ashamed, but in spite of that I did all right in school. Starting with the second grade you had to fight your way up to get your place in the class hierarchy. I fought my way up to number two in the second grade. Also, I broke my nose, or someone did. I was better at wrestling than at fisticuffs. I fought all through lunch with Dr. Jones' fat son. I suppose I had been scheduled to go home for lunch, because Mother showed up just before one o'clock when I was scheduled to go back into class. We were still in the middle of the fight, so I caught something at home in addition.

We lived well, and we were healthy. We all worked hard; each had his little chores and his share in the general work. One had to chop and bring in the wood, another milked the cow, while another fed the horses, and all helped with the turkeys and chickens. So, while we were better off than most, because Father had some outside income, we all had to work hard. God was good to us, and so was Grandfather Faries, who left Father income by his will.

In 1905, the Colorado River changed its course. It cut across

California's Imperial County and flowed into the Salton Sea, then listed on the map as 264 feet below sea level. At that time the Imperial Valley was being nourished by water brought through a canal from the Colorado. The town of Coachella, then the largest in the Valley, was about one hundred feet above the level of the Salton Sea. The rampaging river, cutting a new path through centuries of desert silt, washed out thousands of feet of the Southern Pacific Railway's track. The SP, running from Los Angeles through New Orleans and beyond, was Southern California's main freight and passenger line, competing with the Santa Fe which ran north of it. Father read of the river's damage to the SP tracks, and being a man of some vision, realized that the line was too important to abandon, and that they would find a way to divert the river to the gulf as before.

Father had never abandoned his dream of returning to the mission field as soon as his health was restored. Most of the family felt he would never be able to do so, as he had not succeeded in curing his malaria. The Coachella Valley desert was very hot, and land was cheap; there could be no better place for his recovery. Father went to see for himself. God's work loomed more important than personal, or even family, comfort. In 1906, while the river was still flowing into the Salton, he went to the Coachella area. When he returned, sure enough, he had bought a ranch! It was some eighty acres almost squarely at the right angle of the triangle area between Indio and Coachella. Only a few acres of it had been graded, perhaps four or five, but there were about twenty acres to the east, somewhat higher, that could be graded. To the west there were some gradable acres, and beyond that about forty acres of mesquite and sagebrush.

Father told us he had bought the Coachella Valley ranch and was going to move there. Mother, a dedicated woman, did not swear, but I am sure we boys at least muttered an impropriety or two. Culbert was preparing to go in the fall of 1907 to Occidental Academy. At that time, David, having finished the Academy, was ready to go to Occidental College. I was starting the sixth grade, and Van was in grammar school.

Father wanted to go immediately to Coachella and get the ranch under way. We boys were to help during the summer school vacation periods. The house on the ranch was not suitable for occupancy, so arrangements had to be made. Funds were a bit short, and Father traded the Orange County ranch for a home in the Highland Park section of Los Angeles, about six blocks from Occidental College.

Before moving to Los Angeles, there was the final summer in Orange and the trip to Coachella. I still fondly remember the Santa Ana River. It ran down next to the home and ranch of Madame Modjeska, the celebrated Polish-American actress. We went there to play in the stream, and I went to her house a few times, where she would give me a piece of cake.

For the trip to Coachella we fixed up the wagon with boxes along each side of the wagon bed. Over the bed was a set of bows covered with canvas. The rig was almost identical to the great old Conestogas and similar covered wagons, which crossed the plains and mountains to the West in the pre- and post-Civil War periods. We were going to plan and begin the development of the ranch, and be back just in time to start school.

We went via the Santa Ana River Canyon, Riverside, and the Jackrabbit Grade, making about twenty-five miles a day. Evenings we would stop and camp where there was water. We'd put out the Army cots, make our fire, cook, eat, wash the dishes, and then sit by the fire for awhile while the bright-eyed coyotes, waiting for garbage, kept their distance. Very early, we would turn in. This method of travel was tremendous fun for us. It took five days, during which we learned a lot about organizing.

Father forbade travel on Sunday, so we rested among the rocks and willows by a small stream. This was my idea of heaven; the stream and the evening breeze seemed to be whispering Indian lore.

On the morning after, the moon, the skulking coyotes and snakes and lizards were gone. On we drove to "Indio and the Ranch!"

Indio lay alongside the tracks. There was a station, an ice plant for refrigerating the produce cars, two general merchandise stores and a white-steepled Presbyterian church, all with hitching rails for the patient horses. There was also a public school and a pool hall with lunch room.

At the ranch, only about four acres had been graded. The house, when we first saw it, looked like pictures from the "dust bowl" of the thirties. It was about 24 by 15 or 18 feet, and had two rooms. It stood on rocks, with no foundation, and was built of one-by-twelve-inch redwood boards running up and down. There was no plumbing, and the outhouse lay on its side. There was no barn, and the corral was broken. The wind blew thirty miles an hour and was full of dust. Did

Father's vision, even then, allow him to see what a showplace this desolate and windswept acreage would one day become? Now, when I visit the place almost seventy years later, there are forty acres of the best offshoot dates, mulched and interset with golden citrus. Some of the northern Africa offshoots that I had set out are seventy feet tall. Windbreaks keep out the strong, dusty winds from San Gorgonio Pass. The cow yard is a truck garden; the shaded bungalow is air-conditioned. Even though we sold the place in the thirties, all this was largely accomplished by the Faries family.

Since his primary objective was to regain his health in order to return to his missionary work, Father was eager to settle on the ranch and begin work. However, many arrangements had to be made, so, after a couple of days, we returned to Los Angeles.

After a couple of months in a rented house, we were able to move into the house for which the Orange ranch had been traded. We lived there for nine years. David went to Occidental College, while Culbert went to Occidental Academy, and I went to Monte Vista Street Grammar School.

I rather think we got the worst of the trade of our property for this house, but I guess it was the thing to do in the circumstances. The house was not too well completed when we moved in, though people had been living in it.

Much to the horror of all of us, when we moved in, we found the place infested with fleas, or perhaps bedbugs. Well, we were in, and the deal was through, so we weren't going to get into litigation. It was necessary to remove all the moldings, take out all the beds and wash everything—floors, walls, back of the baseboards—everything, with kerosene. So, it became home for us, although it took me several years to be over pining for the good old life in Orange.

Father spent a considerable amount of time at the ranch, and later, we boys gradually made the place more livable, but it was nine years before the family actually moved there. So Orange was gone, the ranch not ready, and Los Angeles, for better or worse, was home.

The Monte Vista Street School was a good elementary school, and only about two and a half blocks from where we lived. Of course we walked from the top of the hill. At noon, Mr. Jackson brought his ice cream and tamale wagon to the back of the school so the horse could stand in the shade of a big tree there. He had two kinds of ice cream, cones or dishes, five or ten cents, and it was good. He had two kinds of tamales, Texas tamales which were wrapped in corn husks, and large Mexican tamales which were wrapped in corn husks, but with layers of corn meal in between and a big center of Texas chile. I liked these best. Tamales and ice cream may not have been a very good lunch by today's standards, but we thought it all right and had it often.

During the noon hour there were baseball games. There was a girls' diamond, and the girls from Garvanza School played the girls from Highland Park. The Garvanza girls were unwilling to play, though, when the Duncan sisters, Rosetta and Vivian, played. Rosetta was the rougher one. The "Highland Parks" were the better players and usually won.

A few years later, in high school, the Duncan girls began to work on a musical. They completed it after they were through high school, and I remember going to see it at the Morosco Theatre in Los Angeles. It was called "Topsy and Eva" and was based upon the Harriet Beecher Stowe novel. It became a big hit, and the sisters toured the country with it for many years. It had a number of songs, one of which was called "Rememb'ring," which is what I am doing now, and what I have called this book.

After the seventh grade I made a decision to go to summer school in order to skip half a year and graduate early. There were about twenty students in the class. So I went back to school in the upper half, which graduated in February. I also learned to swim in the YMCA pool.

Finishing school in February made it possible for me that year to spend a full spring and summer working on the ranch. I spent a lot of time working on the ranch during school years, including one period of fifteen uninterrupted months. I came to feel, with rather wry humor, that going to school was my vacation time.

Yes, like so many American boys of song and story, I had a paper route. We carriers rode our bicycles from school or home to the livery stable in the afternoons to pick up our papers. The livery stable, a rough-lumber red building, stored hay, rented horses and buggies, and was a general feed and fertilizer store. The owner's daughter, Hannah Baker, went to school in South Pasadena and was a year ahead of my class, very pretty and about the most popular girl in the school. I had the pleasure of escorting her on a few occasions. On one such occasion, we were in the back of the red streetcar when I asked her about a girl sitting near us. She said, "That's Lois Shorten. She is from Garvanza and goes to South Pasadena. She's a good friend of mine, and I'll introduce you." She did—and to her surprise, I left her and sat with Lois, whom I later married.

When I was ready to enter high school, by family custom that meant Occidental Academy. However, it had been decided at that time to close the Academy, which was cloased halfway through my first year, so I transferred to South Pasadena High School. I enjoyed South Pasadena High, and went there for two and a half years. I went out for athletics, but only made track, and did pretty well in the shorter races.

The real hub of Highland Park in those days was Occidental College, though the Ebell Club was, after the college center, the number two social center. The young folks of our group had "Christian Endeavor" every Sunday afternoon, after which we'd go, boys and girls together, to someone's home for Sunday evening cake and ice cream and other nonalcoholic refreshment. We'd play the piano and sing songs, play games and otherwise have a good time until about 8:30, when the boys took the girls home—unless we snuck off to a movie or something of that sort.

One of the members, though not a regular member of our group at this time, was Louis Bundy. He may have been a bit older than I, but was in my class at school and at Occidental Academy. He was a brilliant boy, stocky and broad of shoulder, and played better football than any high schooler; and, he was something of a split personality.

One night Louis Bundy made a phone call to the local drugstore. He said he was calling from the home of a lady who lived the other side of the Santa Fe tracks in a quiet area with several pepper trees and nice, well-kept homes. Louis said the lady couldn't get out, and needed something sent from the drug store, and that the delivery person should bring some change for a bill—I think ten dollars. Bruno Zeishe, then delivering for the store, was sent over on his bicycle. When Bruno got to a group of trees, Louis Bundy stepped out and killed him. All he took was the money—less than ten dollars! Soon there was an all-points out for Louis Bundy. At his trial he was defended by Earl Rogers, one of the greatest criminal lawyers we ever had in Los Angeles, or perhaps I should say he was defended by Roger's firm, though the general talk was that Rogers was to represent him. No person under eighteen had ever been hanged, but Louis

Bundy was convicted and hanged. He may have passed his eighteenth birthday before he was executed, but hanged he was, though Earl Rogers' daughter, Adela Rogers St. John, stated in her book that no client of her father's had ever been hanged.

After grammar school, life became a back-and-forth run for me: a heavy academic schedule carried between periods of work on the Coachella Valley ranch. The ranch work was actually spread over two long periods of eight and fifteen months, and a couple of summers with school coming between.

Much of my work concerned the house and living area. The house was small, about 18 by 24 feet, built of rough redwood siding one inch by twelve inches, placed vertically with two-inch battens nailed over the cracks between the boards. The floors were white pine, tongue and grooved. The roof, on a V-frame, was shingled. The bedrooms were tiny and held cots. There was no plumbing at first; we were fortunate to have the little four-inch well, from which we carried water for the house. Our new well had a pit around it, some twenty feet deep. It was railed at the top and had a ladder. It was covered and was quite cool at the bottom. This was where we kept our butter and other perishables. Before long we installed electricity. Also, we installed a hand pump. After the big twelve-inch well was dug, we had a tank high above the ground to provide pressure.

I mentioned that the house was raised on blocks. This provided a shady resting place for the dogs and chickens, but also for scorpions and tarantulas, not to mention harmless lizards. And there were large red ants with stingers. They'd get into your shoes at night, as would spiders, and unless we remembered to remove them before putting on our shoes, we'd get a sting that would make big, painful, itching lumps.

Anyone not familiar with this, or a similar area, cannot imagine how hot and dry it was. One had to be careful about turning over rocks, because a scorpion or a sidewinder might be under any rock. I once captured a very small rattlesnake, perhaps six inches long. I put it in a glass jar, with nail holes punched in the cap for air. I'm not sure what I intended to do with it, but in the morning my snake was gone. Well, that meant turning the house upside down, unmaking all the beds, searching everywhere to make sure it wasn't in the house. A young rattler's bite is just as deadly as a full-grown one, and these sidewinders, who grow only to about three feet, are as deadly as the big diamondbacks.

Father became one of the first large-scale date growers in the country. He noted that the pollen of the male dates ripened earlier on the sunny side, provided the leaves did not shade the bud spathes which provided the pollen. He, therefore, cut back the leaves so as to get early pollen for the early blooming female dates. He also noted a considerable number of leaves were required to absorb the elements from sun and soil, so he started counting and working on this before most growers did. He was the first, or one of the first, to dust the female branches with pollen shaken off into a bag, or with little twigs of the male palm. He would also tie a few male blossoms right into the buds on the female dates so as to make a better setting of dates. He noted, too, that if a female bunch of dates was too long, those below would not be good, and would have to be cut off. He worked on many things, including a Mexican lemon, so sweet it could be eaten with enjoyment.

Father was one of the largest purchasers of the "first shipment" of date offshoots from North Africa. These had been brought in by a newly-formed date growers' association. The Department of Agriculture was very anxious that the date business get started in the Coachella Valley, but they were rightfully afraid of the scales which infested the North African date palms. They used sheep dip to kill the parleaeri and other scales, and, unfortunately, killed a lot of the offshoots. These were mostly Deglet Noors, a staple, and we also had Mactoom dates. I think before we sold the ranch our date production was up to over two hundred tons annually.

All the work done on the house was eventually nullified by a disastrous fire which took place after Mother and the boys had moved there. Perhaps even worse than the damage to the house was the loss of Father's extensive and unique collection of Chinese memorabilia. We had barrels and boxes of artifacts: great honorary scrolls, antiques of various kinds, even Chinese mud money from very long ago. All were lost.

Working on the ranch was a wonderful experience and, in spite of the hard work, I would not have missed Father's "Arabah Farm."

# Chapter 3
## School Days

*I* had one more year of high school, and I thought of going back to South Pasadena, but apparently they decided they no longer needed the Highland Park students and raised our tuition. Most of my friends decided on other schools, and a number of my close friends in Highland Park were going to Los Angeles High School. I decided to go there. My particular girlfriend and future bride, Lois Shorten, decided on Hollywood High.

I suppose the senior year in high school is the time when youngsters have the most fun; they don't yet have the cares of the world, nor the financial woes of a family. Certainly, it was a great time for me.

We used to call the 1915 class the last good graduating class at the old site. I believe the new school opened in 1917; the old building, thereafter, was used for adult education, and is today the headquarters of the Board of Education. The old tower was taken down after the 1933 earthquake. We Highland Park students got off the streetcar at Sunset Boulevard, crossed the street and ran up the steps—about 130 steps—no small feat, when one was in a hurry and had a load of books.

I attended the 100th anniversary of the Los Angeles High Alumni Association, organized in 1876. The Alumni Building has an interesting story: One day the great motion picture lawyer, George Cohen, got a call from a lady, asking him to come to the rest home where she lived. It seems she wanted his services in drawing her will. Mr. Cohen was a very busy man, and for such a relatively unimportant job, he sent a young lawyer. The old lady in the rest home left her estate to the Los Angeles High Alumni Association. To everyone's surprise, the amount involved was in excess of half a million dollars, a tremendous fortune in those days. This gift enabled the Alumni Building to be constructed, a number of scholarships to be established, and other benefits to be provided. This gift was indicative of the spirit of L.A. High, so many of whose graduates have gone on to fame and service, some of them in the entertainment field. Zion Meyers had a beautiful sister, Carmel, who became a popular film star. A girl named Edith Spare became known to the world as Edith Head, undoubtedly the best-known film costume designer. Then there was Douglas Shearer, Norma Shearer's brother, whose name has appeared among the technical credits on many films. He started with stage management at L.A. High while a student. Rube Wolf, a year or two below me, always wanted to lead the high school orchestra, and he later became a popular band leader. His brother, Marcus, and sister, Fanny, became Fanchon and Marco, one of the most famous dance teams. Another girl, Juanita Horton, became a film star known as Bessie Love. There were several students who became well-known musicians, and others made their mark in other fields.

And so, farewell to high school years, and to my friends and neighbors of that period. "Proudly upon..." as we used to start the famous Los Angeles High School hymn.

My younger brother, Van, died in 1912. This handsome, likeable boy contracted polio and died within twenty-four hours after contracting the disease.

I entered Occidental College in the autumn of 1915 at the then-new campus. There were, at that time, only three buildings: Fowler and Johnson halls, opposite each other, and Swan Hall down next to the athletic field. Swan Hall was then the men's dormitory. Certainly the campus today is entirely different from my time there. I enjoyed myself at Occidental; I felt right at home.

"Rope Rush," as they called it, occurred at the start of the school year. In today's atmosphere this sort of thing may seem inappropriate, but a very sound perception lay at the bottom of all this apparent nonsense. Prior to "Rope Rush," the new freshmen were strangers, having neither acquaintance with most of our classmates, nor the means of making their acquaintance. After all this roughhousing, we were relaxed with each other; we had a common identity and a common purpose; we became a unit, and functioned thereafter as a group. I am not at all sure that something of considerable value has not been lost in today's abhorrence of this kind of strenuous and, admittedly, sometimes risky activity among young students.

The contest was between the sophomores and the new frosh. An area, perhaps 100 feet square, was roped off on the athletic field, and each of us was given several lengths of cotton rope. The object was to capture and tie up as many opponents as possible within a preset time period. At the gun, whoever had the most prisoners was the victor. As I seemed to have some familiarity with Occidental, and was in pretty good trim from all the work at the ranch, I was chosen captain of our freshman team. We organized our strategy pretty well, I think. We chose three of our biggest fellows to do the tying up, while the rest of us worked at defending our men and capturing theirs, which we piled in a corner and kept from untying themselves or each other. I don't remember how much we won, but win we did. We won the next year, too, when I was on the sophomore side of the contest, though I wasn't captain. Of course there were other activities, including the "Book Rush," in which we fought to get a copy of the annual. I was successful in this, though in the struggle I wound up face down in the gravel between Johnson and Fowler halls, and was pretty well cut up.

I was elected to be president of the junior class, which ordinarily meant going on to be president of the student body the following year. This was the expectancy of my fraternity, the Owl and Key, which I had joined as a sophomore. This later became Phi Gamma Delta at Occidental.

Great changes took place in my life during my sophomore year in 1916. Money being rather tight, it was decided to sell the Highland Park house and move the family to the ranch. And it was at this time that Father told me I would have to assume responsibility for my own education, since the family could no longer afford to do so. However, I did get five shares of stock in the American Exchange Bank of Duluth, which came to me from my grandfather and would help carry me for awhile. I decided to go to Stanford, where brother Culbert was, and did go there and was about to join the Phi Gamma fraternity, but just at that time Father had a heart attack, so I came back to Occidental. I lived for awhile at David's house near the college.

In April of 1917, President Wilson, after all his promises to keep us out of what became known as World War I, decided that we must go in to save Great Britain and the world from the Germans under Kaiser Wilhelm.

It was soon decided to start a Reserve Officers' Training Corps (ROTC) at Occidental, and very soon I was doing "squads right" with a gun. The weather was very hot, and it was dusty, dirty work. I thought to myself that it would certainly be much worse in the trenches of France. I decided I'd prefer the navy. However, not being 21, I wasn't quite ready for this yet. We were given the right to leave college early that year, to work the farm crops, so along in May, I went down to the ranch for a couple of months and helped Father.

# Chapter 4
# "You're In The Navy Now"

Deciding to get in before being drafted, and still preferring the Navy, I got an introduction to "Bud" Hill, then counsel to the county in civil matters. Bud Hill gave me a letter to Commander Eugene Overton, a lawyer of the firm of Overton, Lyman and Plum. Overton was executive officer of the Naval Training Center located at Pier 7 at the San Pedro Harbor. I took my letter to Overton's office. He read it, and asked, "You want to join the Navy?" I said, "Yes, Sir." He told me to raise my right hand, and swore me in, just like that! No physical, nothing! I went into the Naval Coast Defense Reserve. There were about seven hundred young men in the warehouse where they were located, divided into companies. I was put in Company B, headed by a Stanford long distance runner named Wilson! His nickname was "Skin." He assigned me a cot, got my uniform, and made necessary arrangements. I wasn't called out for a few days. I went there, permanently, about July 30, 1917.

The young men of the Naval Defense Reserve felt they would be defending the coast from German submarines. For this purpose they had a converted yacht. Actually, many of them were yachtsmen. Nearly all of them were college or university men, and they were a good company. Soon, however, all were required to "sign over" to the regular navy. I had never expected anything else, but some few refused to sign over. Because of their refusal they were put on lightships. There was one of these at the entrance to San Francisco Bay, next to the Faralone Islands. These ships stayed out for weeks on end, coming in only for supplies, and they would roll and roll and roll. That lightship assignment, and one or two others, was enough to break the will of practically all the college boys who had refused to sign over. I had signed over at the beginning, so I was in the regular Navy. I was given a uniform of blue serge and the regular navy style "sailor hat," which had to be made "seagoing."

The big corrugated iron warehouse where we were stationed contained several hundred cots for the various platoons of men training there. At one side were showers and toilets, and at the end, the big kitchen. The officers, who lived ashore, had a separate mess, as did the chief petty officers. The rest of us ate in a big hallway. I later got a job of "hashing," as they called it, in the chief petty officers' mess, which meant I could eat what they hadn't put on their plates. They fed themselves pretty well, since they paid for their food and had their own cook. I did regular drills, but didn't have to go through all the things that were assigned later, such as the butch haircut, policing the grounds, KP, and so forth. I was glad to miss all that. There was no boot camp at the time, no quarantine, and we could leave for the weekends.

Our commanding officer, John Mel, was an Annapolis man, a retired captain, and he did not spend much time there. Commander Overton, our "exec," was pretty much in charge; of course he had a staff of officers. Even at the beginning, the Naval Training Station was a popular place. There was a parade on the fairground every Saturday morning, with a band and lots of marching, countermarching and inspections. We were occasionally inspected by visiting officers, sometimes an admiral. Yes, there were lots of girls who came down, and some fine times were had on weekends. It wasn't long before I was put on the "accepted" list for special rates at hotels, and I often spent a weekend at one of them. They put us up in available spare rooms, charging us fifty cents or a dollar a night. There were parties arranged by the hotel hostesses and attended by invited young ladies. It was a well-planned social time all around, and I enjoyed it. However, we did have work to do, some of it of much value. We had to study the "Bluejacket's Manual," a big, thick book. Anyone learning all of it would certainly have been a better sailor than I ever was. Of course one needed practical experience, but all basic Navy knowhow was in that manual, from knot-tying to sail-rigging to care of the injured. I studied it quite diligently.

I started out by learning to be a signalman. This required good proficiency in Morse Code and other codes, knowledge of flags and pennants, and the ability to send out and receive messages by flag and pennant. These were primarily based on dots and dashes. I wasn't, perhaps, really good at it, but I did work hard and passed the examination for signalman. I also had small arms practice, and got to be a marksman. This was rather difficult for me, since I was required to shoot right-handed so as not to get in other people's way; so I had to use the left eye to sight, and at the same time learn to manage to sling using the right shoulder. I remember being examined in signals by the chief boatswain's mate. He asked, "On Sunday morning, what do you think about the pennant flying?" I said, "Well, a church pennant is the only one allowed to fly above the American flag, so I presume the church pennant is flown." This was the right answer. He asked, "What does the chaplain do on Sunday morning aboard a ship at sea?" "Well," I said, "The chaplain on a battleship comes up onto the main deck, walks around and goes below. Then he says, 'On account of the inclement weather, there will be no religious service this date. Pass the word, Boatswain,'" He thought this a good joke, and I suppose it was. I certainly remember that when I was on the battleship *Mississippi*, we had divine service about once in three months.

While at San Pedro, we had various duties in addition to our training. One was standing guard on some of the passenger ships. I got to be a platoon leader, and then, temporarily, a company commander. I enjoyed it all, but at times got terribly bored; there really wasn't much to do. I got away from base on weekends, but I seldom went back to Highland Park because our home there was gone and so were my friends. It was a slow life until I got into officers' training class.

Prior to this, officers had been "made" by selection. A man was told, "Tag, you're an ensign," bought himself an officer's uniform, and shipped out. I recall one young fellow I knew who had family connections; he was given a stripe and a half, just like that. It was "Tag, you're a junior lieutenant." He was a good-looking fellow, and his uniform sported a staff tassel over the shoulder because he was made an aide to the commander of the 12th Naval District. Then came the time when, for some reason, he was called on to take charge of a small naval vessel at night, across San Francisco Bay. He ran a red light, nearly bringing about a terrible accident, and that is when they discovered he was color-blind.

I decided that, even though I was only twenty-one and had no math higher than trigonometry, nor any astronomy or navigation, I would try for officers' class. I went to the officer of the day and asked how to go about it. He pointed to a little house at the end of the dock and told me to go there and tell whomever was there that I wanted to try for officers' school. When I walked in, a couple of young officers were there, doing nothing, sitting with their feet on the desk, gossiping. I saluted them, and told them why I was there. I was handed a form, which I filled out, and then they began asking me questions—the silliest, most foolish questions, I thought, that I was ever asked, but I answered them courteously. They said then, "That's all, we will let you know."

A few weeks passed, and in came the battleship *Oregon*. This old ship, built about 1898, had not been in the Spanish-American War. She had steamed around through the canal and arrived on the Pacific coast after the war was over. She sat extremely low in the water and, when she came in, was crowded with men all over the deck. The ship had been in mothballs up to World War I, and was then outfitted; whether it was ever commissioned, I don't know. But I was posted to her as a signal boy, so I was told to pack my dunnage. While I was doing this, someone came and told me I was on the list of those who had made the grade to go to officers' training. I went over, and sure enough, there it was. Some 150 of us had tested, and I think about forty made it. So, I went to the officer of the day and told him, "I have been posted as signal boy on the *Oregon*, but I just saw my name on the Officers' Training Camp list. What should I do?" He said, "Signalmen come a dime a dozen. Just unpack your dunnage. You're going to officers' training."

The course was three months, with an examination every month which was called the "flunk out test." We got rid of several students, perhaps a fourth, who flunked out. Some students were brought up from the San Diego Naval Base to fill the vacancies. About forty took the final examination. I stood number 26. The top few got to go on to Annapolis. Well, I passed, and there was nothing in particular for me to do. We were sent to San Francisco to get our commissions as ensigns, U.S.N.R.F. We were reserve ensigns, not regular Navy; our rank was not confirmed until after three months of successful service on board ship. I was first assigned to the old gunboat, *Vicksburg*. We were sent to the Gulf of Lower (Baja) California, sometimes called the Sea of Cortez. I was a watch officer, having to stand one watch in three, and also assistant to the navigator. I was assistant in charge of codes and secret information, which meant I got to know a bit more than the other ensigns and enlisted men about what was going on in the war. We were supposedly, and in fact, training gun crews, although we had another secret mission. This was looking for German wirelesses in Mexico. Many Germans had dual Mexican citizenship, and some of them were in contact with Germany. We put in to every little bay or port, and sent one or more officers with a few enlisted men ashore. I went ashore in a number of places.

On one of the occasions when we were at Guaymas, I said to a friend, "I'm going ashore to look up my old friend, Miss Morales." She was half German and half Mexican, and I knew the family lived somewhere back of Guaymas, and had a business in Guaymas. Miss Morales had been the close friend of a girl I used to take out as a senior in high school. My friend went along, but reluctantly. I had some high school Spanish, and had learned some at the ranch, so I learned from the local citizens that the Morales' place of business was at the end of the street, past the main part of town. It was a hay, grain and farm implement store. My friend, Joe, refused to go in with me. As I walked in, several men jumped to their feet and stood at attention. This surprised me, because we were generally not too well received in Mexico. I explained my visit in my high school Spanish, and was told that the Morales family was at the ranch. I said I had known Miss Morales at Westlake School for Girls, and wished to pay my respects to her and her family. They thanked me, and said they would convey them. Through the windows in front, I could see that Joe was pacing distractedly and beckoning me to come out. I made my exit after the exchange of various courtesies, including bows. Mexicans are very courteous people, and these were even more so than average. Joe hurried me down the street, and I asked why he was so shaken. He turned me around and said, "What do you see?" There flew the German flag on the building I had been in! I had been in a German Consulate, and Mr. Morales was a German consul! I suppose it might have made an international incident, but I told no one and heard nothing more about it.

A little later, relations improved, and the president of Mexico (or perhaps of the province) gave a big party for our officers at the hotel in Guaymas. At that time there were about five of our ships in the harbor.

So we beat our way up the coast of lower California and returned. We had about three weeks of heavy rain, fog and clouds, and only made about five knots through all this.

When we reached San Francisco, I found I had orders to the *U.S.S. Chew*, Destroyer No. 106. The ship was to have been ready to go out in September, but was several months behind schedule. In the meantime, I had two duties. First, I was assigned as an inspector at the Union Iron Works in San Francisco. They were building destroyers, among them the *Chew*. What I knew about being an inspector you could put, as Mom used to say, "In your ear," but I did my best. I went from there almost every morning during these first few months to get the crew together. I lived on Mare Island. Secondly, my permanent duty was to the *Chew*. I was to put together a crew for that destroyer at the Mare Island Naval Training Station, near Vallejo. I had a skeleton crew of about twenty experienced or semi-experienced men, though only one was topflight. This was the quartermaster chief petty officer, who had done duty in the English Channel and in the Atlantic. We had to add about a hundred men to this skeleton crew.

We got to know some very nice girls. I recall with pleasure a girl I went out with several times. She was one of the most beautiful girls I have ever seen. Her family was socially prominent, and I was invited to their home. I went out to the Twin Peaks area and found the location. As I neared the address, it was hard to credit that this was the home of such a cultured young woman. The house was old and weather-beaten, with a lot of steps leading up to it. A servant—Chinese, I believe—opened the door, and I nearly gasped aloud. There was a wealth of the most beautiful Chinese tapestries, antiques, oriental rugs, paintings, a regally handsome grand piano—no one ever saw a more artistically or magnificently-furnished home.

One Monday morning when I arrived at Mare Island, I thought, "Boy, something is very wrong!" It was, too. The men from my destroyer group had broken into a warehouse and found a five-gallon container of alcohol-based paint thinner. Though it was marked "poison," they drank it. Some twenty of the men were in the brig, and five were in the hospital, having gone blind from drinking that horrible stuff. I had to get the men out of the brig to report to

Washington, and report to my captain, Jacob H. Klein, Jr.—"Jakey," as we called him. Fortunately all of the men recovered, including those who had gone blind. All "did" ten days or so for their escapade.

I got to know the commandant of the Naval Training Station quite well, a man by the name of Miller. Captain Miller loved good music and had a first-class musician in charge of his orchestra, a very fat man who did not always wear his uniform as chief petty officer. His name was Paul Whiteman, the Paul Whiteman who was to become the first of the bandleaders of the so-called "Big Band Era." He was a fine musician, able to play not only the jazz that later made him famous, but excellent classical music, and his orchestra at the training camp was well trained in the classics.

When the war ended, Paul Whiteman was the first to ask to be relieved from active duty. He had the offer of a job that would pay him $1,500 a week. The request went to Captain Miller, who said, "Nothing doing. He'll wait his turn like everyone else." However, he was overturned by Washington, and in about three weeks Paul Whiteman was en route to his job at the Brown Palace Hotel in Denver.

One Sunday, a number of us, being a bit bored, wanted to get away and, having no car, we got one of the Crocker boys from the banking family to take us in his car to see the geysers in Geyserville, to the Petrified Forest, where we picked up some agate, and to other places. Someone suggested we go to a roadhouse near Vallejo which served wild duck. We had to wait awhile, but it was a beautiful place, and the duck was excellent. Unfortunately, I found my jaws were beginning to hurt, and I couldn't open them to eat. When I got back aboard the *Intrepid*, I looked in the mirror, and sure enough, my jaws were swollen. I realized I must have the mumps. I went to sick bay and was told to pack my bag, without speaking to anyone, and check into the hospital immediately. I was there about three weeks.

In time the *U.S.S. Chew* was completed. I was in the destroyer camp, and stood watch there. The influenza epidemic was on, one of the worst epidemics in our country's history. Everyone in the San Francisco area wore flu masks. It was a very virulent form of flu, often fatal.

During this period, part of the watch officer's duty was to make the rounds twice a night with some hospital apprentices and look into every tent. In fact, they were required to keep the sides of the tents up, whether for observation, ventilation, or as part of the treatment, I don't know. We woke everyone up to make sure he didn't have a temperature and felt all right. On one of my duty nights, there were twenty-four dead; on another night the death toll was thirty. Bodies were virtually stacked in the morgue.

After it was just about all over, I came down with the flu; unfortunately, I was in the flu ward when the ship was ready to leave. I was to have been assistant to Commander Pierce, the navigation officer, in charge of code books. But at embarkation time, I had a temperature of 102°; so, after all my work, I was left behind. They went directly around, then over to Turkey, where they were based on the Bosphorus until much later, about the time the treaty was signed. I felt very down about not being able to go; I really didn't think I was sick enough to have been left behind, and I greatly regretted losing my chance for a real war experience.

I had lost a lot of weight as a consequence of the mumps and flu. I was down to about 135 pounds, and they wanted me to build myself up. They recommended that I drink beer, or near beer, but I couldn't stand either. I did take a little wine, or hard liquor occasionally, but I've never been able to like beer. Well, they said I should play golf. The officers had a 9-hole golf course in back of the hospital area; they also had a ship's cook who was a golf instructor. It turned out he was no cook; he had been given the rating and the pay in order to keep him there. He was a professional golf instructor, and the officers were determined to keep him. It was dangerous to send him out as a ship's cook, but it was decided that was the only way he could get out. The chief yeoman, Glasgow, was the key to the situation, for Captain Miller certainly wouldn't allow his golf expert to get away. Well, one night after hours, a call came in for a ship's cook; he was to go out with the ship that same night. So, through Glasgow's enlisted men, we got our expert's papers, got him aboard a launch, and the ship was gone with our golf expert. I'm sorry about those who had to eat his cooking. I thought I might get caught in an investigation, but I was away for awhile, and the war was winding down.

After my destroyer had left without me, the war being in its final stages, it wasn't thought worthwhile to reassign me. I applied for discharge, wanting to get back to college. So, I was sent to the Port Guard at San Francisco, which operated from one of the piers. We were sent out as a routine matter to check every ship that entered San Francisco Harbor.

Three weeks later, my discharge came through, and I said goodbye to active service. I'd served a year and nine months, more than many or most who served in World War I, but I had had no chance to be a hero of any sort. I received a benefit of $60 on leaving the service. There were no schooling benefits or anything of the sort. I had no place to live, a few hundred dollars, and my decision to finish college and go on to law school.

# Chapter 5
## Back To School
## & Back To The Navy

*A* crying need at the time of my mustering out of the Navy was civilian clothes, specifically a couple of suits, since all I had were Navy uniforms. Fortunately, my Navy equipment included a fine overcoat. I had very little money at the time. My friend, Roy Carver, son of Los Angeles' most expensive tailor, was at Mare Island at the time, and he urged me to go to his father who, he said, would treat me well. I did so, and Mr. Carver was glad to see me, wanting, of course, to hear all about his boy. I mentioned my need of a couple of suits, and Mr. Carver assured me he'd make them for me at cost. We looked at various swatches of material, and I chose two, neither the least nor the most expensive. Mr. Carver would be happy to make up the suits for me, at only $175 for one and $225 for the other. I said I would think it over. I went downtown to Foreman and Clark, looked over what they had, and emerged with two suits which did me for quite a time. They cost me $35.

I found my old friend, Malcolm Morlan, and his new bride, Kit, living in a little bungalow in Highland Park. They were glad to see me, as I, them. His mother and father still lived in their old home, and Malcolm's room was vacant. Well, nothing would do but I move in there, and Mother and Father Morlan would take care of me. You bet! The room was on the second floor, dormers on the side, and with no ceiling. The windows had no glass, but there were screens, and canvas curtains to keep out the rain. There was a washbasin, but no toilet or shower; these were downstairs. The door led to steep back stairs. It was a nice room, and I moved in at the price of $18 a month for room and breakfast, not nearly enough, even then. We got it up to

$25. Sometimes I had dinner with them. They were very good to me, seeing that I had clean linen and giving sort of general supervision. I stayed there, going to college and law school, for three and a half years, until my marriage in 1922.

At that time, a pre-law degree was not required; that is to say, one could go to law school and take the bar examinations without having earned a liberal arts degree. I felt, though, that I wanted the educational rounding-out provided by a liberal arts course, as well as the professional degree, and I have never regretted this, although it meant a lot more work and time. So, I returned to Occidental, and eventually wound up with a schedule consisting of college classes in the morning, work at the Automobile Club of Southern California in the afternoon, and law school at night. The fact that I had lost a year and a half put me somewhat behind my classmates, though I had gained a little maturity, which helped me in buckling down to work.

At Occidental, the practice was to award eleven credits to returning servicemen in recognition of their service. Enrolling in February 1919, I had had nineteen months of service, whereas some of the returnees had as little as ninety days. I felt entitled to more than this minimal credit, and said so. They asked if I had done work or had schooling in the Navy that I could show or be examined for to receive extra credit. I took in my navigation notebooks, star, moon and sun sights, coastal sailing—all that I had been required to learn and to do in navigation. Dr. Smiley, of the mathematics department, looked them over and awarded me an additional eleven credits, with which I was quite satisfied, since it meant I could finish college in a year and a half. I must say that, in my new-found maturity, I had some regrets about my first two years in college. Had I realized then the importance of grades, or that I might have been Phi Beta Kappa, I would have worked harder. But I'd had a good time those first years.

Brother David was general counsel for the Automobile Club of Southern California, and building a large department. David said to me, "If you're going back to school, wait a few days. I've got a job for you to do in San Diego." The job he assigned me became not only my first work for the Auto Club, but my introduction to the law, and a very good one.

Still in naval officer's uniform, I went to San Diego with the assignment of locating and subpoenaing a sergeant and several men who had been stationed at Camp Kearney. It seems there had been some sort of gala in Oceanside, and most of the men from Camp Kearney, the nearby Army base, had been there watching the events. The sergeant and the men I sought had been standing on a corner when a little girl rushed out in front of them. A line of cars was approaching and one of them, though the driver jammed on his brakes, struck the child, badly injuring her. We had reason to think the child was mentally deficient, spastic or something of the sort. The plaintiff, however, contended that the child's mental problem was a result of the accident, and that the driver was solely negligent.

The war was over, the men were gone from Camp Kearney, and it was quite a difficult job to locate the sergeant. I finally found him driving a mail truck on the route between San Diego and Jolon, in the mountains on the route to Imperial Valley. He proved to have considerable respect for the uniform I still wore, and helped me locate the other men I sought. We subpoenaed them, and they were present at the trial. I was not, but the trial was good for me in a couple of ways. First, it showed me some things one should never do, and I've remembered the lessons. Second, it helped make my name as an investigator, and it wasn't too long before I found my pay raised at the Auto Club.

David, as chief counsel for the defense, put the sergeant on the stand first. After he had testified, the plaintiff's attorney (who should have known better, as he was an experienced trial lawyer) leaned back and said to the sergeant, "Now, just relax. I want to ask you a few questions. You saw everything, did you?" The sergeant replied in the affirmative. "Well, tell me again what you saw." This was, of course, the old trick of getting repetition in the hope of eliciting a different story the second time. The sergeant said, "I saw the cars coming down the street, and this little girl ran in front of them. The man in the car that hit her didn't have time to stop. The child was injured, and somebody grabbed her up and took her to the hospital. My men and I stayed and gave our names and addresses. This was while we were stationed at Camp Kearney."

Q.   How fast was the car coming?
     "Objection!"
Q.   Well, how far ahead did you see him?
A.   He would have been about 75 feet down the road when I saw him first. The child ran out at the last second, and the driver didn't have time to more than jam on his brakes.

Q.  Did you see him before the child ran out?
A.  Yes, I saw him coming.
Q.  Well, how fast was he going?
A.  I think it was about 35 miles an hour.
NOTE: Cars of that day had two-wheel brakes.
Q.  You're sure it wasn't 36?
A.  No, I don't think it was a bit over 35.
Q.  You seem very positive about that.
A.  Yes, sir.
Q.  Well, young man, just think of it, now. You say this man was driving about 35 miles an hour?
A.  Yes, I think that's the top estimate of his speed.
Q.  How far away did you see him?
A.  About 75 feet.
Q.  Well, now, suppose you just sit there and tell the court what you know about judging speed.

(One of the oldest of rules is that you never ask a question to which you do not know the answer). The sergeant proceeded:

A.  When I got out of high school, I went to work in a speedometer factory in Detroit. I worked there for two or three years, got into other mechanical work and started riding as a mechanic; those were the days of two-man teams, driver and mechanic. I tested various cars, particularly racing cars, then got to driving racing cars myself. Of course these all had speedometers, and it was very important that we watch and understand them. I drove in a lot of races, including the Indianapolis Road Races of (here he named the years), and became a timer at the Indianapolis Raceway, handling the checkered flag. I flagged down the winners and others in several races.

At this point the lawyer could have died, realizing how far he had put his foot into his mouth. But the sergeant went on:

I've also driven for every bigwig who came to Camp Kearney in the past year and a half. I've been official driver for all dignitaries, whether generals or nice old ladies, whether in a hurry or wanting to be driven slowly. If you'd like more of my qualifications for judging speed, perhaps I can think of some.

Q.  Well, that's enough.

They asked the sergeant if he had children of his own, which he did. However, when asked if he had been driving, and his own child had run out, whether he could have avoided him, the court ruled that he not answer. The Auto Club for the defense won the case, and all were very pleased. If anyone had thought of objecting to my being hired as an investigator, being the general counsel's brother, this changed their minds. So, after I came back from San Diego, I started in half-days for the Auto Club at $25 a month.

After mornings at Occidental, I'd study on the streetcar on the way to the Auto Club, where I worked from 1:00 to 5:00. Then, I'd head for law school, first at Southwestern because it had classes starting at 5:15. Later, I got to taking some classes at the University of Southern California, which had its classes starting at 7:00. The earlier evening class was more to my liking, since I could get through at 8:00 or half past, and then go home for a couple hours of study, or perhaps visit my young lady, Lois Shorten, until 10:00 or so before getting down to the books. Strange as it seems, I was getting better grades than I had gotten before the Navy, when I had nothing on my mind except college. I was beginning to hit my stride.

The Auto Club let me use a skinny little car; I think it was an Overland. They were supposed to be good for about 12,500 miles. I drove this in doing my work of drawing maps of accidents, seeing witnesses and so forth. After a while I graduated to a Dodge. It was secondhand, but better. I did not have it overnight. The Dodge had very hard tires; they carried about ninety pounds of pressure, and when one blew, it really blew!

As a rule when I got home at night, I'd find Mr. Morlan still up. We were good friends, and at times I would sit and play cribbage with him, which was a pleasure. I have very fond memories of the Morlans; they were the kind of people we call "the salt of the earth."

I had been doing pretty well with both my studies and my work, and had, in fact, been raised to $50 a month for half-days at the Auto Club, when the opportunity came to join a naval exercise as a reserve officer. The Pacific Fleet was to steam to the Panama Canal Zone, and there join the Atlantic Fleet for exercises off Panama and on down off the South American coast. So, from January to March, I was a reserve ensign in the junior ward room with the regular junior officers of the *U.S.S. Mississippi.* She was one of three new battleships, the others were the *Idaho* and the *Missouri,* that were the pride of the fleet. Each was over six hundred feet long and displaced in excess of thirty thousand tons. They had not been completed in time to see action in World War I.

Our captain was Captain Powers Symington, of the family which produced our Senator Stuart Symington. As a member of the junior wardroom and mess, I paid for my food and things of that sort. In addition to drills, navigation watches and normal desk work, I supervised two or three batteries of 5" guns portside. Our record in battle practice was not the best, but decidedly not the worst.

So down we cruised, and met the Atlantic Fleet at the Canal Zone.

I went across through the Canal on a Navy supply ship, just to say I had been to the Atlantic. Others did the same, and I recall that the supply ship's officers, not expecting us, had not prepared food for us. They had the galley make up an unbelievable number of ham sandwiches. Unhappily for me, the beverage was beer which I never liked.

The two fleets cruised down the Central and South American coasts, performing maneuvers on the way. Some of these I didn't fully understand. It may be that, as a reserve ensign, I was not taken fully into the admiral's confidence, but we heard later that the maneuvers were a success.

We ran into a heavy hurricane, with winds of more than seventy miles per hour. It became necessary for the destroyers to move from their screening positions into the lee of the battleships. Destroyers roll badly in heavy weather. I recall, from having taken out destroyers earlier, that a destroyer could roll 63 degrees and still right itself. I was on one in 1918–19, watching the gauges on our destroyer in a storm, and marking a roll of 53 degrees. These appeared to be rolling even further, and it seemed they could go clear over. They didn't— but it was a terrible storm.

Valparaiso, which we called Valpo, is quite interesting. As you approach along the coast of Chile, there are extremely precipitous mountains, bare and very high. These run all the way along the coast from Peru to Valpo, where there begins to be more rainfall, and foliage and trees become apparent on the mountains. But Valpo itself is quite dry. It is about as far south of the equator as Los Angeles is north. Down all that bare stretch of coast, there are only two things found that provide any reason to live or work there: the copper mines for which Chile is famous; and the guano, or bird droppings, which is highly profitable, the guano being perhaps the finest fertilizer in the world.

We had to drop anchor quite far out; there wasn't much of a bay nor much of a beach, though there was a fair-sized pier. Immediately past the beach are the vertical cliffs, which one goes up by means of asencions—elevators—which run all day and are very cheap to ride. The streets were dirty; little outhouses sat along the streets. These were for the general public, and were not segregated as to sex.

Although there were some business areas on the beach level, the people lived on top, and, at that time, Valpo had a population of a couple hundred thousand.

We officers were allowed to go ashore as we pleased when not on duty. Enlisted men were allowed to go ashore under supervision, supposedly, of the petty officers and shore patrols; the Navy did attempt to maintain some degree of order. At this time Prohibition was in force in the United States, and some of our enlisted men went too far, being able to get liquor freely in South America. There would be, literally, hundreds of them lying on the deck or passed out altogether. Elsewhere, many continuously hurled sexual inferences at girls. There were quite a number of such girls. On one occasion, another officer and I were in a shoe store when two came in and tried to strike up a conversation. Having a little Spanish, I could talk to them a bit, but the shoe store man was very amused; it seems they wanted us to come up to their rooms. Well, we didn't go.

In the capital city of Santiago, we put on a parade of sailors and marines. We were treated very courteously by the Chilean people, and I could get along better than most of our people because of my Spanish and some French learned in college. Spanish, of course, is the native tongue, but the French helped, too.

Most of Santiago's buildings were of adobe brick, and some of the better buildings appeared to have poured concrete walls. On one occasion I went to a department store. It was a beautiful building of some four or five stories. While I was there an earthquake struck. It rolled and rolled for about four minutes, while the clerks went on waiting on people, and no one paid any attention. I thought the walls, which were very thick, would crack, but no damage was done. Apparently, this was a very common occurrence. I bought a few remembrances to send back to Mother and some friends, including a Chaopina Indian rug which we had for many years.

I caught the night train back to Valparaiso on what we'd call a "milk train" that moved at about eight or ten miles an hour and made many stops. There was a passenger car that was full. A Chinese sat next to me and slept on my shoulder; I don't think I slept at all. The train was behind schedule and got into Valpo at about 6:30. With the help of the shore patrol, I got to my shipboard duties at 8:00.

I struck up an acquaintance in Valparaiso with the representative of an American tire company. He was from Akron, Ohio, and told me he had been down there a year and a half, and was very tired of it. He invited me to dinner at the best hotel in Valparaiso. People would go there for dinner at around ten o'clock and stay until midnight or so, the meal being served on and off through this period, with a long wait between courses. The orchestra played chiefly our popular American melodies. In these long waits there was nothing to do but sit, talk and smoke. He gave me an excellent cigar, the first I ever smoked. Well, that several-course Chilean meal was fine, but when I finally left, I was hungrier than when I'd gone in. Walking down the street, I passed a bakery; they were closed, but the men were there, cleaning and mopping up. I banged on the door, and they let me in. In a glass case there were some cookies and cakes. I pointed to some that looked good, and they said, "Si, Biscochos!" I bought a dozen and walked down the dock, stuffing them into my mouth. Really, they were wonderful—the best food I ever tasted!

I was surprised and upset by the contrast between the wealthy and the poor. A strike was brewing while we were there, and after we left, the longshoremen and other laborers did go out. They were terribly poor, and should have had better wages. Also, we learned the tariff was peculiar: while there was no tariff on diamonds and many other forms of luxuries, there was a tariff on shoes, locally-made or imported, and on wine, certainly both necessities. Yes, wine is a necessity there.

I'll always remember the day we left. All the senior officers wanted to go ashore. It was their last opportunity, so I was officer of the day on the *U.S.S. Mississippi*, that is, I was in charge. It was a long day, longer than the usual watch period. And, the *Mississippi* being one of the fine, big, new ships, we had open house for the local citizens. The Navy's shore boats plied back and forth to the beach, as did local harbor craft. The Chileans were most courteous, bowing, trying hard to make themselves understood, expressing their appreciation for being allowed on board. They were shown over a large part of the ship;

enlisted men guided them about, and petty officers explained the workings of various gear. I was, as I said, in charge when a big lighter came alongside loaded with "chocolate." I sent for the chief store-keeper, who looked at the shipping orders and said all was in order, that the load should be brought aboard and stowed in such-and-such a hold. He said it was for the senior officers' mess. I looked rather askance at the whole transaction, because the "chocolate" was packed in wooden crates in which one could see straw wrapping. Some of the boxes were labelled, "Se Tapa, Muy Buena," giving me the idea it was liquor. I suspected Chilean wines, which were very much in demand, and as I've said, this was the time when the United States had Prohibition. Well, I was only a reserve member of the junior mess. I began to suspect this might be why I was in charge, and no one else was there. So, what was I to do? Well, after all, I was doing my job, and the steward apparently expected it, saying it was chocolate. I let them bring it aboard and stow it in the hold; the steward signed for it, as did I, and away they went. The shipment was locked up and I forgot about it; that is, until I was back in Los Angeles. I believe I was in Coachella when there was an investigation. I couldn't be found for that investigation, either, and I wonder— did they really want me?

There were hundreds of visitors aboard, when in late afternoon people were just starting to leave, and somehow a story got around that the fleet was going to up-anchor at 5:00, regardless of whether the visitors were all off or not. I had the word spread that they would all be taken ashore, but for some reason there was panic. You never saw so many fine, courteous people turn so wild! They were like wild animals. I had to station armed men with fixed bayonets alongside the gangplank and by the gangplank entrance, because they couldn't be allowed off any faster than the boats could pick them up. There were a few minor incidents, but no serious problems. I was surprised, and greatly relieved, that we didn't have more trouble, because these people were truly panic-stricken.

We headed back up the coast toward Panama. On a very hot morning, we heard the cry, "Man overboard!" All the ships maneuvered in search pattern, but he was never seen. The story was that this man, who was on an oiler or supply ship, had reported to his Officer of the Deck that he was sick and couldn't stand watch. He was sent to the doctor who examined him and said, "You're all right. Here, take this pill and go back to work." Instead of going back to his watch, the man went to the stern of the ship and jumped overboard. So far as is known, he never came to the surface.

In the afternoon, from another ship came the cry, "Man overboard!" Maneuvers were made as before, and this man was never sighted, either. There were many sharks in those waters, and perhaps one got him; he was listed as "lost." With two men overboard, everyone was in a most disturbed state of mind. Officers were pacing up and down all of the ships. Sure enough, at about 5:30 p.m., again came the cry, and number three was lost. Like the other two, he was never found, or even seen, though boats were lowered and an extra wide search was made. Still, strangely, with the third man gone, the nervousness subsided, and the pacing stopped; everything soon returned to normal. The old superstition that things happen in threes seemed to have been fulfilled.

At night the battleships steamed "in line." Each ship had a blue stern light to mark its position; otherwise they were completely dark. They steamed at an interval of about 100 feet, and engine revolutions had to be carefully synchronized to maintain interval. We reserve officers stood one watch in three, besides doing our regular location sights, moon and star sights, keeping our notebooks, seeing to the watertight doors, keeping everything properly policed, and so on. At night, we had to assist the Chief Watch Officer as directed, which included keeping watch that the interval was maintained. One night I was on watch when I observed that the enlisted man who stood bow watch did not seem to be watching; his duty was to keep watch on the ship ahead. These men stood watch of only an hour or so at a time, because they had to be constantly alert. I called this to the attention of the Officer of the Deck, and he agreed I should investigate. I went up to the man and passed my hand in front of his eyes. Sure enough, he was asleep, though his eyes were open. This was serious; a crash would have terrible consequences in damage to the ships, and would undoubtedly bring about a general court-martial. I shook him awake and talked to him for a few moments to make sure he was back in our part of the universe. I then reported to the watch officer, who relieved the man immediately and sent him below. He could have been in serious trouble, but our executive officer decided on a deck court, which can only issue a maximum of ten days' punishment. So, he got off fairly lightly. I tried to be as easy as I could, but I had to testify against the man.

Another night when I was on duty, a gale-force wind came up. It was my duty to get the deck awnings "housed," that is, taken down and properly stowed away. I broke out the boatswain's mate, a chief petty officer, and he got the men out of bunks to house the awnings. Well, they were sleepy and tired, and perhaps thought they could get away with something; in any case, they were doing a very poor job of folding and stowing. I got hold of the bosun's mate and "chewed him out" a bit, reminding him that it was his job to see that the men did the job properly, used proper knots and so forth. I did it rather quietly, but I also reported the incident. Later, he came to me and apologized, and I let him off easily. But there was some satisfaction in showing him that one of the "insects" as they used to call us, knew what to do, and could, and would, tell him off. Perhaps he thought he could get away with it because I was only a reserve. The Officer of the Deck backed me up, as was proper.

On our return to Panama, we spent about ten days there. Several times I went in to Colon. One day another officer and I went by small boat to a nearby island. Coming back, our engine conked out, and we were becalmed in Panama Bay; the ship sent out another boat to tow us in. Another time it rained on us three times during the trip from ship to shore, a distance of about three miles. It is quite a climate.

When we got back to Long Beach Harbor, I learned that my father had had another heart attack at the ranch in Coachella, and I was therefore excused from going on to Bremerton with the ship. I went down to the ranch and helped out for about three weeks, until Father was able to be up and around.

Returning from the desert, I reported to the ship and to Captain Symington. He was very considerate, saying they were always willing to grant leave under such circumstances.

Before returning to school, I had a chance for a vacation trip. Thinking I might, very probably, never have a chance for a trip of the kind again, I took it. With a college friend named Howard Edgecomb, I went to the mountains. We both loved to fish, and we rented a couple of burros at Hume, California, where we had gone from Fresno. At Hume, there were a sawmill, a store and the big trees–Sequoia Gigantea, the mountain redwood. We had gone to Fresno by train and taken a bus from there. This bus was an old Packard with a twelve-cylinder engine. The driver told me it had been old when he got it, and he had driven it 400,000 miles. It still sounded good.

As you will have gathered from my accounts of trips with Father, we had to work a lot harder for our fun in those days than one does today, what with cars, off-road vehicles, campers and the like. We took two burros and went up the Kings River Canyon. Amid the giant sequoias, they were growing young sequoias, and they were beautiful, as was the entire area. The young trees were ten to twelve feet tall; they stood along the trail, and a stream kept them constantly wet. We went up the trail alongside the Kings River for perhaps seven miles.

Kings Canyon is sometimes called "Little Yosemite." There were high cliffs on each side of this beautiful stream, the main of three branches of the Kings River. On each side there was room to walk, but not a lot more. Streams made falls from the high cliffs on either side, which looked to me to be several thousand feet high. We followed the Kings Canyon trail to the branching trail that led to Bubb's Creek, following our geodetic survey maps. We wanted to fish for golden trout, so we had to climb up the side, switching back and forth across several small streams until we got to the pass, then over the pass to Woods Creek. We went to Corral Meadow, but it seemed a little dry; also, it was sort of a packing station, so we moved back to Bubb's Creek to camp and to fish, and it was very good.

The first night we tied the burros down by the grassy meadow, thinking they would be very content with the lush grass by the stream. They were, as it turned out, very unhappy, and we soon learned why. There were enormous mosquitoes near the stream, and they bit the soft noses of the burros. We took them up the side of the mountain for the night, and soon the braying stopped.

Even though we never fished all day, we caught far more fish than we could eat, so, having brought plenty of salt, we dried a lot of fish, hanging them in the sun after cleaning and covering them with salt. They were beautiful fish, most of them of the golden variety. We picked a lot of the spiny, prickly gooseberries and made jam of them. We had brought far more sugar than we needed, and we made quarts of the jam.

I let my beard grow, and it was red. I was surprised to see that I was, even then, beginning to get some gray.

It was, too soon, time to return. My leave of absence was over, and

I went back to the Auto Club and to school. I felt all had worked out well; I had had my cruise and, probably, my last big fishing trip. It was time now to take up the main threads of life again.

# Chapter 6
# The Auto Club
# & The Law

1922 was quite a year. In that year, I finished my work at Occidental, went to work full time at the Auto Club, took, and passed, my bar examinations, became engaged, and got married. Lois Shorten had been brought into the Auto Club by David, then its chief counsel, and was actually making more at the time than I—$175 per month, while I was making $150. We had agreed, though, that she would give up her job when we were married, and after the October wedding she did so, to take care of the much more demanding job of homemaker. She had the care of her very ill mother, who lived with us until her death a few months after we were married. I continued my work at the Auto Club, and, of course, my responsibilities increased rapidly.

At that time one did not have to be a lawyer to try cases in justice court, that is, before a justice of the peace. I tried a few such cases, but not many, before I was admitted to practice. It was good training. These were not personal injury cases, but accident cases involving damage to automobiles. Actually, during this period I had offers from two or three other places, but preferred for the time to stay with the Auto Club. I got to the place where I was preparing the investigations of all cases involving uninsured automobiles, and this was quite an assignment. We tried to settle all such cases, and if we couldn't settle them, we advised the client to go elsewhere. But we did the investigations, located the witnesses, took their statements and did whatever else was required, including drawings of the locations involved. This was part of the service at the time; however, shortly after I left, a disagreement arose with the Bar Association, or State Bar. Their contention was that our investigating and "advising" the individual to get his own lawyer, when we couldn't arrange a settlement, was practicing law.

There were a great number of cases involving streetcars at this time. These were usually of no great importance; often a fender would be torn off by the steps, or cowcatcher, of a streetcar. The steps, at front and rear entrances to the streetcars, tore off quite easily. They were made of wood and so constructed as to sever readily. It didn't cost a great deal of money to replace them, and automobile fenders in those days were not too expensive. They could be unscrewed, taken off, pounded out and run through a flattening machine, painted, the paint baked on, and then the fender replaced, for about six to ten dollars.

One day I had a call from a man waiting for service in a garage. He reported that a man in the garage, having had his fender damaged, was demanding a new fender. The garage man told him the damage didn't warrant a new fender; the old one could be repaired. He explained that under his auto insurance contract, he was obliged to repair a fender if its condition made that feasible. Obviously, this would be cheaper. The man insisted, "No, I am to have a new fender. I want a new fender." This was refused, whereupon the man picked up a baseball bat lying nearby, and went to work on the fender. After smashing it thoroughly, he said, "Now, give me a new fender!" It was at this point that my caller phoned me at the Auto Club. I rushed down to the garage, but, unfortunately, the man had left, so we didn't catch him. I never did know the final outcome.

The head of the Claims Department of the Los Angeles Railway was the father of a fellow I had known at Occidental. Mr. McRoberts was an adjuster, and he and I used to stack up our files and cases in our respective offices until we had about fifty matters each. We would meet about every six weeks to go over the files. We were very frank with each other, opening our files to each other's inspection, and were able to settle most matters. I found it was a standard practice of the L.A. Railway (which is to say, McRoberts) to offer about 50% under the then-laws of negligence. We didn't have "comparative negligence" then; one had to be entirely free from causal negligence in order to recover. So, the temptation was to double the expense and thus get an amount sufficient to cover the true amount of the bill. We didn't do that, but we joked about it.

It was my duty to open a file on each automobile accident, and I had temporary charge of two to four hundred new cases every month. In each case, the report would be taken, by me or another, and I would then look it over and decide what was needed to start the investigation and complete the file. I would make notes for my secretary; I had a highly capable one at the time, and she had two or three girls under her. As I went through a file and made instructions as to what was to be done, I would put each file on the desk for the secretary. She would note in the book the times for each to be done; e.g., we allowed eight days for bills to be in, so many days for a reply from our member, so many for a reply from the other side, and so on.

I have a type of mind that served me well in this assignment. One glance at a file would recall all the particulars of a case to me. This ability, or gift, was very helpful in college, too. On reading a book or attending a lecture, I made notes of what I thought important. I found that, before examinations, a few minutes with my notes would pretty well bring back what I needed to know. I'm afraid I was guilty of trying to outguess my teachers as to what they would figure important and make the subject of later exams. But, in truth, I usually guessed right. After the exam, or later, after handling the matter in the file in question, the subject would leave my mind again. Considering the volume of work that had to be done, this proved a very happy talent. I tried very few cases as the work kept me more than busy. I did take charge of the work with certain insurance companies and with the Los Angeles Railway.

My first civil case was before I was admitted to practice. There had been a motor car collision, with considerable property damage, right in the center of Camarillo, California, then a little town. At that time, there was no municipal court, and the justice of the peace of Camarillo was the barber. We (the Auto Club) sued a Camarillo resident for loss of use damages to our client's car. The Auto Club subrogated to the right of the man insured by it. I suppose they thought it would be a good case for me to try my wings on, since it looked "open and shut."

The insured, now my client, and I went up on the morning of the case. We found that a room adjoining and opening into the barber shop had been turned into a courtroom. There were about fifty seats, all full, and people standing all along the walls. The defendant was not present. The barber, as justice of the peace, sat at the head of a table. The defendant was a well-thought-of fellow who had answered in pro per; that is, for himself, without a lawyer. He was not present, so the barber took us into his shop, where we talked for a time and returned to the courtroom, crowded by reason of local publicity. By ten o'clock, the defendant had not appeared, so we talked and killed time until about ten to eleven. I then got up and moved the judge to enter judgment for me by default, saying I would put my witness on the stand and prove the case to show we were right. The barber was a quiet old man, a farmer type, and apparently a man of good judgment. He looked at me and said, "Well, it's ten o'clock until it gets to be eleven o'clock. I know he's going to be here. He told me he was going to the public library to the law section." I thought this a bit strange, but agreed to wait, and shortly, in came the defendant. He had a lot of papers which he had copied out by hand, including a demurrer. He had copied out all the grounds for a demurrer that he found in a law book—very long—stating all the reasons recognized by law, but not in any way specific. He passed this up to the barber-judge, and I looked it over, too. The judge said to me, "What about it?" I replied, "Well, he has merely stated a lot of grounds from the textbook; it is not in proper form. In any case, he is too late in filing the demurrer; it has to be done before answering, or with his answer, and within ten days of the time he was served the papers in that County." I read the applicable section to the judge, and he said, "Well, that's right, it has to be done within ten days if served in the County or thirty days if served outside." And the judge ruled with me, saying, "Let's go ahead and try the case."

We did so, and finished a little before noon. Several witnesses testified as to how the accident happened, and I questioned a repairman as to the damage and time necessary to repair the car. The judge simply sat there, and it got to be around 12:30. Finally I said to my client, "What do you think we ought to do? Shall we take him out and show him where the accident happened?" He agreed, it being only about a block to the scene. We got one of the townsmen to suggest this, and all trooped out. The various witnesses then pointed out the places where the rubble had been found, where they had been standing, where the accident occurred and so on. On the way back, the judge took me by the arm, and we walked away from the other people. He said, "You're entitled to recover, but I feel kind of sorry for this fellow. Can't you cut down the amount a little?" I said, "Well, we'll cut out the claim for loss of use. I have no authority to go beyond that."

Actually, I didn't know whether we'd proved any damage by loss of use, so we may not even have been entitled to collect that part of the claim. He got up on the bench and announced, "Well, this has been a difficult case, a very difficult case." I thought, without saying, that it hadn't seemed so to me. He went on, "I have been giving it a great deal of thought. The defendant was wrong, and the plaintiff is entitled to recover, and is awarded the amount of his bills." I think there were one or two other little items. I stood after this, and said, "Your Honor, while I am up here, may I have a judgment entered, and a writ of execution issued? I have the papers ready." He asked, "What's this all about? Why do you need this?" I explained that I didn't want to have to travel back and forth, get a writ of execution, levy on the defendant's ranch, and take all those steps to collect. But the justice of the peace said, "Oh, you don't have to do those things. I've known this fellow for years, and I'll get his check and send it to you." Sure enough, in a few days in came the check. Included was a note from the justice of the peace, saying, "I have made entry that the judgment has been paid in full." So, perhaps, he had a good way to handle these matters; better than the formalities we go through in downtown Los Angeles.

I continued with the Auto Club for two more years after Lois and I were married. However, it was increasingly borne in upon me that, as a trained lawyer, I belonged in the practice of my profession. I had decided that the best entree, and perhaps the best practical training, was to be had in the field of public practice, and to that end I laid my plans.

Before Lois and I were married, I had bought a lot on Pine Street in South Pasadena. Claude Faithfull, the architect, married a woman who had lived with the Albert Shortens while going through Normal School. He gave us the plans and the supervision of construction of our new house as a wedding present. Faithfull was, I think, head of the architecture department at USC at the time, and the stubbornest man you ever saw. Nothing would do but that he build us the kind of house that he knew we should have. Well, the house cost more than we'd planned, yet it didn't have a downstairs bedroom. This posed a problem, because Lois had to care for her ill mother. Nevertheless, the house was an attractive one, an architect's house so to speak. We had hoped to move right in upon our marriage, but it wasn't finished, so we had to wait a few weeks. When we did move in, we put a bed in the living room for Lois' mother. Unhappily, she lived only a few weeks after that.

I was admitted to practice in 1922. In December of 1923, I wanted to go into the county counsel's office, but at the time there were no openings. I spoke to the "boss" there, Edward T. Bishop. He said he could do nothing for me since he had to take his new deputies from the list of eligibles. He suggested that I take the examination for deputy public defender, which was being given in three weeks. He said I might later get into the county counsel's office by transfer. So, I signed up for the examination. In law school, we had not been required to take Criminal Procedure, and I had not taken it. I had taken Criminal Law, as required. So, I studied Criminal Procedure for those three weeks, not only reading the code, but reading Charles Fricke's book on Criminal Law. Fricke had written the book while an assistant district attorney, and he later became a judge. The book was then in about its third or fourth printing, and there were more; the last one or two were brought up to date and edited after Judge Fricke's death. He was on our Los Angeles County court for a number of years, and was considered the dean of the criminal judges. I got to know him quite well.

I believe I stood third in the examination of some forty who took it. George Benedict, who was number one, was immediately appointed. Thanks to an action by the Board of Supervisors, two more positions were created in the Public Defender's Office almost immediately, so Charles Fulcher (who had stood second) and I were appointed. This was early 1924, and I continued in that office until 1926, when I took the examination for county counsel. Here I stood second, and soon was appointed. I stayed there about a year and a half, until 1927, when I went with the firm of Faries and Williamson. During that period, I taught for about a year, part time, at Southwestern University Law School.

The first criminal case I tried was a "hopeless" one. I think this may have been office practice; that is, to give the new man such cases. In this way he wouldn't be accused of having "lost a good case," nor would the records of the older men be impaired. My first criminal client, then, was a little old man who had been discovered by the police while "beating the bushes" down in the old Los Angeles River bed. At that time, before the flood control measures, a lot of brush, including wild tobacco trees grew down there. The head of the arresting officers was a corporal or sergeant named Stone. They had come upon this person who was, I believe, a narcotics addict. He had a long nail on one thumb, under which he had cocaine. I called attention to this. He was quite dirty as to appearance. He had had with him two young children, boys of about five and seven, and was charged with having committed lewd and lascivious acts upon the bodies of both. Stone had apparently been enraged, and had beaten the fellow on the spot, which he should never have done. So, I was required to defend this apparently open-and-shut case. Because of his age, which disqualified him as a witness, I succeeded in keeping out of the trial the testimony of the younger boy. However, there was a conviction of such acts upon the older boy. I believe the judge instructed the jury to find the defendant not guilty with respect to the younger boy. These cases are very inflammatory, and the judge, district attorney, and defense counsel must be very careful.

The whole record of what took place went up to the California Adult Authority, who would then know the entire story. Thus, the single conviction didn't make too much difference, nor did the district attorney mind it. The entire story would be considered by the Authority in determining the length of the offender's sentence.

The judge in the case was Walton J. Wood. He had been the first public defender of Los Angeles County; this, I believe, meant he was the first public defender in the United States. He said to me, "Well, Faries, it was pretty bad. You certainly didn't do well on that case, but I think you ought to be a good lawyer some day. Just keep working at it, and you'll get there; you'll be all right." I took his compliment and his evaluation to heart, and I believe it helped me, even though my first criminal case hadn't exactly covered me with glory.

Another early case was that of a young man charged with being party to robbery committed by an older man, which is to say accessory before the fact. His defense was that he had not been acquainted with the man committing the robberies, but a victim of circumstances. He said he had been parking his car when the man appeared, stuck a gun in his side, and said he would kill the defendant unless he did as told. They drove some distance; then the man had the defendant stop and wait while he got out and robbed a person, then got back in the car. This was repeated. The defendant said he had never seen the robber before and had been afraid the fellow would shoot him unless he complied with orders.

In the first trial, the jury disagreed. Parenthetically, in those days jurors were kept at their deliberations in the evening. Today, they are locked up in a hotel, have their meal and recreation, and don't deliberate until the following morning. On the occasion of the second trial, I happened to walk down a side hall past the jury room while deliberations were going on. I saw my friend, James Costello, the deputy district attorney, standing on a chair by an open transom, listening to what went on in the jury room. Well, this was not right, so I got in touch with the judge and took him around and showed him what was happening. He then called everybody in and, to my surprise, declared a mistrial.

The case came up for trial the third time, and again, the jury disagreed. On the fourth trial, there was a change in tactics. The district attorney was very anxious to convict this young man, as were the police, so the district attorney held back a lot of evidence, thinking to use it in rebuttal after I had made my defense. However, feeling that the district attorney had not shown sufficient evidence to convict, I thought it wise to rest, giving no evidence. This I did, but to my surprise, the jury returned a verdict of guilty.

I immediately filed an appeal, my first. I worked very hard on my briefs, and had four points I thought were excellent. The case was assigned to Justice Lewis R. Works, presiding justice of the Criminal Court of Appeal for our district.

The decision of Justice Works came down, and I hastened to read it. As was his custom, he had written a very short decision. He said, "The plaintiff (that is the people) failed to connect the young man with the gun found in the back of the car. Therefore, a new trial must be had in this case." He didn't even consider any of the four points I had made, all of which were good. The decision went on, "Therefore, it is not necessary to consider any of the other points raised by the defense." I was quite crushed, though, of course, happy that I had won my first case in appellate court.

In the final outcome, we compromised by not sending the young man to the penitentiary, but instead, having him sent to the county jail for some lesser offense than robbery. I believe he was sentenced to two years, and served approximately one.

Very often defense counsel is in such a position. Any person has a right to be defended if he insists he is innocent. He must not be allowed to go on the stand and perjure himself when his counsel knows the testimony to be perjury. He should be kept off the stand if, for instance, he has admitted the crime to his lawyer. Even so, he is entitled to have a jury decide guilt or innocence, and not the lawyer assigned to his case.

Often the most interesting cases are not those reported by the media. The newspaper reporters would make their rounds, stopping for a few minutes in each court. They would go to the clerk and ask if there was anything of interest going on . Having to cover perhaps fifty courts each day, they could spend only five or ten minutes, even where there was a story that might be of interest to them. *Time Magazine*, I think, said at one time, "The story is the thing." This would seem to indicate that facts and accuracy are secondary.

It was, and is, common police procedure to put out dragnets when something seems to be in the wind. Perhaps irregularly, they go through the cheaper hotels. It is common for young men, who come to the city to look for work, to stay in such places. Having nothing to do, they may sit around and talk to the people there. It may happen that one of them says to such a young man, "I'm going away for a few days. May I put my suitcase in your closet so I won't have to pay rent on my room while I'm gone?" Perhaps the fellow has taken the young man out to dinner, or otherwise, seemed to befriend him. So, he agrees to keep the property. About that time the police go through the hotel, and it turns out the suitcase contains burglar's tools, or other stolen goods. The young man is arrested and charged with possession of the material. Oh, one knows about constitutional rights, warrants, the showing required, and all those things. Warrants, including "John Doe" warrants, were not, and are not, too difficult to get, particularly when the persons involved are probably suspects. The youth involved might be quite innocent, having no background that would cause suspicion, but is lacking an adequate explanation. He is called upon to explain how he earns his living and pays the rent. If not working, he is very liable to be found guilty of possession of burglar's tools or stolen goods. The presumption is, as a rule, that one not working and in possession of such things has used or intends to use them, so very often, young men were arrested when guilty of nothing more than consorting with the wrong people. Isn't the old saying, "Evil communications corrupt good morals?" There is also the fact, that since these persons have been in the company of criminals, the police want them to talk, perhaps making their job easier. In light of these things, we in the public defender's office were very scrupulous in trying to weed out those who should be pleaded "guilty" and those who should be pleaded "not guilty." Yes, we did, even in those days, use "plea bargaining."

I really did not enjoy working in the public defender's office. I had never intended to practice criminal law. I was doing it while awaiting a chance to get into the county counsel's office.

Bill Aggeler, the head of the public defender's office while I was there, later became a judge. Few judges were more strict or gave more severe sentences than William Tell Aggeler. Bill was much loved; juries would become very fond of him. He was the lawyer in the Mary Pickford kidnapping case, when he had five of the jurors crying.

That picture of five jurors weeping as they sat in the box and listened to arguments in favor of the young man who had gone wrong by associating with the kidnappers in the Pickford case, will always be with me. They did convict him, but he was given a lesser sentence than the older members of the gang. Does it seem strange that jurors will convict, even when their emotions are so torn that they are in tears? I don't find it so. Jurors, as a rule, try very hard to do justice. Contrary to what I've heard people say, they are usually very hard to sway from what they think is right. It is always a tip-off to a judge when lawyers, at the start of a trial, begin excusing people of apparent common sense and capability. He knows the lawyer trying to get rid of such people must have a reason; generally, that there is some weakness in his case, and he is going to try to befuddle the jury, or gain their sympathy.

At the time Bill was heading the public defender's office, a "hot" subject was the creation of an Adult Authority to determine the time prisoners should be held after minimum sentence had been served. The statute proposed was adopted, and the Adult Authority is still with us, though under a different name, I believe, and its power has been diminished by statute. At the time, everyone was talking about the subject. Under the statute being considered, a prisoner's whole record would go up when they were sentenced to the penitentiary, and would be reviewed after they had served their minimum time. The Adult Authority was in charge of this review. They would consider the entire record and then fix the balance of time to be served before parole, or the amount of time on parole, or both. The subject was an important one, and the Los Angeles Bar Association scheduled a debate. The spokesman opposing the Adult Authority, and the indeterminate sentence, was Judge Carlos Hardy, who took the position that the judge who had heard the case and listened to the witnesses and looked into the eyes of the defendant should, as an experienced man, a well-qualified judge of human nature, be the one to pronounce the time to be served. He maintained that the public would prefer the giving of definite sentences. When Bill Aggeler spoke, he seemed to be going all around the subject, but toward the end, the parts of his humorous recital began to fall into place, and all could see what he was getting at. Without question, he won the debate hands-down. He had been better prepared, and along the way he had his audience thinking with him. I am sure this is one of the reasons that the indeterminate sentence was adopted at the time. It was shortly thereafter that Aggeler was appointed to the bench, and rightly so.

It was a common thing on my part, and on the part of many lawyers, to become well acquainted with the court clerks, because in this way one could learn a great deal not only about the judge, but about the trying of cases. Judge Walton J. Wood's clerk was a quiet sort, but he told me, "If you try a case before Judge Wood, remember two things. First, he is a little deaf and won't admit it, so always be sure he is looking at you and you at him when you speak—and speak up. Secondly, he is an excellent lawyer, and too fast for most lawyers, so when he starts to say something, you shut up. Don't say a word until you know he is through with what he is going to talk about." I followed his advice, and it worked very well with Walton Wood—in fact, it is a good practice with any judge.

There was a period during which I was called upon to "clear out the jail" daily. In other words, I had the job in the public defender's office of answering all the jail inmates' requests for legal advice which came into that office. There was a box in which prisoners could put these requests, and I picked them up daily. On request, I would talk to these people personally. One who called on me was a very intelligent older gentleman, in jail for shooting over the heads or, perhaps at, the people in a Willowbrook area restaurant. The neighborhood was quite poor and very populous. It seemed this gentleman had been put out of the restaurant and told not to come back.

They told him to stay out, in no uncertain terms. He went home and got his .22 automatic rifle, which was equipped with a silencer. He shot, he claimed, over the top of the restaurant, after calling the people out and threatening them with being shot if they again bothered him. The operators of the restaurant contended he had shot at them, but I doubted it, because he was undoubtedly an excellent rifleman. It also developed, that at night this man would walk the area streets, carrying a Philippine blowgun, some six feet long. He claimed to have learned its use in the Philippines in the 1898 war, and could kill a person with a blown dart. So far as we knew, he had never done so.

However, the sheriff's people had told me that two children in the vicinity had been killed by bullets from a .22 rifle, and that no shots were heard at the time of the killings. In those days, the science of ballistics was not so well understood as today, and we could not tell if a bullet was from a particular gun unless it was "fresh." In any event, the sheriff's office was anxious to have this man behind bars for as long as possible, because they believed him responsible for the deaths of the children. I became well acquainted with this man. He was highly intelligent, and he was impressively capable of handling figures. One could reel off a dozen four-digit numbers and, without paper or pencil, he would rattle off their sum.

He claimed to be a first class telegrapher, and I believed him. He said he had won prizes as the fastest and best telegrapher in large areas. But as he talked, he began to tell me some very peculiar things. For example, he said that his brain worked best when the moon is directly between the earth and sun, or directly opposite the sun on a line through the earth. He said he enjoyed those periods of time, and would walk the streets all night long, his brain exceedingly active. I pleaded him not guilty, and contrary to his wishes, not guilty by reason of insanity. The trial on the subject of his guilt was before a jury; that on the subject of his insanity, before a judge. The same judge served in both matters; both were tried at the same time. The judge, Edwin Hahn, insisted on different lawyers for each matter. So Franklin Paden, of the defender's office, a very capable man, represented him on the insanity plea, while I appeared for him in the matter of shooting with intent to kill—that is to say, assault with intent to commit murder. The jury found him guilty of a lesser charge, that of assault with a deadly weapon, and the judge found him to be insane. Assault with a deadly weapon does not carry a long penitentiary sentence; it is in the discretion of the judge whether to send the convicted man to the penitentiary or to the county jail. The judge took us into chambers after the trial; he said that the man was unquestionably insane, at least at times, and experts had so testified. However, he felt that the psychiatric hospitals of the state were not really safe. No judgment was entered on the insanity, or it was set aside, and the defendant was sent to the penitentiary. After going there, he used to write to me about every month. I don't know how he got the letters out, but they got to me, telling me he was going to "get me" upon his release. The letters finally ceased, and I never saw him.

Although one hears most about judges being threatened, they are seldom killed by people they have sentenced. I believe the record will bear me out in saying that there is much more danger in defending or in prosecuting a criminal than in being the judge at his trial. The defense lawyer faces frequent danger; this is particularly true in domestic cases. Fairly often, lawyers are shot by people angered by a result of a domestic action. As an example, a husband is grieved by what happened with respect to his property, and the children go and shoot the lawyer. There is less trouble with that since the law which came into effect at about the time I officially left the bench. Now that marriages are dissolved, instead of being granted on evidence of extreme cruelty and the like, there is not so much vile testimony. But, there are still dangerous cases, and dangerous individuals.

I recall one case in which a very able woman lawyer was shot while she was taking a shower, and her career was ended. I believe her assailant was never discovered. Then, there was a friend, a very fine lawyer and a very fine man, who was killed by the husband of a client; and I can think of others.

# Chapter 7
# Jail Personalities
# & The Law

*I* have found in some of my old folders, a number of verbal sketches of interesting persons and cases collected from my days as a deputy public defender. Neither these persons nor their stories are of great significance in the march of human affairs. They do, however, throw some interesting sidelights on what a writer and commentator of the early days of radio called "The Passing Parade."

Gabriel Perez was brown-eyed, slender and of medium height, with impassive face, heavy lips and a thick, but well-groomed mustache. His hair was blue-black, and combed off the forehead back to the nape of his neck, where it was chopped off at right angles to his spine, as though with a butcher's cleaver. Having received a public defender slip from him, I gave the turnkey in charge of the cell gates a slip with his name and the numeral 4. This told the turnkey that Perez, in Tank 4, was wanted in "the screen." This was a wire cage extending out into the visiting room of the jail. After a few minutes' chat with Scotty, the deputy sheriff on the gate, I saw Perez approaching. This "screen" was actually composed of bars covered with a close netting of wire. The net was supposed to be sufficiently fine to prevent anything being passed to or from prisoners. Unfortunately, the man who first put it up did not know his business; soon a prisoner was caught at the rear "blowing snow" (dope) through it, so a second screen was added, 14 inches outside the first. The prisoner had to talk to his guest through the double screen, but as a deputy public defender, and perhaps the man's lawyer-to-be, I was allowed to talk to him inside the screen. We sat at a table, prisoner on one side, counsel on the other. An upright board between

supposedly prevented anything being passed. This was not too efficient, but did at least have a dampening effect on passing anything. I
felt sure Perez had talked with a lawyer there before. I asked, "Se
habla Ingles?" He indicated that he wanted an interpreter, so I called
to Scotty, "Let me have a two-way talker in Spanish." Out came a
prisoner, dressed not in the conventional blue denim, but in khaki,
denoting that he was a "trusty." This, by the way, is sometimes written "trustie" and "trustee." Such a person, however, is not a "trustee"
of anything, but a prisoner who has convinced the wardens that he
can be trusted, and is used in noncustodial jobs, generally being
allowed extra privileges. The man seated himself beside Perez, and
our conversation went like this:

Faries: Do you remember that this morning Judge Keyes
appointed me to be your lawyer?

Perez: (through Interpreter) Yes.

Faries: I read the charges and the information filed against you
by the district attorney, and the transcript of the testimony given at the preliminary hearing. (This was
repeated to Perez by the interpreter.)

Perez: Si, si.

Faries: Also, I talked to the deputy district attorney about your
case. Do you know what they say you did?
(All my statements were repeated to Perez, and all his to
me, through the interpreter.)

Perez: Yes, but I didn't do it.

Faries: You were charged with passing a fictitious, that is, a bad
check; in fact, several of them. Mr. Billeke says that in
June, eight months ago, you came into his grocery store in
the evening while he was eating dinner. He says his wife
was tending the store, and she called to him that you had
gotten a lot of groceries and wanted them to take a check
for about $36.00 for them. You said it was a paycheck.
They say this check was not paid, and they have told the
police that you got a lot of groceries once before; the
police say that they found a gun in your house. The district attorney has had a handwriting expert examine the
check and samples of your handwriting, and he says that
the endorsement on the check is in your handwriting.

Perez:     It could not have been; I didn't pass that check. I don't know him. I don't know that store, and I'm not guilty.

Faries:    All right, when the case goes to trial we'll plead you not guilty.

Perez:     Si, Senor. I have a wife and four children, and they are hungry. I want to care for them. Can you get me out of here, so I can care for them?

Faries:    No. You must tell me how to win this case, then you will get out after the trial. You have no money to make bail. What is your defense?

Perez:     I don't know; I did not pass that check.

Faries:    Do you remember where you were last June? Do you remember that month?

Perez:     Si. I was working. Putting out an advertising paper, little papers for a medicine man over in Mara Villa Park (a Mexican district about 10 miles east of Los Angeles).

Faries:    Fine, who were you working for?

Perez:     A man named Fillipe Renteria. There was another man working with us. I can't remember his name, but the medicine man we were talking about in the papers was Dr. Juan de Dios Garay. He prepared the medicine the papers talked about.

Faries:    Where did Garay get his mail?

Perez:     128 North Main Street, Los Angeles.

Faries:    Where did Renteria get his mail?

Perez:     The same place.

Faries:    Is professor Garay there now?

Perez:     I don't know.

Faries:    As a matter of fact, you do know that Juan de Dios Garay is not here, don't you?

Perez:     I heard he had gone to Mexico.

Faries:    Did you work with him on June 6th, the day the check was passed?

Perez:     Si, Senor.

Faries:    What hours did you work?

Perez:     All day.

Faries:    Did you work in the evening?

Perez:     No, not as a rule.

Faries:    What day of the week was June 6?

Perez:     I don't know.

Faries:    Do you think these men would testify for you? Would they testify you were working at 7:00 that evening, the evening of June 6?

Perez:     I haven't talked to them, but I'm…but if they remember they would.

Faries:    How long since you've seen these men?

Perez:     Not since last summer.

Faries:    Could they testify as to your good character?

Perez:     Oh, si, si.

Faries:    I wanted to ask you something else. Do you know Carabajal?

Perez:     Si. I knew him in El Paso.

Faries:    And you know that he is here. Have you known him here?

Perez:     A little.

Faries:    Do you know he is charged with two checks in the same court as you are? And that the amount of the checks in each case is within a few cents of the ones you're charged with passing? Did you know that?

Perez:     I don't know anything about that.

Faries:    Now, Perez, I'm sorry for you and your family. I want to do the best I can, but if you go to trial, you'll be convicted. It looks to me as though you haven't told me the straight story, and I'm going to tell you why. Dr. Juan de Dios Garay came to me some time before I took this job, as a proposed client in a civil matter. This was before your arrest. Also, he was convicted here, under his own name, in the federal court for this district. The conviction was for using United States mails in an attempt to defraud. I saw him leave for Leavenworth Penitentiary. As for Fillipe Renteria, he left here last summer and went to Chicago. He was convicted there of forging a number of checks, and he is now in the Illinois State Penitentiary. He confessed to giving and spending the money from false checks written out here, and he told about you and Jose Carabajal. That's how they found and arrested both of you. Carabajal is the man who worked with you, and whose name you could not remember. Right?

Perez:    I can't remember it.

Faries:   Well, I'm not trying to get a confession out of you. The district attorney told me that he felt sorry for you and Carabajal, because you were used by Renteria and de Dios Garay. I'm going to see how he feels about my recommending that you be allowed to plead guilty to obtaining money under false pretenses. That's a lesser offense, and under it you could get a county jail sentence. You could work on the Road Gang and earn a little money for your family. That would be better than the penitentiary, wouldn't it? No, don't make up your mind now; I'll see the D.A., and he'll consider it and let us know before Thursday. And we must enter a plea on that day. Is that all right?

Perez:    (In English, directly to me) Yes. Thank you very much.

I smiled a bit, and he saw the point. Well, I didn't mention it to the district attorney. However, later the district attorney said, "Absolutely not! He's a bad actor, and we will not reduce the charge." I never did ask anyone who stole the printed checks. I was always curious about it, but I was too busy to follow up on it. The things that happen in and around courts and go unpublished are often the most amusing.

•  •  •

Joseph Fainer, Esq., whose son became a fine judge, was a brash, fearless, "try-anything" kind of lawyer—the very prototype of the flamboyant courtroom personality. He had a big shock of graying hair, a mobile mouth, and a tendency to strut in court. For years, he represented Amie Semple McPherson, the controversial evangelist who built the great tabernacle near Echo Park. It will be remembered that she disappeared for a time, and the story was that she dove into the ocean near Carmel, California, and came up in the Arizona desert. She said she had had to walk many miles to civilization. I was among those many people who saw her when she arrived and was taken to the district attorney's office. She did, indeed, look very bedraggled, but I couldn't help noticing her shoes; not only were they not worn, they weren't even dusty!

At the time of my story, Joe was practicing criminal law, and was defending a young man. I don't recall the nature of the charge, but Joe was in his final argument for the defense. Suddenly, while addressing the jury, he knelt on one knee, exactly as Al Jolson did while singing "Mammy." He opened his mouth and, in a fine tenor, proceeded to sing, "Where is my wond'ring boy tonight? The child of my heart's tender care. My heart overflows, for I love him, he knows. Oh, where is my boy tonight?"

Of course, all this showmanship was a blatant attempt to play upon the sympathies of the jury, and certainly not proper. Had I been sitting as judge, I would have rebuked him, but I was not, and he got away with it.

• • •

The prisoner, Louis Wong, was a Chinese man of the old school. He was a typical opium-eater, thin and hipless, with the carriage of the letter "S" and very bad breath. He was being returned to jail from court, and on such occasions it is the duty of the turnkey at the wicket to "fan down" the prisoner; that is, search him for weapons, narcotics or contraband of any sort.

The turnkey first examined Wong's hat, then started fanning him down—feeling him from shoulders to bottoms of pantlegs. Suddenly, a transformation! Wong's eyes became slit-like; his lips drew back over his brown, loose teeth and his bad breath filled the air. The turnkey jumped back, "What's the matter, Wong?" "Me too ticklish!"

• • •

Chung Seng (or perhaps Hung Lee—there was some doubt as to his true name), though perhaps not guilty, had pleaded guilty to a charge of receiving stolen property, and made application for probation. He was charged with having purchased sacks of beans, knowing them to have been stolen. One would not have believed it to look at him. He was short, fat, smiling, had weak eyes for which he wore glasses with thin, iron frames; and he had the wit associated with his calling of vegetable peddler. These peddlers were fast disappearing, even in those days; we old Californians knew and liked their banal good nature.

Well, it developed that Chung, as he called himself, was a pillar of a local Methodist church. He had been in Los Angeles for twenty-five years, and in one place of business for sixteen years. He had money, good credit, a host of Caucasian friends, and no police record. "People vs. Chung on Application," said Judge Avery. "Is the defendant in court?" "He is, your Honor," said his counsel, Ray Cheesboro, later to become Judge Cheesboro.

Judge:   Come forward, Chung Seng.
            (Chung goes up from the empty jury box where he has
            been sitting.)
Chung:  Good morning, Judge Avery (bows as he speaks).
Judge:   (smiling back) Good morning, Chung Seng. Take that seat
            over there (points to witness box).
            (Chung Seng beams all over as he looks through his
            rimmed glasses at the courtroom.)
Judge:   How old are you, Chung?
Chung:  I think about 54 years American, 55 Chinese.
Judge:   How long have you been in this country?
Chung:  I think about 44 years.
Judge:   Have you ever been arrested before?
Chung:  (soberly) Yes, one time.
Judge:   Tell us about that.
            (The rows of attorneys at counsel table lean forward to
            hear.)
Chung:  Twenty-six years ago in San Diego. $2.00 fine. Ride bicycle
            too fast.
            (The bailiff made no attempt to quell the courtroom
            laughter for some time.)

● ● ●

Juan Castro was short, round-faced, heavy of lip and quick of eye. Of Mexican ancestry, he was not yet eighteen, or said he was not. He had an awful time getting corroboration of this, so as to have himself sent to juvenile court on his first offense. That court had put him on probation, and he was put on the train to go back to Mexico where, he said, he had relatives and friends. This was on April 1. About May 1, I received word that he was in jail and wanted me to come and see him again. Our conversation went like this:

Faries:   I thought when you left here that I was done with you for
            good. I had done you a good turn, and was glad to be rid
            of you. Do you like it here in jail?
Castro:  No, Senor, but my people are proud people, and they
            don't want me. So, I made my way back.
Faries:   Well, what are you in for this time?
Castro:  Stealing, same as last time.
Faries:   Why did you do it?

Castro:  Senor, you are my friend, and I will not lie to you. All my life I have lived by stealing. I don't know how to work. I want to, but I can't make myself do it.

Faries:  Did you commit this burglary to get back in jail?

Castro:  (shrugs his shoulders) No, Senor, I am here again, and I am guilty.

I saw Juan again, on his departure for reform school, where he had been committed for two years.

Faries:  What are you going to do up there?

Castro:  I will learn to work.

Faries:  (looks at him unsmiling) That's right. But if I find you in this jail again, I'll see that you get the Big House.

Castro:  Senor, I will not lie to you; you are my American friend. I would like to see you personally, but I will not do so again.

• • •

The following story was told to me by my then-boss, Bill Aggeler, and I believe it to be true. I have some doubt about the name, though Aggeler's word was always good, even when telling a funny story.

The unlawful appropriation of a horse, regardless of its value, was, under California statute, grand larceny and a felony. It made no difference whether the horse was a thoroughbred or a skinny plowhorse, insofar as the law was concerned. All this has its roots in earlier times, when a horse was much more important to a man's livelihood, or even to his life. Of course, the judge in a given case might take into account the actual value of the horse when handing down his sentence. This story, though, is about a spavined, swayback belonging to Captain Jim, a California Indian. It was not much of a horse, but probably important to Captain Jim.

Juego Bromo, a Mexican national who lived near the railroad tracks in Whittier, had spent Saturday evening and some of his wages in Jimtown. Jimtown was a Mexican area with a pool hall, and Juego had probably spent his time and money there. He was arrested, and the officers testified that he had stolen Captain Jim's horse on the Saturday night in question. In due course he appeared in Superior Court for arraignment and plea. He had no money or counsel, so Bill Aggeler was appointed to represent him. Juego was suspicious of his lawyer and insisted on pleading not guilty, but refused to tell his story (that is, the facts of the case) to Aggeler. He said, "I will tell it all when the time comes." This was through an interpreter, and later, in court, his testimony was via interpreter.

Clerk: State your name.

Bromo: Bromo, Juego Bromo.

D.A.: Where do you live?

Bromo: In Whittier, California, by the railroad tracks.

D.A.: What is your occupation?

Bromo: I work for a living, at anything.

D.A.: You have heard all the testimony against you?

Bromo: Yes, but it is not right.

D.A.: Well, what, if anything, took place on the evening of October 11?

Bromo: Sir, I speak only the truth. I was in Jimtown, eating and playing pool with my friends until late in the evening. The moon was gone down when I started home, and I walked up the railroad tracks. The night was cool and very quiet. I was passing a eucalyptus grove when I heard something behind me. It sounded like this (illustrates with foot and mouth): clump, clump, clump…getting louder. I was very frightened, for I knew there were bad men in the neighborhood, so I walked fast. I thought it would stop when I got out beyond the grove, but it did not. I was afraid until I heard a horse whinny. I hid my money under the lapel of my coat, pinning it into a bag, and then I turned to look. What was following me was the horse the officers were talking about. It had on a halter. I knew the horse was old Captain Jim's, and I tried to chase it back down the tracks, but it would not go, and I did not want to hurt it. Also, I thought a train might come along and hurt it. Three times I tried to chase it back. The fourth time it was almost up to me, and I saw there was a rope hanging from the halter ring. I thought how foolish I was; I should have noticed the rope before. I had reached the road leading to my house, and he was almost stepping on my heels. There was an Automobile Club sign and a stop sign near the railroad crossing, and I thought I would tie him to the signpost, so he would not get lost. So I took hold of the rope, and just as I did, the officers came along the road and arrested me. So, that is the proof that I am not guilty.

The jury found that there was reasonable doubt. He was found not guilty and released.

•  •  •

Joe Galang was a Filipino. In my experience with them, they are emotional people, easily aroused, with quick tempers and standards of their own. I have known a number of them well because of my Naval service. Many of them served as our messboys and cabin stewards.

Joe had been schooled by eight years in Uncle Sam's Navy and three years as a houseboy. I think, though, that at the time I met him he was working as some sort of helper at Huntington Memorial Hospital. He told me his story in jail, and his voice broke as he spoke of his mother and sister. Was he acting? I thought not. Well, Judge Charles Burnell, sometimes known as "Foul-Mouthed Burnell," had appointed me to represent Joe, and I was going to do so to the best of my ability. He was charged with larceny from the person, grand larceny, punishable under the indeterminate sentence law by from one to ten years in the penitentiary.

The charge stated that Joe had taken from Wong Ark, a Chinese, the sum of $27. Wong said the defendant was playing Chinese dominoes or checkers with him and two other Chinese, in Chinatown, when suddenly the defendant snatched $27 from Wong's coat pocket and ran away. This was corroborated by Song Sun, one of the other Chinese. They chased him, they said, and he ran up a back stairway and onto a roof and hid under the eaves. The Chinese called the police.

The police officer testified that he had received the call at about 1:00 a.m. and had gone to the old building in Chinatown. The defendant was pulled from under the eaves, took $27 from his pocket and said, "Here's the money." It looked like a pretty good case for the plaintiff—in this case, the People.

Joe said he had been walking along Alameda Street in the Chinese section. The Chinese, standing in front of his place, said to him, "Gamble, gamble?" Joe said he understood a little Chinese, and had some money, so he went in with the man. He paid the banker $17 and entered the game. He lost, and thought the game looked crooked. Nevertheless, he sold the banker his watch for $10 and put that in. He was convinced that the game was crooked, and getting more so. Finally, he grabbed the money from the pocket of the

Chinese banker and ran off. He didn't, he said, want any more—just his own $27. I find from my notes that the banker still had the watch. The decision? Case dismissed.

• • •

I have mentioned Judge "Foul-Mouthed" Burnell who was a brilliant man, but not familiar with criminal law. I was assigned to his court the first day he was on the bench. Judge Burnell came in after we had arrived and took his place on the bench. Before him on the desk was a big stack of transcripts, each with recommendations from the probation officer. This, in short, was "Probation and Sentence Day." Now, it seems to me that most judges always look these reports over–certainly I always did when I was on the bench. But it was apparent that Judge Burnell had not done so. Well, he picked up the first one, and he read and read and read. The first two or three defendants called were some Navy boys, still in uniform, who had been arrested for "shacking up" with some minors. The girls in question were well under sixteen, probably 13 or 14, and the sailors were charged with rape. The judge looked them over. He did not go through the customary formalities of ascertaining their true names, etc., but merely looked down and said, "Probation granted. Next time, get 'em older." This was the way he started making his record, and he made it obvious that he was not in favor of sending up young sailors, even for having relations with young girls.

Personally, I felt they should have been sentenced, since the girls were obviously so very young. But, that was his decision. He went through several more cases in this manner, and finally we took him into chambers; that is, we asked for a conference in chambers, and explained to him the procedure necessary to make a correct record. This must be interpretable by anyone, and must show that the rights of prisoners were granted to them. Also, if a prisoner was sent to jail or penitentiary, the record must follow them and be complete enough to be of guidance there.

• • •

Almost the same thing happened with Judge Charles S. Crail. When appointed to the bench, I don't think he had ever handled any criminal work. I was his department's public defender. He was a rather deliberate sort of fellow, a self-reliant and opinionated man. He apparently did not care about "minor requirements." He said to us, "I'll do it my way, and then you fellows go ahead and fix up the record so it is proper." Well, we would hardly do that; we were officers of the court and had to go along with the requirement for a reported record, a full and accurate transcript by the court reporter.

On one occasion I sat before Judge Crail, representing a defendant among a group of IWWs (Independent Workers of the World, a strong union then, with definite Communist leanings). When nineteen of them came into court, seventeen of them elected to represent themselves. One was represented by a smooth-talking and able lawyer, and one by me, so as to have the benefit of the public defender's office. So, each of the seventeen who was representing himself insisted on making his own statement; it became a very lengthy business. Also, each made his own objections. One of them, in fact, asked to have Judge Crail disqualified. Crail asked his reason. He said, "I can see by the smirk on your face that you're against me, and you're prejudiced." Judge Crail's face was, in fact, drawn up on one side. He said to the defendant, "I am not responsible for the shape of my face or the twist of my mouth. I was in Alaska after the 1898 gold rush, and there I froze my face. It has been this way ever since. Your challenge is denied."

• • •

I took a call one day in the public defender's office. The feminine voice on the phone said, "This is nurse Jones in the county hospital, Ward 110 (this was the jail ward). I'm not speaking officially, but just for the sake of humanity. We have a Jacob Limon, a Mexican, who has valvular heart trouble. He was sent from Lincoln Heights jail; we don't know the charge. He has only a short time to live, a couple of months at the most. He couldn't possibly run away if he wanted to. I'm wondering if we could find a way to get him out of this ward and over to where he can have proper treatment and can at least be made comfortable. I don't know what to do, so I'm calling the public defender's office to see if you can have something done."

I said, "All right, I'll see what can be done."

Now, my job was entirely in connection with criminal cases in Superior Court; I had nothing to do with Municipal Court. But, I had said I'd do what I could, so I talked it over with my superior. At his suggestion, I went to the presiding judge of the Municipal Court and explained the situation to him. He issued an order transferring the man from Ward 110 to the proper ward of the hospital "on his own recognizance"—that is, without even bail. I don't know how long the man lived, but I am sure he was much better off.

Yes even courts and judges are human.

# Chapter 8
## Deputy County Counsel

In 1925, while I was in the public defender's office and we were living in our first home in South Pasadena, our daughter, Barbara, was born. She was a healthy child for her first six months, but when she was about six months and her mother began to wean her, her health declined. We tried to tell the doctors about it, but looking Barbara over they all said she was a fine, healthy child. She continued to fail until she could scarcely raise her head and was flat on her back. We had two sets of doctors, and finally persuaded a third to come to the house. As soon as he walked in the door, he said, "This child is suffering from protein poisoning; I can tell by the odor." It was true; she could not digest cow's milk or any other, other than human. So, he put her on strained vegetables and in a little while she got so she could drink buttermilk and, later, skim milk. She gradually became better, but then came down with whooping cough. The doctor said it might be better if we went to the beach for a year or so. He felt a moist climate would help.

So, we sold the house and leased a house in Hermosa Beach. It was a big beachfront house, and we stayed there for a year. I commuted daily on the big red cars, and Barbara grew healthy. The commuting took an hour each way, but I enjoyed visiting with a number of the men I knew. Sometimes we played cards on the way up.

Friends used to come down and visit us. This got to be something of a nuisance because it seemed every weekend there was a party with lots of guests. We came up for Thanksgiving and, because it was foggy and cold at the beach, and Barbara was now quite well, we decided to move back. We rented a house near the Oneonta School, so we again became part of South Pasadena, and loved it.

I had been in the public defender's office for about two years when I went over to the county counsel, Ed Bishop. He was the man who had earlier advised me to take the examination and go into the public defender's office, which I had successfully done. However, I had never wanted to practice criminal law and had wanted to work in the county counsel's office from the beginning. I asked Ed about getting transferred, and I believe there was a way this could have legally been done. However, Ed was very straitlaced, and he told me I'd have to take the examination along with everyone else. There was to be an examination in a short time; however, Ed said they badly needed a man who was familiar with the work of the Road Department. He said there was a lawyer who worked in that department, and he would probably get the first appointment if he passed the exam. I decided to take the examination anyway. I think I stood second out of ten. The man in the Road Department had stood first.

But, again, a second vacancy came up very soon, and I was moved into the county counsel's office.

I had to approve all county warrants and expenditures, except payment for services–that is, employees' salaries. I was attorney for the county firemen, the Health Department, the sheriff's office, the justices of the peace, the municipal judges and so forth.

I remember one time when I was acting as attorney for the sheriff. Our sheriff was Big Bill Traeger. He was a big, likable fellow, apparently not disturbed by things that should disturb him. However, little things that should not have bothered him disturbed him very much. Bill had an undersheriff, Eugene Biscailuz, who was already a well-known character, and became even more beloved and favored in the vicinity after he became sheriff. The chief civil deputy, with whom I had to work a great deal, was Captain Arthur Jewell. Art had passed the bar, though I don't know if he was ever admitted. Sheriff Traeger paid less attention than he should, no doubt, to the civil work, because Art Jewell was such a capable man, entirely familiar with the department over the years. This department had to do with the serving of papers, attachments, writs and so forth. These matters are often quite technical. Unfortunately, Jewell was involved in an accident and broke his kneecap very severely, taking him out of the office for about ten months. Just at that time, his assistant, "Doc" Pfaffle, also capable and qualified, had an accident; he was crushed between two cars and seriously injured, so he was not available. There were others who had worked in the department before retirement, but none could be called back because they were not well enough. So, the sheriff went to the Board of Supervisors for help. They, in turn, sent me over to run the Civil Department of the sheriff's office. This was quite natural, as I was the attorney for the office.

Well, when I came to running that office, I soon found I was a "Babe in the Woods." And, there was a dearth of experienced men to whom I could turn for help or advice.

One afternoon a writ was brought in, served on the sheriff, demanding that he take all the furniture out of a 300-room furnished apartment building. I was aghast, because there were many people living there, probably some of them old or sick. Apparently, the furniture was being bought on time, and payments had not been made. The seller, who still had title, had put up a bond and was going to repossess it. What was I to do? Turn these people out into the street? I was in a quandary and called an office conference on the subject. The bond was apparently from a good bonding company and calculated to reimburse in the event of loss by wrongful taking of possession of the furniture, drapes and so forth. Our discussion brought forth no ideas.

A young fellow was working on some books back in the corner. He waggled a finger at me, so I went over to him. He said, "Pardon me, but I couldn't help overhearing. You know what I think I would do if I were in your position?" I said, "No, by all means, tell me." "Well," he said, "I would except to the amount and surety on the bond—that is, the company that has gone on the bond. That would require a hearing in ten days. You could thus gain time, and perhaps something can be worked out in the meantime." I objected, "But the bonding company is unquestionably good." "Makes no difference," he said. "Hard cases make bad law, and that's what I'd do in your situation." To make a long story short, I did as he suggested, and the case was settled within the time thus gained.

I had many more duties in the county counsel's office. I learned about buying bulls for the County Farm, Rancho Los Amigos. This is now a county hospital rehabilitation center, near Downey. And, I learned about flood control work, and about street bonds—many things to do with the operation of civil government. It became my job, under the Health Department, to order the roping off of Olvera

Street when the bubonic plague struck there. It was at that time that I first met Mrs. Christine Sterling.

I learned a good deal, too, about the bail bond business, and how it was conducted. In those times, I had to collect forfeited bail bonds. There was, for example, a lady named Lizzie Sax, the owner of a lot of property in San Bernardino County. It was being used by bail bondsmen to qualify for bonds, and she was making a considerable amount of money in this fashion. She was a terrible-looking character, dirty and dressed in dirty old clothes. I found that this property, being used as security for hundreds of thousands of dollars worth of bail bonds, was simply raw land, of little or no value. I did clean up that situation. It was shortly thereafter that the bonding laws were changed.

So ended my period of public service. I felt I had been both a good public defender and a good county counsel; not the best of either, perhaps, but a comfortable way above the worst. Certainly, I had gained a great deal from experience. But, it was again time to move on, this time to private practice and community service, chosen on the basis of my interest and what I felt to be the value of the given project.

# Chapter 9
# Los Angeles
# Before 1930

*A*round the end of 1927, or the beginning of 1928, my brother David's firm, Faries and Williamson, had taken on a good deal of work in the area of real estate and financing, both public and private. They also had as clients some small bond houses. It was a time of considerable expansion among private entrepreneurs and on the part of Los Angeles, both city and county. I had rather specialized in these areas insofar as my studies were concerned, and my time in the county counsel's office had been of immeasurable value, both in learning how things worked and in becoming acquainted with those in charge. My expertise was of potential value to the firm, and they had the clients for whom I could put that expertise to work. It was time for me to enter private practice.

The arrangement made was that I would have a drawing account and would share in two "pots"; I would have a small percentage of the total business earnings and a larger percentage of earnings from business which I brought in.

At this period, building and planning were going on at a great rate in Los Angeles. It was decided in 1926 that the city had to have a new City Hall. This was built at the northeast corner of First and Main streets. It was a 29-story building of some 328 feet and was dedicated in 1928. The city attorney had been found by the judiciary to be correct in his decision that the 150-foot limit placed by ordinance on buildings in Los Angeles did not have to be observed by the city itself. It was a most attractive building and a landmark; until the height-limiting ordinance was removed years later, it could be seen from any direction. One could orient himself from any direction by

*The Faries brothers, Culbert William, David Reid and McIntyre*

looking for City Hall. The underlying reason for the 150-foot limitation had to do with water pressure, the fighting of fire, and the possibility of earthquakes. The new building was severely damaged in the earthquake of 1933; I don't think the public was ever told quite the extent of the damage.

Some years after the completion of City Hall, the old Bank of Italy building was destroyed and the area began to take on the look of a civic center. The growth of this area, from First Street to Olympic Boulevard and from Main to Figueroa Street was the business growth feature as well as the municipal growth feature of the years from about 1919 to 1929. I believe that during much of this period this was the fastest-growing business area in North America.

To round out the picture of this area's growth, it is necessary to consider the Bunker Hill area. At the turn of the century and for a time thereafter, this had been a choice residential area. It ran from 5th Street and Olive Street, bordering Hill Street, up to Temple Street, and west from Hill to Figueroa. It was considerably higher than the neighboring areas and blocked the western growth of the business area; traffic had to go around it. By 1927, the area was seriously run down. The famous old Melrose Hotel, once the finest residential hotel in the city, had become an eyesore. All the houses had lost their glory, and most of them, their paint.

An ambitious project was considered; why not cut down Bunker Hill to the level of Hill Street, which it bordered, thus allowing growth to go through, rather than around? This project was proposed to an excellent firm of engineers in Chicago, Babcock and Sons, whom the firm of Faries and Williamson represented, and for whom I did a good deal of work. They had mapped the progress of the business district of Los Angeles from about 1890 to that time, and showed the way business and traffic were dispersing. Business had originally started down around Temple and Alameda, then moved toward Temple and Broadway, continuing south, skirting around Bunker Hill. The upshot of their engineering work was to show that the idea was impractical. One big point was that the addition of all this area, if put on the market at once, would adversely affect land values in the downtown area because it was too much to absorb. To put this much land on the market at once would destroy mortgage values.

The people who had engaged Babcock and Sons didn't like the outcome very well. At any rate, we, the firm, had to represent Babcock and Sons in litigation, or proposed litigation, regarding their fee, and the idea of cutting down Bunker Hill was abandoned. The hill was cut down a little, then a little more in the '50s as a government rehabilitation project.

At the time I entered private practice, the boom was in full swing. These were the days of the subdivider—that period from about 1926 to 1932 or early 1933; the Great Depression did not affect our area's surging growth and boundless optimism for a long time after that stock market debacle in October 1929.

Faries and Williamson did not practice criminal law. This does not mean, however, that the firm did not have some clients who ran pretty close to the edge of prosecutable acts. I can recall our Fred Fuller, who ran the department advising on subdivision matters, shaking his fist at one of these high pressure fellows and saying, "That's criminal; that's a felony! You can go to the penitentiary for that, and I'll not represent you!"

About the time I joined Faries and Williamson, they were handling an interesting case. The litigant was a well-to-do manufacturer from Danzig. Danzig was a German territory prior to the Treaty of Versailles which, after World War I, established the so-called Polish Corridor. This gentleman had a son who had been a lieutenant in the German army during the war. The son had been gassed, seriously injuring his lungs. Tuberculosis threatened, and their doctor suggested that he might benefit from the climate of California. So, the fond father sold his business, which was a considerable one, and with the money, purchased annuities from German insurance companies. The family moved to Los Angeles and rented a large home in the Hancock Park area. They brought with them all their possessions, which included a great chest full of valuable artifacts and a number of paintings by recognized masters.

The family entertained widely, and became accepted and respected. As was common, they frequently had house guests. One of these was a German baron, who stayed quite a long time. The family had, or leased, an ocean-going pleasure craft on which they often spent weekends. They enjoyed, in short, a very pleasant and quite expensive life-style. But, it will be remembered that throughout this period the German mark was going down in value, finally, in fact, reaching the point at which it was literally not worth the paper it was written on.

One weekend the family went out on their yacht, leaving the baron behind. When they returned, the baron was gone. Gone, too, were the great chest with its valuable contents and the paintings, which had been cut from their frames. The police investigation turned up no clues, and no part of the loot was ever traced. As a rule, such things surface in time, often in South America. The insurance company, knowing this, delayed payment, hoping some of the objects would show up.

The family had immediately reported their loss, cooperated in the police investigation, and done everything they should have. They went to their Los Angeles insurance broker, who had been to their house and seen the paintings before writing their policy. Now arose the problem. The family, our clients, said they had asked for, and should have received, a "valued" policy. This is one which sets a fixed value on the insured items, such as the paintings involved. What they had gotten, instead, was a policy for some $200,000 covering the paintings as a whole, with no agreed figure on any of them.

So, there was a dispute, largely based on this misunderstanding, particularly as all the paintings had been viewed and listed. They discussed their claim on several occasions with the broker, who was a reputable man and well thought of. No agreement was reached, and the insurance company refused to pay until that subject was cleared up. They offered a much lesser amount, around $100,000, but this, the family considered insufficient. A suit resulted, brought by Faries and Williamson.

The insurer was Lloyds of London. In those days, Lloyds could not be sued in California, even though they sold insurance here. They had to be sued in London. This has now been changed by statute, but at the time, jurisdiction could not be obtained over Lloyds of London except by suing them in London. Thus, in addition to the suit here, we brought suit there. The local insurance agent was also sued, and that suit went forward in the Los Angeles court. Depositions were taken, both here and in England, and experts were called in. Sir Joseph Duveen, said to be the greatest art expert at the time, was called upon, and testified by deposition. Some of the experts put the value of the paintings at considerably above three hundred thousand; others put it as low as one hundred thousand. It is strange how widely "experts" in the same field differ on the same thing. It also bears note that expert witnesses seem invariably to think along the same lines as their employer. To me, at least, it was very apparent that the insurance carrier was dragging things out in the hope that something would turn up. What was the correct valuation? Nobody knows. Did the baron show up? Never. Were the paintings ever found? Not as far as I know.

The suit dragged on. Meantime, the value of the family's German annuities was diminishing as the mark went down. Finally, on the actual date of the hearing in London, Fred Williamson, in London, reached a settlement "on the courthouse steps," as it were. I think the recovery, in American money, was $196,000, which included costs. We considered this a good settlement in all the circumstances. Our client was paid off in British pounds, which were then the standard of the world, and he, therefore, netted a great deal of money.

The client received his money and went back to Danzig where he repurchased his former business. This he could do at most favorable terms, by virtue of paying in British pounds rather than German marks. Germany started to boom, and his business prospered. The son, who had recovered, returned several times to California, as did the father. Neither the baron nor the paintings were ever found.

Another rather peculiar case involved the interests of Harry Chandler. Fred Williamson had married Harry's daughter, Ruth, and it had been through Chandler's influence that David had taken Fred into the firm as a partner.

In this matter, we represented the family who were the owners, or at least had majority control, of the great TeJon Ranch. This was one of the last of the great California ranches, most of the others having, by then, been broken up. It stretched from just beyond Gorman, on the Ridge Route (then U.S. Highway 99, today also I-5), to Bakersfield, and then to an area about eleven miles down the plain, north of the Tehachapi Mountains. The road over the mountains was not the fine, divided highway it is today, but narrow, curving and dangerous, particularly so in the old Grapevine portion. It was then only a single lane in each direction and not divided.

It seems that the chief of police of an Orange County city was on his way to a convention to be held in Fresno. He had left wife and children at home, and was driving at night. He was driving a rather small car, a convertible with a cloth or canvas top. All was fine, except that with him in the car was neither his wife nor his child, but a young woman.

The Reserve Oil Company was drilling some exploratory wells on that part of the ranch, and a company employee had left a gate open in the fence that lined the road. A yearling heifer got through this gate and wandered onto the road. The car came around a curve, going fast, and hit the yearling. The heifer's body was thrown into the air and came down upon, and through, the cloth top of the car. One of its hoofs went into the young woman's body, badly injuring her. I was sent out by the firm to investigate, and did so, taking notes on the various distances and probable path, seeking and taking testimony from possible witnesses, and learning all I could about the occurrence. I spent several days at the ranch house.

Bakersfield was the county seat of Kern County, and there the young woman filed suit, asking a tremendous amount in damages. I don't recall how much, nor what the contention was as to punitive damages. Bakersfield was very much a union town, and counsel for the young woman were from that city. They seized upon the idea of making the action a trial of Harry Chandler, the wealthy *Los Angeles Times,* and any others who might have an interest in the TeJon Ranch.

Counsel for the defense were put to emphasizing the impropriety that had occurred, the character of the young woman, et cetera. But the other side had a field day trying Harry Chandler and the *Times.* Now, neither of these matters had anything to do with the right to recover, or with the amount of recovery that should be set. I'm not sure exactly why our office tried the case, but as I recall, there was no insurance covering this sort of suit. David, an excellent trial lawyer, headed the defense. The first difficulty was trying to impanel a jury which would not be in any way biased or prejudiced. This, in such a thorough-going union town, proved impossible. And, of course, the other side wanted people of anti-*Times* or anti-Chandler feelings or opinions. All challenges, both for cause and preemption, were exhausted; the jury, finally chosen, was satisfactory to neither side, and the result was a hung jury. They hung just about on the lines that had been indicated by the challenges—seven for one side and five for the other. What happened? As is often the case in such matters, the case was settled before a second trial could be called.

I got a call that the son of one of our very good clients was in the county jail. He had been in an automobile accident, and the officer who came on the scene said he was just plain drunk. I went down to the old jail, and the young man was there with a bad hang-over as well as a bruise on his head and two black eyes. I bailed him out, and before the case came up for hearing, the district attorney agreed with us that he was unlikely to get a conviction because of the injuries he had sustained, and he therefore dismissed the action.

But, it was interesting being down at the jail on that Monday morning. The room was full, and the holding tanks behind the room were more than full of various types and races of people. An amusing thing took place among the drunks and prostitutes, the biters and fighters, and those caught driving under the influence of alcohol or drugs. Before the court was a very large, quite slender and patrician-looking woman, wearing a big and expensive fur coat. Probably she had imbibed a bit too much; at any rate, she was in court. She gave her name as Jane Doe, and, along with the drunks, fallen women and others, she pleaded not guilty. The bail was set, and she had the cash, or someone had brought it to her. She put up the cash bail and then proceeded to put up cash bail for six other women who had been in the cell with her. She "took them out" on bail, and I was told she paid for their defense and threw a big dinner for them afterward.

I concerned myself primarily with business law, with bond matters, property settlements, savings and loans, and the like, but there were some "personal" cases, too.

One day when our offices were in the Subway Terminal Building, Will Curtiss, my father-in-law's brother-in-law, came in to see me. He wanted me to go with him to meet a man who was bidding on plans for the construction of the Union Station in Los Angeles. Will said that this man needed about $35,000 to complete his payroll for the station plans he was going to submit. The man had told him he had good reason to think he would be the successful bidder, and would therefore be willing to pay handsomely for the short-term loan of $35,000.

So, I went with him to see this man, who had a small furnished office suite on one of the lower floors of the Terminal Building. He was a very busy man. The problem was that I recognized him. I had seen him in the county jail some time before, when I was with the public defender's office, and I knew he had been sent on to the penitentiary. He was a good-looking man, with a turned-up grey mustache and a nice smile, but I knew him for a felon. We talked for awhile, then I asked Curtiss to go back to the office with me, as we were working on another matter. We agreed to return at two o'clock.

In the meantime, I got ahold of Forrest Murphy, Esq. He had been a deputy district attorney when I was a public defender, and we had worked together on a number of cases. I described the would-be borrower to him, since I couldn't recall his name. Forrest did, though, and said, "I sent that man to the penitentiary."

We returned to the man's office at two o'clock, taking with us some investigators, who we left outside the door. The entire office had been cleaned out. The floor was bare; there were no desks, no typewriters, no telephones, no sign of occupancy. It would appear that, though I had tried to cover my recognition of him, he must have recognized me from the days when he was a prisoner in the county jail.

This, then, is how it was in Los Angeles at the end of the 1920s, at least from the standpoint of a law office. What was to come—that is, the Great Depression—was so cataclysmic and so far-reaching in its effects, and lasted so long, as to constitute almost a story of a different world, with different people.

# Chapter 10
## Depression Days

*I*t is difficult for anyone who has not been through such a time to imagine what the Great Depression was like. Certainly no one raised in the unprecedented material affluence our country has enjoyed since the end of World War II can have any conception of the poverty, the misery and despair which was the lot of so many. This was not confined to the so-called working class, though they, undoubtedly, suffered most. Those of us who enjoyed a continuous income during that harsh time were indeed fortunate, and for the most part, at least, we counted our blessings and tried to do what we could to help.

There was no Social Security; there was no Medicare or Medicaid, either. State and county aid provided a little relief here and there, but that was all, and could not begin to take care of all the needy. Some unemployment relief plans had been started by the state and county, but fell far short of doing the job. So, various communities formed committees. I was chairman of the committee for South Pasadena, a portion of Alhambra, and a part of Los Angeles. I was convinced that the little we could do with the part-time jobs was not really worthwhile, and that federal aid had somehow to be obtained. Many good people gave their time and effort to this project.

About the time this crisis was coming to a close, one day in 1935, I came home to our Primrose Avenue rental house and said, "Well, we've been talking about moving for a long time, and finances have held us up, but if you want anything to say about the new house, you'd better speak up; Johnny Douglas is starting to draw plans."

John Douglas was an architect friend of ours, and Lois pitched in

*McIntyre and Lois Faries, 1938*

with him on the design, the room plan, and the like. Soon he had drawn a reasonably-priced house which he superintended as the contractor. The house was a bit small, but the location was just fine. Ridgeway Road was a wide, curving, quiet street that was far enough from Huntington Drive so we didn't get the highway noise. Barbara then attended the junior high school in South Pasadena; and our second daughter, Midge, started school in the Huntington Elementary School. She had been through kindergarten and first grade, so she started there in the second grade. Well, she came home the first day, like Niobe, all tears. The trouble? She didn't know anybody! Moreover, they had called her Midge in South Pasadena, and she could only spell Midge, not Marjorie. Next day, she was in tears again because they said her real name was Marjorie, not Midge. She didn't see why her name should be different on the books than what she was called. Well, we found that there were already three Marjories in the class. We suggested that we call her Margaret, and she like the suggestion. There was, in fact, some question as to whether she hadn't been christened Margaret; Marjorie was just the diminutive.

Well, the third day she was again back home in tears, because she hadn't been able to spell Marjorie Ann Faries. The teacher had told her she should be able to spell her own name. But, after the third day of tears, things began to get better, and she was happy there. It was a question whether she wasn't a bit too happy; she soon had too many friends, and the teachers liked her so much that they didn't press her to work. So, the children grew up there. I think it was a worthwhile community and family life we all loved and enjoyed. I do regret that I was so busy with law and politics that I did not give the time I should have to life with my family.

In 1940, the county counsel ruled that the three-man school board should be increased to five. There was tacit agreement that the two new members should be residents of San Marino, the other three being from South Pasadena. The people of San Marino held two or three meetings, and decided to ask William G. Paul, president of the Los Angeles Stock Exchange, and me, to run. At the last minute, a man from South Pasadena filed his petition. The people, particularly those of San Marino, were angry about this, and a group was put together to go from door to door, with the result that William G. Paul and I were elected by the biggest percentage turnout of voters for a school board election ever recorded. I was elected for three three-year terms, serving from 1940 to 1949, inclusive.

There was great satisfaction in my service on the school board, though there were times when it was not so pleasant. We did, of course, get complaints from some people. There were frequent money problems; the fixing of salaries incurred difficulties. But it was greatly rewarding to give out the diplomas and to see the fine children of so many friends graduating.

There is a story of the depression period, the memory of which has given me much satisfaction over the years. The story is about a young fellow who was after my time at Occidental, but whom I had known slightly. He was a bit older than the other students because he had drifted awhile before college. At this time he was washing dishes for a living and on this occasion was lying around on the beach down at Long Beach. He got to talking with a lady—not a bikini-clad one—but an elderly lady. Somehow, in their conversation, she struck a chord in him, with the result that she persuaded him to go on to college and try to make something of himself. So, he enrolled at Occidental, riding a motorcycle back and forth from Long Beach. He found a night watchman job to support himself while in college, and graduated. He went on, took advanced work, and became a teacher of English in a high school. He had come from a Southern mountain area. There were still, in those days, pockets in the mountains whose people had virtually no contact with the outside world since coming to America—mainly from England and Scotland in the 1600s. They just "got lost" and still kept alive the traditions of the 17th century and largely spoke Elizabethan English.

The young man told me he had grown up in one of these little communities. On Sundays, he said, all would go to church, and after church they would picnic together. The young men would draw a line in the dust down the middle of the street; they would divide each side of the line and fight with their fists. The old men would watch them, give them pointers, and tell them what they should or should not have done—in short, train them to be fighters. It was a hardening and toughening process. They were so poor, he said, that they saved and re-molded the lead bullets used in their firearms. They were taught, and required, to be excellent shots; squirrels must be shot in the head, to save the meat for squirrel pie, and the bullet found, to be reused.

The young man decided he was going to see the world; he didn't want to stay in the mountains all his life. He knew his parents would be very much against such a move, if they learned of his intention, so he planned his movements. Some miles from his community, a railway ran down through the mountains. There was a freight which ran through nightly, just before dawn. His plan was to catch this train as it slowed for a curve, and one night he slipped away and ran for the track. Just as he hopped aboard the freight car, a bullet whistled over his head. His father had followed him. He looked back and saw his father wave the gun. The father could have easily hit him had he chosen, and the boy knew what that shot over his head meant: it was a warning never to return. The young man told me, "I'm going back, but not until my father dies. I am a teacher, and I'm going to go back and start a school for the people in that place. I've been saving money, and when my father dies, I'm going to do it."

About this time, there was an amusing incident I witnessed in Santa Barbara. I was acquainted with District Attorney Ward of Santa Barbara County. At that time he was allowed a private civil practice while serving as district attorney. One judge handled all the probate matters of the court; his name was Crowe. It was a current joke that he looked and sat like a crow. He had a large nose and sat very quietly on the bench. He was elderly and thin and said—or cawed— very little.

I was there on some law and motion matters. Before my matter on the calendar was that of my friend, Ward, who was probating a will. He brought to the stand one of the head men of the local bank, and I thought his questioning of the witness sufficient. But after Ward had finished questioning the man, the judge simply sat there. And sat there. Finally, Ward said, "Has your Honor any questions?" The judge said, "No. Have you anything more that you want to ask this man?" Ward replied that he had not. "Well, then," said the judge, "I guess you'd better have him step down." Ward, looking embarrassed, asked, "Have I omitted something?" "How," asked the judge, looking quietly but sharply at Ward, "do you know that the man is dead?"

Ward was, of course, a bit taken aback. He stammered, "Well, uh, his funeral was yesterday, and I think everybody in town was there. It was a big funeral."

"That's true," said the judge. "In fact, I was at the funeral myself. But I didn't look into the coffin. So, in fact, I couldn't say from a legal standpoint whether or not he was dead."

A titter ran through the courtroom, and the judge asked Ward, "Would you want to testify? Do you know he's dead?"

The district attorney thought a moment. "If your Honor would please put the matter over to two o'clock, we can bring in the coroner to prove he is dead."

Few people outside the legal profession have any real idea of the variety of things a lawyer can be called upon to do. The following story illustrates some of them. "Mankind United" was a church group of sorts. The group was engaged in a number of activities, most of which came about through their rather unusual method of recruiting converts.

The head and, I believe, founder of the organization was a Mr. Bell. He was not a large man, but of great presence. He had the appearance of vibrant health, and compelling, hypnotic eyes. He also had a fine speaking voice; he was, in fact, often referred to as "the Voice."

The creed of the church was based upon the period told about in the Acts of the Apostles, which is to say, the period immediately after Christ had risen from the dead. The story of Ananias and his wife, Sapphira, in Acts 5:1-5, was basic to their operation. You will recall that Ananias and his wife were members of the Apostolic Church. They sold some property, but kept some of the money. Questioned by the elders, they lied about the amount of money they had received. Ananias was rebuked by Peter, and thereupon fell dead. Thus, when new believers joined Bell's church, they were required to give all they had to the church. They joined as probationers, not as full members. If, for example, the convert owned a gas station, the church would take the property and, in turn, give the convert a job, perhaps working in that gas station. The property would belong to the church, presumably to the benefit of all the believers.

They had had great success in a number of ways, and they had a great number of properties: farms, ranches, gas stations, eating houses, a necktie factory, several little old hotels and other items. Most of the members were of European background. They were good people and honest in their belief.

They had various governing committees, managers chosen by the church, who conducted the day-to-day business affairs.

They had acquired the old Continental Building at Fourth and Spring streets in Los Angeles. The building was beginning to be run down, and the church set about making it a paying proposition. The first thing they did was get rid of the outside cleaning help. Church members took over the task of nightly cleaning and other needed janitorial work. In this way, they served the church. But the discharged cleaning workers belonged to a union. They complained to the church, but the workers were let go. Eventually, the union brought the matter to the attention of Robert Walker Kenny, then attorney general of the state of California. In his capacity as attorney general he looked into the matter of Mankind United group or church. He found they were not paying, and had not paid, any taxes on the meals they served, the neckties they made and sold, and the like. Nor were they accounting for monies paid to their members. The contention of Mankind United was that, as a religious organization, they could not be held accountable, nor made to pay taxes of any kind.

Their information was a little faulty. Some time before this, the United States Supreme Court had held that, while a church's religious activities are, indeed, not accountable to the state, any business run for profit by a church is liable in the same way as any lay business. So Kenny, as attorney general, promptly filed what is known as a "jeopardy assessment" for back California taxes against the church. He filed an amount of several million dollars, which prompted Uncle Sam to immediately do likewise. The church was thereupon faced with liens for many thousands of dollars.

The church, on advice of counsel, filed a proceeding in "protective bankruptcy" to hold off the liens and get an opportunity to come up with a plan of reorganization, while keeping control. This would also give them a breathing space in which to fight the taxes, if granted. But when the matter came for hearing before the federal district judge, they had not yet worked out their reorganization plan. The judge, bankruptcy referee or both, evidently thought differently from counsel for the church. Instead of putting them into protective bankruptcy, the judge put them into regular bankruptcy, saying that they were, in fact, bankrupt and should be liquidated. He appointed three trustees to carry this out.

The people of the church were hurt and infuriated. It was Kenny who took the heat, along with the trustees whom he had been responsible for getting appointed. The trustees decided to divide the work; one had the main area in Southern California, one had Northern California, and the third, who had Oregon, was also in charge of "outside work" and assets. He had charge of the attempt to fight the taxes, or get them compromised.

Frederick Napoleon Howser became the new attorney general, and he thought of me and got in touch. He asked me to take the place of one of the trustees named McKee who had become ill. As the situation now stood, the group had a pretty strong management committee, which was more and more taking over activities from Mr. Bell. I agreed, so I had the state of Oregon and some work in Northern California, along with the tax problems.

Being a business lawyer, though not a tax specialist, and having by this time gained a degree of political sophistication, I was aware that neither the state nor the national government would be anxious to get tangled in a great deal of litigation. What with the First Amendment rights and other considerations, it would undoubtedly, if not settled, have to go all the way to the United States Supreme Court. This made me think that I might well be successful in negotiating a settlement.

There were numerous properties in Oregon. There was the aforementioned necktie factory, some small hotels and gas stations, and a cheese factory. There was also a beautiful ranch of some fifteen to seventeen hundred acres, a highly valuable property. It was well-watered, rich land, and well cared for. The cheese factory worked in well with the ranch. The factory was run by a water wheel, and produced some of the finest cheddar cheese I have ever tasted. The church's largest business was the growing and selling of gladiolus bulbs. This business, based in Oregon, was also under my supervision. At this time, the church had the world's largest gladiolus operation. The church people did all the work themselves—men, women, and children. Their workdays were not eight hours, but from first light to sundown, each day except Sunday. The children, who attended the public schools, worked in the fields before and after school hours.

The local farmers and agriculturists liked these church people; they were a source of cheap and honest labor, willing to work hard and always law-abiding. In turn, for their services, some of the ranchers allowed the church people to glean their pear orchards after harvest, this being a pear area. The church people put up a great deal of canned fruit—not only pears, but other fruit. These were not only for themselves, but for other church members throughout the western states. I once saw, at one of the motels, some eight thousand jars of fruit which they had put up. All the fruit had come from gleanings; they had purchased none of it.

Gradually, we sold off portions of various assets and pieces of property. Gradually, also, Mr. Bell was pushed into the background, and the managing committee of the church took almost complete control.

We three trustees were still in general charge. Paying off the debt had taken most of the better properties, but there were a few good ones left. The committee seemed quite pleased that the matter had been straightened out, and that they would still have the church and some property intact.

Having completed the settlements with federal and state authorities, and having had them approved by the courts, it was time for me to get out. They didn't need me any longer, and I was becoming increasingly active in other law business and politics.

# Chapter 11
# Olvera Street

*L*et me lay some historical and geographical groundwork before getting on with the story of the Los Angeles Plaza area, and its restoration and preservation. The Los Angeles business district around 1890 had moved away from the old area which was generally from the Plaza on the north to Third Street on the south. The federal post office and federal court buildings were built much later. City Hall was on Broadway between Second and Third. The old county jail was in the red brick building at Temple and New High streets, and this building housed a couple of criminal superior courts. The courthouse of red sandstone at Temple and North Broadway had been built around 1887, and continued to be used until the 1933 earthquake rendered it unfit for occupancy. There had been an outside caged elevator going up the back, alongside the Hall of Records. To the south was the *Los Angeles Times* building at the northeast corner of First and Broadway. On the east side of Broadway was the old Chamber of Commerce building.

The Plaza area, considered the birthplace of the city of Los Angeles, was about forty-six acres in size when Gaspar de Portola visited it in 1769. In 1781, Spanish Franciscans under Father Crespi and the military guards officially founded El Pueblo de Neustra Senora, la Reina de Los Angeles de Porciunsula (the town of Our Lady, Queen of Angels of Porziuncola).

It was about 1904 that the old Los Angeles Railway Company, which ran the yellow streetcars, put in a transformer station on a piece of land on Olvera Street, next to the old Avila Adobe, the first real house built in Los Angeles. At one time it had about twenty-one

*Olvera Street, looking south toward the Plaza, before restoration, circa 1926. Note Avila Adobe center left, and the Plaza substation. Sepulveda House is on the right. (used by courtesy of El Pueblo de Los Angeles Historic Park)*

rooms. The Avilas were one of the prominent families among the old Mexican inhabitants, the Californians, as they called themselves. As a boy in 1904 or 1905, I used to come from Orange to visit cousins, and on several occasions, went to watch the workmen putting in the transformer station, laying tracks and so forth.

I paid no further attention to the Olvera Street area until the occasion when I was in the county counsel's office and acting as attorney for the Health Department. This 1927 incident was the second outbreak of Bubonic Plague; there had been one somewhat further east, by the mule market, in 1904. We roped off the Olvera Street area. As I recall, we did not rope off the Pico House, then a Mexican hotel with a lunch room and a pool hall on the lower floor. Ladies of ill repute were in good supply on New High Street.

At that time there was Father John's flophouse on North Main Street, in what is now an Olvera Street building. Nearby was a delicatessen. Across the street were the Atlantic and Pacific hotels, which had been condemned against human habitation, and were demolished at the time of the Olvera Street reconstruction. On the corner was an Italian drugstore, and on the east side of the Plaza was the Chinese area.

The beginning of the area's restoration started when Christine Sterling came down from San Francisco after the breakup of her marriage. She was, she told me, a daughter of a man who had been one of the vigilantes at the time of the great earthquake. She brought with her, her two children, June and Peter.

She saw the Plaza around 1926 and was horrified. Olvera Street was then a muddy, unpaved alley. Sewage ran down the middle and sides of the street, and collected in the depressions. There were some little leased garages, but no business buildings fronted on Olvera Street–only back doors. She tried her best to get public opinion aroused; she put up signs and made every effort, but for a time had no success. Finally, she learned that the way to get things done in Los Angeles, was to enlist the interest of Harry Chandler, owner of the *Times* newspaper. So, she went to the *Times,* got to see Mr. Chandler, and told him in no uncertain terms what she thought. She said that not only should the good people of Los Angeles, and the business interests, be condemned for permitting such a situation to exist, but they were missing a "good bet." She told him some of the background of the historic Plaza area, particularly the Olvera Street part, pointing out the folly of allowing all this to disappear.

Chandler's interest was indeed engaged. He got together a group of his friends for a luncheon–and all knew that when Harry Chandler gave a luncheon one should bring his checkbook. Among those present was my brother, David. There was Lucien Brunswig of the Brunswig Drug Company and General Moses E. Sherman, who owned a lot of land in the San Fernando Valley and who owned the green streetcars and perhaps had an interest in the yellow ones. There was Sherman's right-hand man, Arnold Haskell. At that time General Sherman was largely bedridden, so Haskell did most of the work while the general lay on a davenport and talked all day on the telephone. Then there was Harry Bauer of the Southern California Edison Company, and his son-in-law. There was also Rudolpho Montes, who later went to New Orleans and started the Port Authority and other activities that made New Orleans the great seaport for the Gulf of New Mexico.

The outcome of the luncheon was the formation of the Plaza de Los Angeles Corporation. Faries and Williamson took on the unpaid ("pro bono publico") job of organizing the corporation. This was 1928, and I, being low man on the totem pole, was assigned to advise the new corporation. I kept the minutes and talked with Mrs. Sterling. Harry Chandler was president of the corporation, and I had much contact with him. The street restoration, or rejuvenation, was begun. A suggestion had been made that the corporation be non-profit, but Chandler opposed this. He told me later that he wanted to write off his investment, which was $25,000. At the time, he envisioned restoring and operating Olvera Street and also New China City, which he wanted to see moved to the north of the Mexican restoration.

Olvera Street was, and is, only one block long. It ran between Macy Street and Marchessault Street, named after an old French family. There were many French settlers who came largely to be winegrowers. The people who owned some of the buildings which were on Olvera Street did not always get along with Mrs. Sterling, and even though all could obviously make money by coming in on the Olvera Street project of Plaza de Los Angeles, Inc., they didn't do so. They fought the closing of Olvera Street to vehicular traffic. They were not successful. I assisted the city attorney as co-counsel. We were successful after going through the Superior Court and the Court of Appeals. I think the Supreme Court refused to hear the case after we were upheld by the Court of Appeals.

Going north on Olvera from Marchessault, on the east side of Olvera Street, was the Pelanconi House. This was a substantial old brick edifice, built by Piereo Pelanconi's father. Pietro was an old man, then in his eighties. He said he was born there. He was deeply interested in the preservation project, and was a very interesting person. This property was acquired, as would be all the Olvera Street property, in time. On the ground floor of the next house was a hardware store, owned by the Arconti family. They, too, fought the change. Miss Arconti, one of the daughters, maintained a postcard and trinket store there for some time. She did not get on well with Mrs. Sterling, but she did with me, and all was finally worked out. The state filed to acquire the Sepulveda House; the suit was settled, and the property acquired.

At the corner of Olvera and Main Street was the three-story Italian Hall. In its basement, on Olvera, was a restaurant. I believe it is still there. The building was originally the meeting place for the Italian colony, and they held their dances and parties there. Coming down from Macy Street, on the other side of Olvera Street, were some little old buildings, which were torn down. Then one came to the winery, a very well-built building owned by the Vai family. At the time, the Vai brothers were running the winery, which was the very first winery licensed in California. They made champagne and other wines. The last Mr. Vai was very good about contributing cases of wine when there was a party in connection with the street project. Later, this area was bought, and the portion of it facing Olvera Street is now the El Paseo Cafe, started by Rafael Vega.

Continuing south one comes to the old Avila Adobe, and then to the old L.A. Railway Transformer Building. Next was the Methodist Church, which is still there. The church had the right to use the old building for a number of years at a rental of $1.00 per month. Around the turn to the east of the church was the Methodist Conference Headquarters building, which is now renewed and is called the Biscailuz Building, named after our retired sheriff, Eugene Biscailuz. He had not wanted to quit at the age limit, so his successor, Sheriff Pitchess, and I arranged to move desks from the sheriff's supply over there for him. He maintained an office which he filled with photographs and other old time mementos for some time.

Senora Consuela Castillo de Bonzo was a very able lady. She was a young woman when she heard that Olvera Street was going to be opened by the corporation, Plaza de Los Angeles, Inc., and she immediately put in an application for the Pelanconi House. It was not ready to occupy, so she opened a cafe on Spring Street, then moved La Golondrina to its present site on Olvera Street. Her sons worked there, and her granddaughter, Vivien Consuelo de Bonzo, is still operating it.

The restoration plan required the paving of the pedestrian surfaces of Olvera Street with Padre tile. This is a soft tile, and thinner than bricks. It didn't last well, so later we had to replace it with red brick.

Soon after Mrs. de Bonzo moved in, other businesses came, and only one of them was not Mexican. There was a lady who analyzed or told fortunes by handwriting. Mrs. Sterling was fond of her, and would not let her go. Also, Mrs. Sterling had a relative who painted,

*McIntyre Faries with Mrs. Christine Sterling*

or at any rate, sold paintings. However, Mr. and Mrs. Burroughs were fine people, so in spite of some incongruity, they remained. Otherwise there was a consistent attempt to restore the real old Mexican-American flavor to the community, with some historic truth.

Then came the Great Depression. The magnificent Mrs. Sterling took no fewer than 136 people from Relief and provided work for them. She made herself responsible for them and put them to work in various capacities on the Street. Many became taco stand operators and street vendors; some of those same people still have the booths on the Street. Mrs. Bonzo didn't like street vendors, but Mrs. Sterling overruled her, and Mrs. Sterling was quite definitely in control. The vendors were very colorful and very needy. Mrs. Sterling lent them money to get started. She took on an assistant who was teaching Spanish to Americans. This was Mario Valdez, who later succeeded Mrs. Sterling. After her death, we made him manager of the Street, and he was allowed to keep his little shop.

The Street was levelled and paved through the good offices of Chief James Davis, a very tough, old-time chief of police. With City Council and Police Commission approval, Chief Davis would send down prisoners from Los Angeles City Jail. They would be wearing ball and chain, to discourage any urge to travel, and would work under supervision—grading, laying tile or brick. On one occasion it started to rain around noon, and the prisoners were quartered in the Pelanconi House. Somehow they found an old case of liquor, probably wine, and proceeded to drink it. When the rain ended and staffers went to get them, the whole contingent was drunk as lords. No one knew where the liquor had come from, though there had once been a wine cellar there.

The Avila Adobe lay between the Vai Winery and the Transformer Building on the east side of the Street, and it had been greatly reduced in size. Its yard sloped down 12th or 14th Street to Alameda Street, and at that time had a big billboard. We left this for a time, as it brought in some money. However, the dirt began to slide down onto the Alameda sidewalk. Mario Valdez got a group together, raised the money, and, with a little help from some others, built a high retaining wall, saving the back end of the Avila Adobe lot. The building, owned by the Rimpau family, was soon open to public view for a small fee.

Mrs. Sterling became a close friend of a representative of the old Sepulveda House, Florence de Dodson Schonemann, a member of the Sepulveda family and also of the Dominguez family. She gave an old piano for the House, the second or third piano to be brought around the Horn. She also gave pictures of the first Sepulveda, Kit Carson, and others. I gave a very old picture of Abraham Lincoln. The Mexicans revered President Lincoln for the aid he gave in helping rid the country of Archduke Maximillian, by threatening to send the army.

The people of the Street contributed to furnishing the interior, and there have been gifts from citizens.

The old Zanja Madre, or Mother Ditch, first brought water from the Los Angeles River down around the edge of the cliff, and then over to Olvera Street. It ran down Olvera Street, switching down to the back of the Avila Adobe. The women of those early days used to get water for drinking, washing clothes, etc. from the Zanja Madre as it ran down Olvera Street, turned by the Avila Adobe, and went down again toward the Los Angeles River. Grapes were grown on the flat area below Olvera Street, below Alameda Street. I believe that Olvera Street was once known as Vine or possibly Grape Street.

The present Plaza Square at the south end of Olvera Street was established about 1880. I think it was in 1882 when the Council voted $5,000 to fix it up and plant some trees. President Workman, of the City Council, planted one or both of the fig trees that are now fine old trees.

For a time the area was not maintained well, and in the 1930s the Mexican-American Chamber of Commerce became involved. During the tenure of Dr. Reynaldo Carreon, head of the Chamber, they raised money and built the Kiosko; this is where summer concerts are given and speeches, Blessing of the Animals, and other activities are held. Then, when William Probert was manager of El Pueblo de Los Angeles State Historical Monument (now called state park), the area around the Kiosko was levelled and repaved. I was president in 1968. During that time we started a parking lot plan, and tore down the old Atlantic and Pacific hotels. We agreed on the general plan, which is now worked out in detail by the representatives of the Los Angeles City Park and the State Park Commissions. The ideas for the projects envisioned were those of Mrs. Sterling and of El Pueblo de Los Angeles.

On the south side of the Plaza was the old fire house, which we had to renew. The fire house was remodelled and put back into condition, and this was paid for with the compliments of the fire department. The same was true of the first Masonic Lodge in Los Angeles. When we became active in the restoration, the Pico House was owned by a wealthy Russian immigrant. He had made a lot of money in mining, and had managed to escape with it to America. He was a friend of Mrs. Sterling, and he gave her a written option, for quite a period, to buy the Pico House property for $80,000. We did not have such a sum, and could not get it, so the option ran out. Our main trouble in trying to option or buy a piece of property was that people who owned adjoining property would hear about it and raise their price. For example, just south of the Pico House was the old Merced Theater property, owned by the Mantz family. When they heard about the Pico House option, they doubled their price to us. That was one of the reasons we decided to make, and later did make, the whole area a state park.

Some work had been done on the Merced Theater, but not enough; it should have been completely restored. One problem, manifesting itself in much of the planned restoration, was the argument over required archaeological work. All this area is of archaeological interest; thus, before anything was built, the ground had to be dug up and examined, for some Indian relic could have been found.

Another building of the period was the Garnier Building between the Pico House and Los Angeles Street. It was built for the Chinese, and I recall, as a youth, seeing Chinese sitting on a balcony overlooking Alameda Street. Long streamers of drying vegetables hung down. During the time I was active on Olvera Street, a Chinese woman applied to restore the Joss House when the building was ready to be used again, in memory of her husband; but, at the rate of procedure, she would never live long enough, although the building had been cleaned.

I had been active in politics for some time, and through my various activities I knew every assemblyman from the Los Angeles area, and I was on friendly terms with a number in the Los Angeles Delegation to the State Legislature. Mrs. Sterling knew many others. Mrs. Sterling and I discussed the problems many times, particularly with regard to the fact that each time we would try to option or buy property, the prices would go up on everything around it. Another problem, constantly increasing, was the death of so many of the old-timers who made up the first Board of Directors. Finally, we decided that there was only one feasible way to complete the project. Mrs. Sterling, Mario and I decided against laying out a specific campaign. We felt it should simply evolve; and evolve it did, quite rapidly, to make the area a state park.

Jonathan Hollobaugh, assemblyman from Huntington Park, agreed to present a bill for an appropriation of $1,500,000 to the Assembly for restoration of the park. Los Angeles County had 32 votes out of 80 in the lower house, and we knew them all. Joe headed our county delegation, and they all went on the bill to get the appropriation.

I was well acquainted with J.R. Knowland of the *Oakland Tribune*. J.R. was the 20-year chairman who was known as the "father" to the State Park system. J.R. agreed to the area becoming a state park, and then the commission also agreed. However, they said the State Park Commission could do nothing financially, which I thought would be the case.

A number of others were helpful: Mark Russek and his group, Dr. Carl Dentzel of the Southwest Museum, and a number of people on its board did much. We had a strong friend in Mayor Fletcher Bowron, and also in Supervisors John Anson Ford and Ernest Debs. So it could be said to be a grassroots movement. Jesse Unruh, "Big Daddy" in Democratic politics in the State Assembly, was both friendly and helpful. He got money appropriated for the area south of the Plaza.

The bill was introduced, and all 32 of our assemblymen were on it. It went along beautifully, and we expected no trouble from the governor. It went through the Assembly and then through the Senate Committee. Unfortunately, here it was delayed, to become part of the last group of bills for passage through the Senate. This means it was all approved, and sitting on the pile of those passed by the Assembly, which were to go through the Senate at the last minute. That is often the case, and they "stop the clock" and go on to finish those bills. It usually becomes a mere formality, and we expected this would be the case.

At the last moment, somebody slipped in an amendment which called for taking the money out of the Beach Fund instead of state park funds. Their purpose was to keep the park funds for existing parks, which meant primarily the redwoods. We certainly were all in favor of the redwoods, but Southern California was already getting perhaps less than its share of state park money. Thus, the bill went through on this basis, and it was only a day or two until we heard from the governor. He said that since this was not a beach, he could not take money out of the Beach Funds.

We talked it over with Hal Kennedy, who had brought the governor's message. He said the governor had told him that he would put $750,000 in the 1953 budget for us if the city and county of Los Angeles would each put in $375,000. Well, we had Mayor Bowron on our team, and we had Debs and Ford. These two powerhouses,

*McIntyre Faries (center) named El Gran Hidalgo de Los Angeles. From left, Senora Consuela Castillo de Bonzo, Mayor Sam Yorty, Jerry, and Bishop Ward.*

respectively city and county, went to work; and both appropriations passed, contingent upon the money from the state. The governor kept his word, and the $1,500,000 was appropriated and in hand.

The California attorney general did the condemnation work, and purchased land where the appraisers thought it proper to buy at the price which could be obtained. We did not get all the land we wanted, but what with the city land, the streets, or rights of way over the streets, the city's Plaza land and some few little areas the county had, we were finally in position to go ahead and start the state park.

Then came the question: who should run the Plaza Park? The Board of Supervisors wanted to be in on it, or have a veto. But the City of Los Angeles, particularly the City Council, pointed out that this, after all, was the original city of Los Angeles, these forty-six acres, and that it had been part of the city since 1781. Moreover, they said, the city was already providing the street maintenance and cleaning, police and fire protection, even the toilets in the Plaza, so the city, therefore, should run it.

On the other hand, said the State Park Commission, this is a state park, or monument; therefore, the State Park Commission should run it! However, the commission finally agreed to take the advice of the city and the county on many things.

The first man they sent down to be superintendent (that is, to supervise from this area all the parks in the southern area), was named Hunter. He was a good, conscientious man; but, as might have been expected, the infighting was fierce, and continued for a considerable period of time. It was finally agreed among all three political bodies, that the area to the north of the Plaza Park, north of the Kiosko and the walkways around it, would continue to be operated by our corporation. At the same time, it was decided that the corporation should be converted to nonprofit, stock of the original Plaza de Los Angeles, Inc., being gotten rid of by a merger with the new nonprofit corporation.

Surprisingly, every single one of those people (or their successors, who had stock), agreed to turn in their stock with no recompense, which enabled them to write off the stock as a gift to the state. So, the new corporation was formed, nonprofit, and named "El Pueblo de Los Angeles, Inc." Soon it had a certificate entitling it to accept gifts, which officially entitled the donors of the old stock to their write-off. I was still president of the corporation which ran the Street, with Mario Valdez as manager.

Though few knew it, Mrs. Sterling at this time had developed cancer. She died soon afterward. She had made me promise that I would get the Biscailuz Building fixed up for the Spanish-speaking consuls, and I stayed with this activity. She also made me promise that the go-ahead would be given on the area south of the Plaza. This was done, too, but took more time.

We worked out a general plan, which the commission adopted. I should say we worked out the plan, voted unanimously for it, and put it in the record of the minutes. Of course this required the drafting of detailed plans; unfortunately, that was not accomplished for many years. The State Park Commission, under Governor Reagan, was headed by William Penn Mott, Sr. I retired officially from the bench in December 1967 and was appointed by Reagan to the State Park Commission. Finally, I was persuaded that I should go back on the local Pueblo Commission, which was then going nowhere. So I resigned from the state commission, went on the local, and immediately became its president. No preparation had been made on this, but it went through the City Council in about half an hour; all formalities were waived. So, leaving the City Council at about 10:30, I went down.and, at 11:00, was elected chairman of the Plaza de Los Angeles State Monument Commission. I stayed on for a year. I did not want to serve beyond that.

It was a short time before it became obvious that the three area political groups could not get along, even as well as had been done under the State Park Commission. It was then that the decision was made to form a new commission, with three representatives from the city, three from the county, and three from the state. This was under a law of the state which provided for tri-party agreements of the kind. Years before, when I had been a member of the state's 6th Agricultural District Commission (I was its president for 12 years), we had made use of the tri-party idea. We formed the Coliseum Commission, which is still in operation.

So, the new Commission was formed, but this happy start did not last too long. Now, the State Park Commission threw up its hands and said to the city, "We'll own it, but you run it." Then, the city organized and oversaw a subcommission to advise the city's Recreation and Parks Commission. But there were problems. First, it was very slow to do anything at all. Second, though its planning was good, it was taking a horrible percentage of money received. Third, the merchants were uniformly unhappy. Fourth, it had appeared to us all that there would be enough money to complete the work south of the Plaza, but such had not been the case. And, fifth, a lot of citizens were very dissatisfied. The *Los Angeles Times* wrote a scathing article about the operation in 1979, and it is really no better today. Still, we are thankful for small favors.

I tried very hard, during my short tenure, to get the organization to (1) start collecting old and authentic furniture to be used in the restorations; (2) start an oral history, a collection of taped reminiscences of some of the old residents still living; and (3) start a collection of artifacts, such as old guns, costumes, diaries and the like. I thought of what has been done in other places to preserve and enhance the spirit of the original place. It should have been a colorful and restful reproduction, in all respects possible, of the pueblo of the early days.

The present curator of the park, Mrs. Jean Bruce Poole, is a fine person, who has gathered together a lot of historical information, and I believe she is writing a book about the Plaza. She has a very good lecture with slides, telling the story of the park and surroundings, which are available to the public.

Very early in my time on the Commission, I saw the handwriting on the wall. So did others, among them Hernando Courtright and the Princess Conchita Pignatelli. The latter had been Conchita Sepulveda, and had married Prince Pignatelli of Italy. At my invitation, we three got together for lunch. I suggested the need for a support group to broaden the base of efforts with respect to the cultural aspect of the planned restoration and operation of the area. It seemed to me that many important and influential people, who would have no interest in the political management of the area, would be interested in helping in a social and cultural way, and could be of great assistance in raising funds. They heartily agreed, and thus was born Los Amigos del Pueblo, Inc.

Hernando took the ball, and Conchita was a great help. So, that organization began, and thanks to many others, such as John Bowles, is still very active. It has been very effective in publicizing and getting money for the area, and in stimulating interest in the early California history that is our cultural heritage.

Not long after this, Las Angelitas was formed. This is a group of young women who act as docents. The group was formed under the aegis of the Los Angeles Cultural Heritage Board, headed by Carl Dentzell, curator of the Southwest Museum. They agreed to sponsor conducted tours of places of interest in Los Angeles, particularly the Plaza area.

The earthquake of the sixties virtually destroyed the Avila Adobe. As I have mentioned, much architectural work is required before any sort of construction or reconstruction is permitted in this area, and the cost of that work in this case was around $23,000. Practically all of this was given by Los Amigos del Pueblo. Frankly, we felt that this would put us in a powerful position in connection with the architectural work, particularly in view of our further and much greater contribution.

As treasurer of Los Amigos, I said we would take charge of the costs of rebuilding the Avila Adobe, and Hernando Courtright, then the president, backed me up. William Probert, manager of the Plaza Commission, obtained $50,000 in federal disaster relief funds. At the

*The Avila Adobe fiesta after the restoration.*

time the contract was let, I had in my pocket a check for $85,000 raised by Los Amigos del Pueblo, and we put in some $14,000 more. The merchants of Olvera Street came up with about $20,000, and a few thousand was raised from other sources.

We, of Los Amigos del Pueblo, felt that our architectural suggestions were valid, and that we had more than earned the right to have them considered. After they had our money, they would not, in fact, allow our architect into the reconstruction area. We were thoroughly annoyed, and we certainly were not pleased with the outcome of their arbitrarily-imposed conceptions. Nor were many others satisfied with the outcome. It was determined by the state architectural group. They were advised by "experts" who I'm not sure knew nearly as much about the Mexican homes of 1818–1846 as a number of our people did. I remember that Mario Valdez was terribly disappointed, as were John Bowles, John Roche and most of the rest of us.

There have been a number of such brushes with bureaucracy, and I do occasionally feel a bit discouraged after nearly sixty years of watching this project and trying to "baby it along."

I do feel satisfied that, among us, we have done, or begun, the things Mrs. Sterling dreamed of, and to which she gave so much of her life. John Roche, who followed me as treasurer of Los Amigos del Pueblo (he was also secretary), might well be called the banker of Los Amigos. He told me that Los Amigos has been responsible for around $185,000 in contributions. So, among the three organizations I've referred to, Los Amigos, El Pueblo de Los Angeles, Inc., and Plaza de Los Angeles, Inc., well over half a million dollars has come in from nonprofit patrons. This is far more than has come from any source, except the original appropriation.

# Chapter 12
## Politics &
## Other Matters

M y entry into politics was completely unintentional. But I liked the game and stayed. Along the way, I formed the decision that I would not quit until we had a Republican president, and twenty years later, we did—Dwight D. Eisenhower.

At the bottom of the depression, in 1932, my patient and civic-minded wife, my two lovely girls and I lived in South Pasadena. I worked in my brother's law office, and, though I shared in the earnings, there wasn't much earned. My house rental was $37.50 a month; ground round steak was about 39¢ a pound, and a pound made the meat for a day for four of us.

Well, on a Saturday I was mowing the front lawn with the old-fashioned push mower, when Ted Stearns stopped his car at the curb, and I stepped out to visit with him. Theodore LeGrande Stearns was a bit older than I, a close friend and classmate of my brother, Culbert. Though I didn't know him well, it was nice to visit with him. In the course of our conversation, he said, "The reason I came down to see you was that I want to run for Congress in this 12th District." This was a surprise to me, and a subject quite outside my thoughts at the time, though I was doing some nonpolitical community work. I was the unofficial and unpaid chairman of our relief effort in the area, and chairman of the Civic Affairs Committee of the Oneonta Club.

I said, "Well, I'll vote for you." But he wanted something more. He told me there was to be a meeting of the South Pasadena Republican Club in the meeting room of the City Hall on the following Thursday night. "I need the club's endorsement," he told me. "I would like you to get a group together, go up there and take over that meeting, and

123

get their endorsement for me."

I said, "Why me? I'm not even a member, and anyway, I'm a good friend of Harrison McCall (the club's president), and I wouldn't normally vote against what he might want. Also, Fred Houser, your assemblyman and mine, is probably hoping to get the endorsement, but," I said, "are you sure you want to make the race? Do you think you can win?" "I do," he replied, "And I think I can win."

I thought a moment. "All right," I said, "I'll give you a hand." So, I went to a valuable lady member of the Women's Republican Club, a high school and college classmate, Elizabeth Claflin, now Elizabeth Helter. We discussed the matter, and she helped. Between us, we got about thirty people to go to the meeting, and all joined the South Pasadena Republican Club, paying our own money. This, by the way, was $2.00, a sum of some consideration in those terrible times. It was a very pleasant meeting, and at the end the matter of endorsement came up. I proposed Stearns, with no prejudice toward Fred Houser. Much to my surprise, I walked away from the meeting as president of the South Pasadena Republican Club.

Shortly thereafter, I had a call from our local member of the county Republican Central Committee, Theodore Law. Ted, a South Pasadena real estate man, told me that the Central Committee wanted to try an experiment in our 12th District. They wanted us to have a "grassroots" meeting to hear candidates, and then choose the candidate we would support for the congressional seat of the district. The idea was to hear the thinking of all the candidates for the nomination, and get a look at them. The Central Committee felt that this meeting could come up with an informal agreement on a candidate.

At that time, too, there was a right to cross-file, so there was the possibility that we might pick up some Democrats who would stay with us to the final election. It didn't sound like a bad idea, and it was certainly good for Republicans to get together. The Central Committee felt, and Law agreed, that we might shoot for having a representative from each precinct at the meeting. South Pasadena had 22 precincts, which was small compared with some other areas. So, he asked me to go out and get the representatives from the various precincts. Along with the Republican women and some members of the South Pasadena Republican Club, we took the precinct list and found someone we knew in each precinct. We had a full slate of 22 delegates from South Pasadena, and strange as it seems, they were all for Ted Stearns.

A large tent had been set up in El Monte for the meeting. Each person paid his own share of the expense, including the supper. Five main candidates were nominated. Our group sat together, and, like everyone else, discussed the candidates over dinner; all had previously made their speeches. But Houser had boycotted the meeting, saying this was not the way to do it. He said anybody could run, and the public should not be influenced by previous endorsement of a political group chosen in this manner at the behest of a central committee.

The meeting was deadlocked, and I believe the politically smart boys were about to put in a new dark horse. As I recall, this was Joseph Allard, a lawyer who would have made a good candidate. I knew that when everyone became aware of the deadlock, they would all look around for such a dark horse candidate, and favor him.

We were about to start in again after a recess when, to the consternation of all, Ted Law, as he was rushing down the aisle, fell dead a few feet in front of me. There was some debate about whether the meeting should continue, but it soon took up again. Not, however, before I had a talk with my friend, Frank Rice.

Frank was the chief representative from the mostly Democratic Mexican-American areas. So, after about four ballots, I went to Frank and said, "Frank, if this goes on, we're both going to lose out. So how about lending me four votes on the next ballot? If I don't have any luck, I'll lend you four on the following ballot." We kidded about it a bit, and he agreed.

So, on the next ballot, Ted Stearns became the congressional candidate of the so-called grassroots meeting, and we hoped all would join in backing him. Unfortunately, Fred Houser beat him in the primary and became the Republican nominee. He then proceeded to lose the election to the Democratic nominee in the final election.

As a result, as the front man of the group which had supported Stearns, I became quite well known among 12th District Republicans. The "Republican Assembly," made up of the younger group of Republicans, was started that year, and I became its county vice-chairman. Then the Alhambra group, which had supported Houser, "took me in," and in 1934 I was elected to the county Central Committee. This Republican Assembly was started by about ten young men, possibly some women, who felt that President Hoover and his group had had their day. They felt the Republican Party needed new leadership, and set out to be that leadership.

In the first few weeks after I joined, I brought in some 90 paying members. Then, as I looked at their little newspaper and others, including the *Times*, I realized that while I was getting 90 members, the top man of the assembly had recruited three—and he was president for Los Angeles County. One or two others had recruited five or six members. So I slowed down a bit, and began to look around. The 12th Congressional District, of which I was the head for the Assembly, quickly became the largest group in the County Assembly. Within a short time we had over 550 members, and soon we had the greatest number of any congressional district in the state.

They had an ambitious plan to develop statewide, which they carried out. The first president of the statewide California Republican Assembly was not Ed Shattuck, though he was the driving force. He really chose the man who became president, Sherrill Halbert, later a federal judge. Robert Fenton Craig, a young and politically-minded lawyer, took a year off from his practice. He was paid a small salary, and he "ran the wheels off" his car for that year, going about the state and organizing California Republican Assemblies. Sherrill, the new president went back to talk with Alf Landon. Some of us were not strong for Landon, but that's another story. Leadership expanded and became diversified throughout the State.

Soon the time came to plan to organize a delegation to the 1936 Republican National Convention. Governor Merriam, who had defeated Upton Sinclair in 1934, wanted the delegation pledged to him. He wanted to wield power at the convention, and California was even then a state to be reckoned with—about 4th place at the time. Merriam wanted to control the state as well as the delegates to the convention, since this would unite the people who were not Merriam-minded with the Hoover group, the Hiram Johnson group, the California Republican Assembly, a lot of the Republican Women's Clubs, and others.

A number of Republicans were not favorable to Governor Merriam, and a move was started, amid much newspaper talk, to form an uninstructed delegation. This would have the Republican national committeewoman, Mrs. Williamson of Berkeley. Then there was the old Hiram Johnson group, which included some very fine politicians, notably Frank P. Doherty.

It was thought that the thing to do was pledge the group to Earl Warren, then attorney general. He was considered rather liberal, but very well-connected, being the protege of the powerful J.R. Knowland, publisher of the *Oakland Tribune*. This group, which had organized the delegation, was pretty sure they would have the support of the *Oakland Tribune*, the *Los Angeles Times*, the *San Francisco Chronicle* and the *San Diego Union*. There was also a very strong newspaper organization known as the California Newspaper Publishers Association, to which practically all of the smaller papers belonged. The strong man in that group was Justus Cramer, very close to Merriam. So, adding all these together, it was the Merriam group against the uninstructed delegation, made up of all the other groups. Certainly the women's organizations were with us.

It began to seem a battle of conservatives—that is, the Merriam group—against liberals, but really, it was not all that black-and-white. The Republican Assembly tended to the liberal side of the spectrum. A Mr. Smith, vice president and general manager of the First National Bank of Pomona, became one of the two delegates, while I, from the other end of the 12th Congressional District and from the Republican Assembly, was the second. We would represent the 12th Congressional District on the Earl Warren, uninstructed, delegation to the Republican Convention. At the time, we were, I suppose, a chauvinistic group in a sense, being mostly male-dominated. However, our organization worked largely with the women's groups, and I am bound to say they were well-organized, perhaps better than we were. We, that is, the Assembly, took control of the county Central Committee in our 12th Congressional District, though we didn't have things all our own way; we had about a 4–3 advantage. Much to our surprise, we found that the older members of the county Central Committee, far from being our enemies, were highly pleased with our coming into the group.

Things worked so well that Palmer Conner told Central Committee chairman Ingall Bull, a strong Merriam man, to keep the county Central group and all other groups except our own, out of the 12th Congressional District. He said we would carry it in the primary and finals. And we did, though not for Congress, which we usually lost.

We were very enthusiastic about our success, but about this time I found myself in an unfortunate position. I seemed always to have been one leading the opposition to Ed Shattuck, head of the L.A. County Republican Assembly and really its leader for the whole state. I was personally very fond of Ed, but I felt he was too hidebound in his thinking. It did not seem to me that he understood how to get votes, other than those of the super-conservative Republican groups. I didn't feel that he went over too well with the businessmen; I know he didn't financially. Then there were the conservative Democrats, disgruntled Democrats, and other groups in whom I saw potential support. Remember, cross-filing was permitted in those days. We were a minority party, and I felt I could, if allowed, get the additional necessary votes to win, and get them honestly. I believe I proved this over a period of years.

In 1936, our delegation was nominally pledged to Earl Warren, a good friend of the Republican Assembly and national committeeman, I think, in 1934. I believe it was about this time he began to have higher aspirations; however, he released his delegation in 1936, as he had promised. In 1938, he ran for attorney general, and we supported him. Warren was the good friend and protege of J.R. Knowland who started Earl up the ladder, first as Oakland's assistant city attorney, then as assistant district attorney, and later as district attorney of Alameda County. The friendship between Warren and J.R.'s son, William Knowland, was more than political. For years they were such close friends that Bill even loaned the family linen and silver to Earl when a great occasion called for making a splash. Warren once borrowed linen and silver from Bill when he was governor. Warren had little money of his own; his father had supposedly made a lot, but died without any. Also, though it was not generally known, Earl had to take care of his sister. J.R. was, in my estimation, much smarter, politically, than his sons. Bill had very fine qualities, but had more of the bull than the fox in his makeup. Bill was a most honest man in politics, as much as any man I have ever known.

Arthur Samish was a self-proclaimed lobbyist, and represented a lot of interests. Among them were the glass bottle industry, the wine industry, some racetracks, and perhaps some gambling interests. He was a very able fellow, very courteous, and a Republican. Arty kept a file on everyone—not merely legislators, lobbyists and administrative officers of the state, but politicians and people of wealth. On one occasion, I was sitting in Bill Knowland's office at a time he was running for reelection to the Senate. A check had come in, in the amount of $5,000, marked for Bill's senatorial campaign. The clerk brought it in and asked Bill what he should do with it. Bill grinned, and so did I. He said, "Tell you what; hold on while I write a letter." He wrote a letter addressed to Arty Samish as follows: "Dear Arty, thank you so much for your letter of support for my campaign, and also for the check. At present, though, our finances are in good shape, and we do not need the check. We think it best to send it back to you, and we return it herewith. Cordially, Bill Knowland."

Bill then instructed the clerk to take both the check and letter to have photostatic copies made of each; after this he was to return them to Arty Samish. Thus no connection could be claimed between Samish and the *Tribune* or any of the Knowland family.

Earl Warren began thinking of wider horizons as far back as his national committeeman days, and perhaps by 1936, he was thinking of the presidency. Some of his friends did organize for him in 1940. On the other hand, some of us thought he had a longing to be a justice of the Supreme Court of the United States. I'm not sure where we got that idea, but it was there, that he did have such a longing. Perhaps he wanted that more than the presidency. We thought so, but whether we were right, I cannot say.

Before going back to the convention in 1936, some of us rebelled at the idea of Alf Landon as a candidate. We delegates had nothing against Landon, but felt he did not have a chance against Franklin D. Roosevelt. We were certainly right! We felt that the only man who might have a chance was Senator Arthur Vandenberg of Michigan. He was, at that time, chairman of the Senate Foreign Relations Committee, and was well thought of. Also, he had great strength in the South. He had introduced much worthwhile legislation. I believe he had been the actual author, perhaps with suggestions from Hoover, of the bill setting up the Reconstruction Finance Corporation. This, and several other plans or bills, were held up until Roosevelt was inaugurated. He wanted nothing said or done until he had taken office; then he adopted this and other Vandenberg plans.

When we got to the convention in Cleveland, at least four of us threw our suitcases into the rooms and went in search of Senator Vandenberg. We finally located him sitting alone on a park bench, smoking his pipe. We introduced ourselves and talked to him, asking his permission to start a boom for his nomination as a presidential candidate in the California delegation, and to see if we could spread it elsewhere. He promised to think it over and said he would let us know by 1:00 that night (late hours at conventions!). At 1:00 he found us and told us it was not the thing to do. He said there was no use, that Landon had the convention sewed up; we were not to try to push his candidacy. He thanked us all very politely for our thought of him, but said he had put it out of his mind. We, in turn, thanked him; Senator Vandenberg and I remained friends, corresponding until the end of his life. So, we voted with the others for Landon and Knox, and worked very hard in what turned out to be, perhaps, the most hopeless cause in the history of American presidential politics.

The heart of all political effort is that at the voting level, the so-called "grassroots." This was even more true in those days, when national media meant radio only, and when the state of the country, and the world, was such as to turn all minds to the effort to make conditions better.

It was always considered a good idea to give a new man the "disadvantaged" districts to supervise and try to carry. It fell to my lot to try to get votes in such districts. We had a good working organization in Hollywood and fair ones in Boyle Heights, Highland Park, West Los Angeles, Hancock Park, Santa Monica and some others—in about half the assembly districts I would say. But in many districts there was practically nothing, and it was my duty to try to get an organization and votes there. I spoke a little Spanish, but I was far from fluent, especially in the rapid-fire Mexican dialect. Moreover, one doesn't get these people to vote with him merely by being a "friend" in voting season. I had to do more.

One of my clients was in the San Gabriel Valley Water District, a hidebound conservative organization. They served water to many of the people in the El Monte area and nearby, at $1.25 per month per lot. There were no meters. The soil was sandy, requiring lots of irrigation to grow anything, and many people of the area, in addition to raising families, raised vegetables and other crops to try to make ends meet. So, having abundant and unmetered water was crucially important to these people at this time.

A meeting was called by the Railroad Commission, which was the forerunner of the Public Utilities Commission, to hear public reaction to a plan to put in meters, with a minimum of $1.25 per month per lot. The water company didn't think the objections of these people would amount to much; perhaps they even thought these people didn't use much water. The examiner for the commission was a nice young fellow, an engineer rather than a lawyer—a good, honest man, but not a leader. The district was not entirely peopled by Mexican-Americans, but much to the surprise of my client, when we arrived at the El Monte City Hall for the meeting, there were close to five hundred people in attendance, predominantly women. The meeting hall was packed, and there were many on the steps and walkways as well. The women began chanting, "We want night sessions! We want night sessions!" The crowd paraded in front of the examiner, who simply sat there for about twenty minutes. Finally, a big, heavy Anglo woman stepped up to him, shook her fist under his nose and said, "Do you hear us! We want night sessions!" The examiner said, "Well, madam, I have sent someone to telephone the Commission office in San Francisco to ask if night sessions can be held." She said nothing, and he went on, "You know, we're allowed only a certain amount of time for each session, and then we have to go on to the next place. The work for the month is all scheduled, and we have many other meetings. All of these meetings are announced, just as yours was, for a particular time and date."

The woman had by now gathered her thoughts. She screamed, "What is this, Russia? Is this a free country? Are you bureaucrats going to tell us what to do? We want night sessions because our husbands have to work during the day, and we want them to be here at the meeting!" So, the examiner called another recess.

During one of these recesses, I ran into a Mexican-American friend of mine. I suggested that he take an unofficial poll of these people. So, he agreeing, we took a written poll with questions something like this: "Did you vote for Warren in the last campaign? If so, why? Are you a Republican or a Democrat?" Well, it developed that four out of five at the hearing were Democrats, and on the other hand, about the same percentage had voted for Warren. Nearly everybody responded to the poll, having nothing else to do.

This was very interesting, particularly to my client. He could not understand, as I felt I did, the voting of these people. So, he sent around another set of slips, asking further why they voted for Warren. He tabulated the answers, and they ran about three out of four something like this: "Because he is from our side of the tracks. Because he understands us and is for the things we are for." All this was very hard for my conservative client to understand.

Finally, the word came back that the meeting had to go on, as the examiner had another announced meeting pending. My friend and client had a bad time from these people, and so did I, as his attorney. However, the people did not hold it against me, but against him and the "big corporations." I renewed a number of friendships among the Mexican-Americans, and I believe made some new ones. I still retain some of those friendships.

We always did better in those districts than the registration indicated. I am not sure if this is true today; things are more crystallized now, and we had some ways of proceeding that are different now. And, of course, present-day campaigns are primarily via the media. There are several reasons why we did better then; in the first place, we generally had better-known candidates; secondly, radio at that date was handled better than today—there was no television; third, the newspaper function was handled far better; fourth, we had cross-filing, which was a help because many people neither knew nor cared whether the incumbent was Republican or Democrat; and fifth, we were, I think, more ingenious, and we took the trouble to know and understand the districts to a degree that today's Republican leadership does not seem to approach. We knew how to reach our people, and honesty was drummed into us. With integrity paramount between ourselves and the people of the district, we were received with respect.

I had stayed out, and continued to stay out, of city and county politics while active in Republican Party work. You must remember that, at least in theory, city and county officials are nonpartisan, and the elections to those offices are nonpartisan. At times, the Democratic groups would try to work the word "Democrat" into their campaigns, but we were pretty successful in blocking that. We could, as I say, cross-file and pick up a number of Democrats in the party primaries; generally they would stay with us and provide a nucleus for a Democratic committee, and publicity for our candidate in the finals. I am sure all appreciated our staying out of nonpartisan campaigns. I firmly believe that local politics and partisan state and national politics do not mix well.

In 1936, my brother, Culbert, telephoned me. "Did you know," he said, "that I am not an American citizen?"

"No," I replied. "If you're not, then I suppose I'm not, either. What's it all about?"

Culbert began by telling me that Julia, his wife, had inherited some claims arising out of the Pancho Villa raids. Villa, as you probably know, was a Mexican bandit (or patriot, if one was on his side) who had conducted raids across the Rio Grande into the United States. Afterward, a joint U.S.-Mexican Commission agreed that there should be reparations, and these were duly fixed and awarded. Some of these raids had been on the ranch, near Alice, Texas, which was then owned by Julia's parents, and they were awarded reparation.

In 1936 these awards were finally being heard. Julia had inherited the claims. However, her claim had been disallowed because, said the board, she had married a noncitizen of the United States. Such was the law in 1923, though not any longer. "So," said Culbert, "her claims were refused on the basis of my noncitizenship."

This seemed strange, inasmuch as at the time of their marriage, Culbert had been a second lieutenant in the Armed Forces of the United States. He had been stationed at Brownsville, Texas, just prior to going overseas. I said, "Let me look into it, and we'll talk it over later."

Our mother was still alive, so I explained the situation to her, and she told me, "In 1898 or 1899, the Faries family had a furlough, or sabbatical, as it was the custom of the Missionary Board to grant every seven years. Grandfather Isaiah had been living in Minneapolis, Minnesota, but was definitely failing. That winter, as in other years, he went to California to escape the Minnesota cold. Generally he went to Santa Barbara, but this particular year he was at Pacific Grove, near San Anselmo. I thought it would be very nice to have him baptize our baby, meaning you, and name you after himself. Your father agreed, and this was done."

I never tried to see a baptismal record, but there may well be one at the Pacific Grove Presbyterian church. Mother went on, "Thereafter, we called the children by new names, so as to have Isaiah Faries properly recognized. Just what the names were before that, I'm not sure, but when we came to California because of your father's malaria, we entered the names on the school records as we had named them after your baptism, as Isaiah McIntyre Faries and William Culbert Faries."

In the years we were born, the law required that a child born abroad to American parents must be registered with the American consul nearest the place of his birth. We were born near Che Foo, in

China, but this was not important enough to have an American consul. The British consul was designated acting American consul, and he registered the names as they originally were with the U.S. Department of State. This went to Washington and was recorded there; hence, the names we had grown up and gone to school under did not tally with our names as registered in Washington. This later caused me a good deal of grief. Meantime, however, Culbert's wife's claims had been disallowed because of the mix-up in this case.

Well, I proceeded to take steps in the Los Angeles Superior Court to change our names. I had verified our names with the State Department, and their letter was part of the documentation offered when I filed separate petitions on behalf of Culbert and myself. Included was a deposition of Mother's answers to my questions on the situation.

Immediately, the question of Father's citizenship arose. How could we prove that we had been born to an American citizen? As for Mother, she had been born in England in 1877; her parents came to New York when she was sixteen. Mother had no recollection of ever having been naturalized; Samuel Henry, or Henry Samuel Chittick, had been. It is my impression that, at least at that time, minor children of a father who became naturalized were, by that fact, themselves naturalized.

I knew that Father had been born in Broadalbyn, New York, then the family home. I've seen pictures of the home, a lovely place on Kenyetto Creek, in West Ontario County, New York. I knew, too, that he had been baptized in the Presbyterian church there. So I wrote to the West Ontario County seat, but they replied that they had not, at that time, issued birth certificates. So, I had to try for a baptismal certificate.

Having gotten in touch with the church, I learned that either they had not then issued certificates or that the record was destroyed. There had been a fire at one time, which did burn some records. However, after a considerable search, they located a gentleman of some 91 years who had been a caretaker or custodian of the church at the time. He was very definite as to his recollection of my father's baptism. He said, "Our pew was just behind that of the Faries', and I remember the baptism of William Reid Faries very well. I was a boy at the time." After doing some mental arithmetic, I realized that he quite easily could have recalled the incident, so his deposition was obtained and was among the papers I submitted.

After proper noticing, the matter came up for hearing in the Department of the Presiding Judge of the Los Angeles Superior Court. The presiding judge at the time was Douglas Edmonds, whom I knew. Having looked over the papers, he beckoned me to the bench by crooking a finger. Leaning over, he whispered to me, "This is too good to keep; I'm going to have to give it to the newspapers." I was puzzled. "Why," I asked, "should the newspapers take cognizance of this? What's so interesting about it?"

"Consider," he said, "the headline: Prominent Los Angeles Attorney Practices Law for Sixteen Years Under False Name." We both laughed. He did not give it to the papers, there was no publicity, and the petition was granted and an order made. "Fine," I thought, "we're all set."

Although it might have been fine for Culbert, my troubles were, had I known it, far from over. A few years later, my wife, Lois, and I took a trip to British Columbia, in Canada, by automobile. While there, we purchased for her a beautiful fur coat. We got a slip showing the price and the value they put on it, for customs purposes. We had made our hotel reservations and sent the money in advance, actually more money than was needed, but we failed to get a receipt when we left, showing how long we had stayed.

Coming back we took the ferry; we were given customs forms to fill out, and declared the coat. We actually were not required to pay any duty because the length of our stay had entitled us to bring back goods to that amount free of duty. When we got to our car to leave the ferry in Bremerton, on the windshield was chalked in big red letters the word "Hold." All the other cars went off, and we went to the office. "Yes," they said, "we want to talk to you."

We went inside, where they asked us to produce the coat we had bought. They looked it over, remarking that it was a very nice coat. I said, "Here's the record of what we paid, and what they valued it at, so there should be no tariff."

"Oh," said the official, "we're not governed by what the sellers up there put on things." I said, "Not even the Hudson Bay Company?" "No. How long were you in Canada?" I replied that we had been there several days, and he asked to see the hotel bill. I was forced to say I didn't have one, and explained the situation. "Well," he said again, "that's certainly a very nice coat."

This back and forth went on for a time, and they seemed to be enjoying themselves. Meantime we were standing there, the crowd was waiting for the ferry to go back the other way, and we were holding up the foot traffic. Finally the two men began to laugh. "Look," they said, "we're just having a little fun with you. We're Democrats, and we know your Republican activities. It seemed to be a good chance to have a little fun. Here's your coat; it's a nice one, and of course there is no duty. Now, I'll tell you what to do so this won't happen again. Get yourself a green card from the Department of Immigration." I asked what that might be, and he said to me, "It's what we call a Certificate of Derivative Citizenship. You'll have no trouble if you carry that, but remember, it can't be copied; you must carry the original. With that certificate you'll have no problem getting a passport or anything of the sort." So, I went down to the Los Angeles office of the Department of Immigration. They told me I could get the certificate, but they would require considerable proof, what with the prevalent Communist problem in the country. At their direction, I filled out the application, after which they asked what proof of American citizenship I could show. I told them of the name change order, and they said, "We don't recognize a decision of that sort in state court. You'll have to have something more."

I produced the report cards from the Orange, California, school from about 1903 to 1907, and from the Los Angeles schools after that. They wanted more; they wanted my school records, and they took a lot of letters I had written dating clear back to before we left Wei Hsien in 1903. They had my name, along with those of the rest of the family, from the 1910 U.S. Census. I didn't object to their taking this material, since I wanted this straightened out and thought I would unquestionably get it all back. Such, sadly, was not the case. I tried repeatedly to retrieve these personal records and was repeatedly told they had to have them for evidence.

At any rate, there was, finally, a hearing. I was required to have two witnesses, and I did. Unfortunately, I had brought David T. Chow and my friend Fernando Figueroa, both of whom were naturalized citizens, not born in the United States. They would not allow either of them as a witness, so it had to be held over, and I had to get two native-born witnesses.

When the matter came up for the third time, again under a different examiner, this one went through it all, shook his head and said,

"This is very irregular. I've never had anything like this." And he uttered other readily recognizable cries of minor bureaucrats the world over. As it happened, the United States commissioner of immigration was present on that occasion, so my examiner went in to see him. Soon the commissioner, top man of the department for the entire United States, returned with my examiner.

Looking at the papers and at me, he said, "Haven't I seen that name somewhere?" I replied that this was likely, since I was fairly well-known and had often been in the newspapers. "Well, where have I seen the name?" he asked. Again, I pointed out that I had been around for quite awhile, was a well-known lawyer, and had practiced before several Federal commissions. He asked, "Are you admitted to practice in the federal courts?" I told him I had been so admitted since 1922.

Turning to the hearing officer, the commissioner said, "Call the United States District Court in Los Angeles here. See if you can find this man's name as having been admitted to practice." He went on to say, "One has to be an American citizen to be admitted to federal practice. If you're shown admitted to practice here, I'll sign the order and the certificate." Of course the reply elicited was that I had, indeed, been admitted to practice in the federal district court for the Central District of California, in the 9th Circuit, and also in the United States Supreme Court. So, I got my certificate.

Well, I thought for the second time, "Now everything is fine." At which, no doubt, the gods laughed. They weren't through with me just yet. Upon retirement from Superior Court, it occurred to me that I might be entitled to Social Security. I went to the office, therefore, and inquired. "Why, yes," they said, "you're entitled to receive such and such an amount. You were paying into Social Security from 1936 to 1944." I then recalled that, through my position in the law offices of David R. Faries, and also through being secretary and counsel for Land Escrow and Safe Deposit Company, I had indeed paid contributions to Social Security and was entitled to draw it thereafter.

When I showed my certificate to the Social Security people, they informed me that they did not care to accept the Department of Immigration's assurance that I was a citizen, nor did they recognize my change of name. Curbing my fury, I asked, "Well, what would you recognize?" They said they would check. I was passed around to several people, ending up finally at the desk of some woman lawyer.

She said she had looked everything up, and that I would have to get a derivative certificate of birth. I remarked that to my knowledge that could only be done in the state where one had been born; she informed me that had been changed. I could now get one here in California. Checking, I found that she was right. So, I filed a petition with the Los Angeles Superior Court, reciting all the things I have mentioned here. It was published, the district attorney was notified, and there were no objections. Thus, it came in due course to the Probate Department of our Superior Court. At the time, the presiding judge of the Probate Department was Donald Wright, who had been my friend for many years. Don got a good laugh out of all my troubles, and I showed him the various things I had left, such as my green card and the certified copy of my prior order. He granted the petition, and I obtained the derivative certificate of birth, this being accepted by the Social Security people. But even these last exhibits were retained by the courts, and after ten years, after the mimeographing of the records, such exhibits are destroyed. One way or another, one organization or another, they are all gone now.

At lunch in a Hollywood restaurant one day, I looked out the window at the "HOLLYWOOD" sign on the hill above old Hollywood. Few know its background story, so it seems a fitting one with which to end this part of my story.

S.H. Woodruff was a real estate subdivider who wanted to sell lots in the "Beachwood" subdivision on that hill. Few knew that the land was actually owned by Harry Chandler. I was, at the time, with Faries and Williamson, and we represented Woodruff. Also, Williamson was Chandler's son-in-law.

John Roche was involved in the film business, but he was working with Woodruff, and he got the idea of promoting the subdivision by putting up a big sign, "HOLLYWOODLAND." Everyone knew that Harry Chandler could be interviewed, or talked to, simply by waiting until he had "put the paper to bed" at night, or early in the morning. So John went down to the *Times* and waited until about 2:00 a.m. He put his idea about the sign to Chandler. Chandler listened, then called in old Frank X. Pfaffinger. "Frank," said Chandler, "have we got $50,000 that we could give John Roche to build a sign?" "Why certainly, Mr. Chandler. You recall, we just sold that stock." "Well, give John Roche a check for $50,000."

So Roche got his money that first night. He hired high school football players to do the work. There was no road up that steep hill and no way to get to the sign area except by switching back and forth. They toiled in the bright sun, using burros to carry the sand, cement and so forth. At the location, they mixed the cement in shallow, metal-lined mixing boxes. There were no cement mixers; the cement was mixed, the foundations poured, and the sign built, by human muscle power.

So it stood until time, wind and vandalism made it a pitiful sight. Then, a new idea was born—restore the sign, leaving out the "LAND." The Hollywood Chamber of Commerce and others took up the battle cry, "Save Hollywood's sign!" John Roche was immediately interested, and became treasurer of the project. This was roughly fifty years after the original sign was built, in 1978 and 1979. Letters of the sign were "sold," each selling for $27,000. This time, it would be done with flair. The city Parks and Recreation Department gave its approval, and it was a popular project. The money poured in, and soon there was enough to build the sign and cover all expenses.

I kept in touch with John Roche, whose soul was in the project. He was well over eighty, and his heart was weakening, but he was thrilled by the wonderful cooperation on all sides. By the time the sign was built and was to be dedicated, John was very weak. But he told me with grim determination, "I'm going to live until it's done!"

There was a great storm on the night of the completion celebration, but John Roche was there; he had made it! Three days later, John was on his way to the Beverly Wilshire Hotel to discuss some copy with Hernando Courtright, when his heart, which he forced to see him through the completion and dedication of the sign, finally failed him, and he fell dead on the sidewalk.

Though I was still in private practice, my interest became more and more engrossed in politics. In this I played an increasingly active role until, after the election of President Eisenhower, I was appointed a Superior Court judge, and withdrew from political activity.

# Chapter 13
## The Coliseum &
## Sports Pavilion

*B*usy as I was with politics and the attempt to make a living, it is a source of some satisfaction to recall that I was also able to play a part in civic affairs. Of course, the opportunity arose through my position in political affairs, and my close relations with those in political power.

I have mentioned that I had been chairman of the board of the Sixth Agricultural District. When Olson became governor, I was not reappointed to that position since Olson's philosophy led him to politicize every state office he could. After Earl Warren became governor, he sent Everett Mattoon to me with the request that I go back on that board as chairman. I told him that I could not, or would not do so. He asked my reason, and I said that, as much as I loved the work of the Sixth Agricultural District, it was now a very unhappy situation. The board was badly fragmented, and there was no clear direction. Olson's politicizing had had the effect of placing many in positions of authority who were neither capable of, nor interested in, the work of the district. There were many things to be done that could not be done in that situation, and what existed was an unhappy stalemate.

Later, he returned to me and said in effect, "The governor realizes that you were right in what you said, but he has the matter of control straightened out now, and he promises you his support if you will take the presidency of the Sixth Agricultural District again." So, I was reappointed and served as president until 1953 when I went on the bench. I had to retire then, of course, since no one may hold a judicial position and an administrative post simultaneously in our state. The two do not mix, under our Constitution, and this is, I think, a very good rule.

Not too long after I went back to the commission, our general manager, Louis Venator, came to me with a bright idea. We were very unhappy with the way the Playground Commission of Los Angeles was handling the Coliseum. Also, we wanted to get professional football, which was becoming very popular, and solve the racial problem of playing there. Louis had the idea that we could achieve these things by adding a few words to a section of the California Agricultural Code, Section 80, as I recall. He proposed that we insert in the appropriate section, which defines the rights of the Agricultural District of the state, the power "to condemn leaseholds." Now, the land on which the Coliseum stood was owned by the Sixth Agricultural District, which, in turn, leased it to the City, which, again in turn, ran it through its Playground Commission.

At the time, the University of Southern California and the University of California at Los Angeles used the Coliseum as a home field, and there were occasionally other university and college activities there. The rest of the time it was used as a playground. Also, at the time, local professional football was anathema to the two universities.

We drew a bill, and Louis took it to the Legislature. He was very capable with legislation, and I think he liked being up there. His bill went through the Legislature without any problems, and the words "right to condemn leaseholds" were entered. The bill went to the governor for signature.

Suddenly, William Neal, assistant city attorney of Los Angeles, in charge of legislation for the city, found out about the change and communicated the news to the Los Angeles City Council. They were immediately up in arms, as was Mayor Fletcher Bowron. That very evening, the mayor and two of the councilmen took the train for Sacramento, their objective being to prevent the bill being signed into law. Presumably, they expected to do this by browbeating, or otherwise overwhelming, Governor Earl Warren.

There were and are those who accused Earl Warren of being "wishy-washy." He was nothing of the kind. Warren was a hard-headed Swede, and he had promised us his backing for the Sixth Agricultural District. He signed the bill. This meant that the city of Los Angeles, whose lease still had a few years to run, could have itself condemned right out of the Coliseum. Moreover, the amount of money they would receive, over and above expenses, would, in a condemnation proceeding, be very small.

There was a great furor in the media. However, we had been concerned not to deprive the city of income, but to put the Coliseum to better use, and under much better management. All concerned were public-spirited, and it was finally agreed that the three concerned powers—that is, state, city and county—should run the Coliseum in concert. Under the Joint Powers Act, therefore, we drafted a contract calling for a Joint Powers Commission to run the Coliseum. There would be three from the city, three from the county, and three from the state, plus one alternate for each of the powers. I didn't have much to do with the drafting, though I did go down and talk with Lynn Beebe of O'Melveny and Myers.

Among the early agreements was that a space should be set aside for the building of what later became the sports pavilion. Most important, it was agreed that the commission would get together and hire a good man as manager, to put the Coliseum on a business basis. A contract was drafted, and a call issued for applicants for manager. We had determined a fair salary, and we interviewed some thirty or so people. The three city members of the Commission had in mind a very good man who was either city engineer or assistant city engineer. The county also had a man in mind, as did the state. As might have been expected, the first ballot came up 3-3-3.

One of the members of the commission, from the Sixth Agricultural District, was Standish L. Mitchell, secretary and manager of the Southern California Automobile Club. Stan and I were old friends. He came to see me, and said, "Mac, you know this is going to stay deadlocked unless we do something. I think you agree that the best man they have interviewed, and the best man for the job, is William Nicholas." He had run the Rose Bowl as its manager, and had also run the Pasadena Department of Parks. I agreed with Stan, so we got hold of Roger Jessup, chairman of the Board of Supervisors, who was also on the commission. A deal was struck, with the result that Bill Nicholas went in as general manager by a vote of six to three. A more able fellow in handling the great and near great of the athletic world has never been found anywhere.

The tripartite commission started out with no money at all; what was on hand belonged to the city of Los Angeles and its Playground

Commission. We had to have money, so Bill arranged to borrow some $30,000 for the commission. Thus we started the season. I was on that commission for seven years, serving as president for one year. I think my seventh year, I was an alternate.

Not once did I see anything to be criticized in the way of money matters or acts of political consideration, except possibly the problem of having beer at the Coliseum. The Coliseum made money from the very start, though we never did serve beer.

We got the professional teams, and we kept the universities. All went surprisingly well, and we were able to obtain good concessionaires. I believe it was the year I was president that we built the athletic quarters at a cost of $234,000. We had made a study of other athletic headquarters, and what we built was then considered to be an outstanding facility. These quarters were under the Coliseum seats. I was quite proud of all this, and still am.

At the end of my seven years' service, we had plowed back into buildings and other needs, some $700,000. This included the dressing facilities, facilities for coaches, trainers and the like, the press box, a time clock, a new lighting system and other items. And, we had some $400,000 in the treasury. All this represented a total of well over a million dollars from seats, rentals and concessions. It is an interesting sidelight on how costs have escalated, that the current scoreboard, by itself, cost thirteen million dollars.

A year or two after I went on the Coliseum Commission, Harry Bauer was on the Sixth Agricultural District Commission, though not on the Coliseum Commission. Harry was chairman of the board of Southern California Edison Company. He came to me to talk about the need for a sports pavilion. Bill Nicholas was very much for this idea, and I rather suspect it was he who put the idea in Harry's mind. Bill was not a devious man, but very smart about the ways to get things done. He would have made a good politician! We took the matter up with the Sixth District Commission, and it was agreed that I should propose building a sports pavilion. The idea did not go over very well at the time; a number were hesitant. However, the commission voted the sum of $1,500 and formed a committee, with me as chairman, to make a survey. We were to determine whether such a building would pay, what it would cost and whether we would be able to finance it, since we had no money to finance such a structure ourselves.

We sent Bill Nicholas to look over Madison Square Garden in New York, Maple Leaf Stadium in Toronto, and other such places. He had a professional survey company working with him, who gave attention to the attendance and finances of such places, the overhead, the likely income and such matters. The report was that the project was feasible, and would pay for itself over the period of depreciation, except for restroom facilities, which have a rapid deterioration. The lowest figure we got for the project was $3,500,000. This was from Styles Clements, an excellent architect. His computation was for three million, exclusive of seating and toilets, which came to half a million. His plan called for a partly underground building, thus saving a lot of money. The excavation would be on a slant, and the walls of poured concrete. Clements told us he could raise the money if his firm got the contract.

I thought he probably could raise the money, though I didn't know just how or where, but we felt it should be through public bid. I also had some reservations about allowing the architect to do the financing. Obviously, if we did not permit financing by the architect, then I as chairman of the subcommittee had to find a way to raise the money. I came up with three possible ways to finance the project, the best of which was a combination of a loan and a deal on broadcasting rights. The loan would be from the Bank of America against a pledge of a certain portion of the rentals. The rest would be derived from a ten-year lease of broadcasting rights to the highest bidder. People from the industry advised me that the lowest bid would certainly be enough to cover the amount needed, over and above the Bank of America loan. I reported this back to the Coliseum Commission. We had given no publicity about our plans, except to let it be known that we were discussing the possibility of erecting a sports pavilion on the area reserved for such a building in Exposition Park.

It was just as well that we had announced no definite plans. It was about this time that opera and symphony lovers, along with some downtown businessmen's groups, were becoming very interested in getting an opera house or music center for downtown Los Angeles. Among them was a very influential lady, Mrs. Norman Chandler. There was, at the time, a group (I think a nonprofit corporation) known as Greater Los Angeles Plans. They wanted to build a large municipal auditorium and music center, with parking, in the downtown area. This, they felt, could not only provide opera and other theatrical and musical events, but also exhibitions of various kinds. It was a fine, broad plan and included about four stories of underground parking. As planned, it would cost about twenty-nine million dollars, a staggering sum for those days. Feeling that the structure would serve a multitude of civic purposes, they proposed to raise the money by bond issue; they wanted to put it on the ballot. So this being in the wind, the Coliseum Commission agreed, over my unrecorded objection, to hold up the sports pavilion plan until the voters had the opportunity to express their opinion via the bond issue for the downtown building.

I had serious reservations about their plan. For one thing, the downtown businessmen wanted it closer in than Lafayette Square that some favored. They wanted it where they could use the parking and be handy to the downtown hotels for visitors, restaurants and other businesses, and I felt they had a point. In addition, I did not see how it could possibly pay out as planned, at the cost they envisioned. They put on a fine campaign to put over the bond issue, but it failed by a fairly small margin. They tried again. The second time, they had reduced the proposed amount by several million dollars, but it failed again, this time by a larger majority.

Later, the county Board of Supervisors backed a plan brought by Mrs. Norman Chandler, as the spearhead of a committee consisting of Asa Call, Frank Doherty, Supervisor Jessup and others. This was successful, and the Music Center was realized through the joint effort of outside money, site backing and the Board of Supervisors.

Later on, the Coliseum Commission did go ahead with the sports pavilion. I had left to go on the bench by that time, but they had first-class men who worked hard on the project, and did well. Revenue bonds were possible for the project, by use of the Joint Powers Act, and these men were able to come up with successful ideas and revenue.

The sports pavilion was built almost exactly along the lines we had planned during my tenure. The cost was considerably more than it would have been at the time we first planned the project; I think it was just about double.

# Chapter 14
# Politics

From the late 1880s until around 1909, California politics was dominated by the so-called Southern Pacific Machine. This, in turn, was dominated by the "Big Four," the "Robber Barons" so dear to the hearts of crusading newspaper writers. They were Collis P. Huntington, Mark Hopkins, Adolph Spreckels and Leland Stanford, men of great capacity and tremendous power. The names tie in with railroads, particularly the Central and the Southern Pacific. These men operated largely in San Francisco, and allied with them were others, such as Robert Dollar and Marshall Hale.

The disastrous San Francisco earthquake, and the even more disastrous fire which followed, took place in 1906. In the course of cleaning up and rebuilding the city, it became clear that there was a great deal of graft and allied trouble in San Francisco. There were trials of several members of the Board of Supervisors, and of others, such as the prominent Abe Reuff, attorney and politician. It can be said the cleaning up of California politics really began in 1906; in that sense, perhaps the earthquake and fire were not a total tragedy.

The district attorney, who was prosecuting the graft trials, was shot and killed. He had as his assistant, or deputy district attorney, a young man named Hiram W. Johnson. Johnson was not a large man, though he was quite handsome. He was a very serious fighter, a prosecutor, and above all, a reformer. He inspired confidence, though many mistook his bitter sense of humor for a lack of humor. He became the man of the hour, and it was soon after this that his name began to be mentioned as a candidate for governor. People felt he was the man to "clean up the mess" in Sacramento. However, he demanded that a secret fund be raised which he would administer at his discretion in the drive to clean up the government. So, his friends and supporters raised such a fund–$50,000, I am told—and he had control of it, constantly maintained for the period of his governorship. This was from January 1911 to March 1917.

I have never had any reason to believe that he used any of that money for personal purposes; I think he used it to fund his investigations and for such like purposes. Of course, there was not then the talk about such funds that there has come to be. I would imagine that the so-called "Checkers" fund, raised by and for Nixon in later years, was patterned along the Hiram Johnson line; that is, to use as he saw fit for travel, investigations, whatever he felt necessary. But, Nixon's fund was not properly handled.

Johnson was elected with a large majority, and re-elected. He was supported by the anti-crime people, by those who had a lot at stake in the government of the state. But he was also most enthusiastically supported by the poor and needy; he had a great hold on people, and he did many fine things. During this period many things were adopted which seemed quite radical at the time, such as the Australian ballot and workman's compensation. In his last years, he even gained the support of the migrants who came here during the "Dust Bowl" period.

People thought they had thrown the Southern Pacific out of politics, but I am not at all sure about that. I believe the Southern Pacific had reached the conclusion that overt political activity was bad for its image, and moreover, that the things they wanted done were about completed. Dixwell Pierce and others worked out and proposed a number of financial changes in state government, and Hiram Johnson and his group put through a lot of reforms. People became very pleased with the Republican politics of the day.

It should be remembered that early California politics were primarily Democratic, though sometimes the Republicans got in. A lot of "first families" and wealthy early Californians were from the South, and there was a lot of good leadership among them. But the rise of Hiram Johnson saw a new era, including increased immigration from the north central states. One of the things Hiram Johnson did, perhaps a case of the pendulum swinging the other way, was to see to it that the political parties no longer controlled the state government. He and his group got the law changed so that the state central committee and party county committees, or the respective parties, really became quite impotent. They do not run the state, though most people think they do. The state Central Committee is, and has been for years, set up by the state legislators. It is divided between men and women; the committee and the congressmen have theirs. It is true that the county central committees are on the ballot, but nobody knows or cares who's who among them. They have neither authority nor patronage, and the top people do not seem to want to get into these offices.

In 1938 Republican Governor Merriam, because of his stubbornness and poor appointments, was defeated by Democrat Culbert L. Olson. Actually, there was also at the time a rise in Democratic registration. In any case, Olson tried to go back to the political system of control by patronage from the governor and the party in power, and he went at it the old-fashioned Eastern way. I may cite as an example his dealing with the Sixth Agricultural District, now the Museum of Science and Industry, which should be completely nonpartisan in its activities. Its main function was running a museum, and supervising the Los Angeles Memorial Coliseum and Exposition Park. Obviously, this required a manager who knew something about that type of business, and we (I was on the board) had to find one. Charles Wilson, then manager, became 70 years old, and though we of the commission tried to keep him on, we could not. Governor Olson began "sending down people" to be looked over for the job. The first man he named was a supervisor of laundry routes for Frank Meline. He knew absolutely nothing about dioramas, the operation of a museum, handling of finances or the operation of the Coliseum which was then leased to the Playground Commission. Of course, we just couldn't take that, and I, as chairman, refused him.

The next man that Governor Olson sent down was a fine old doctor from Pasadena who was 69 at the time. I learned in talking to him that he didn't even know there was such a thing as a Sixth Agricultural District. He felt grateful to the governor, but he would have had to retire the following year. He asked how much money the job paid, and when I told him, he said he couldn't possibly get along on that amount of money, having to give up his practice. So we eased him out. Then a newspaper man was proposed along with one or two others. Meantime, the terms of Governor Merriam's appointees—of whom I was one—began to run out, so Olson appointed more

Democrats to the commission. Most of these were not well-known, while the Republicans who were there then were quite well-known and respected people. However, Olson did appoint one good man, Manchester Boddy, the publisher of the *Los Angeles News.* Manchester agreed with us that the management nominees being sent down by the governor were completely unfit, even though they had been approved by the governor, the head of the Democratic Central Committee, by the head of the Democratic Women's Organization, by the Los Angeles County Central Democratic Committee, and by the Young Democrats. This was Olson's system, sending his nominees through all these phases of the Democratic organization to get the approval of people who were merely politicians with no experience bearing on the qualifications of candidates for jobs. Finally, Manchester Boddy went up and saw Governor Olson. He also talked to our state senator from Los Angeles County. Boddy was successful in getting a good man, Louis Venator, nominated. He had been with the *Times,* and had not only newspaper experience but other experience as well. We accepted him as manager, and he did a good job.

Olson's type of politics got him in trouble with the conservative members of the legislature and the "third house." His two boys got him into other trouble, and in 1942 he was succeeded by Earl Warren, then attorney general. The fact was that Olson did not have real political understanding, though he had been, and was, successful as a lawyer. He did not understand that the time to win elections is between elections when people are not thinking about politics. It's like sneaking up on the blind side of a horse. Many Democrats know this today, and play the situation quite well. A good example is Senator Alan Cranston, who works this to perfection. A rather bad illustration was Senator John Tunney, who couldn't understand politics even though he had been so close to the Kennedys since their Massachusetts school days. He seemed to think these connections would carry him, and did not do wise campaigning between elections. The man who understood these matters best was Jesse Unruh, later state treasurer; he was not only knowledgeable, outspoken and able, but streetwise, tough and very humorous.

One of the young Republicans whom I knew in my early days in politics was an organizer of the Republican Assembly named Edmund G. (Pat) Brown. Pat was socially liberal, but conservative in his approach, quite businesslike and a likeable fellow. He was one of those, along with Robert Kenney and Pierson Hall, who switched over to the Democrats. I was invited to join them at the time, but refused. The Republicans were wise in putting up well-known individuals who were liberal insofar as social measures were concerned, but who favored the enterprise system. The Hiram Johnson group had a lot of smart men, such as Earl Warren, so we continued to control the state. It was only after the Republicans stopped putting up these comparatively liberal candidates and began to sponsor fiscal conservatives, who harped on cutting aid to the disadvantaged, that we were in trouble. Just then the Democrats started putting up a few likeable semi-conservatives, such as Pat Brown. But, we continued to control the state, by and large, after I went on the bench in 1953.

By 1963 the liberal Democrats were unquestionably in control of California politics. People don't seem to know or understand that our highly conservative Republicans are humanitarian people. It is necessary at times to recognize and clarify this. There was, for instance, Robert Taft, senator from Ohio, and Republican leader. I knew and loved Robert Taft; we were friends. People think of Taft as a model of conservatism; few remember that he twice voted for public housing and supported many humanitarian causes. Taft told me that he felt public housing was as necessary as county hospitals. He said that as long as workers were as poorly paid as they then were, and while large families continued, there had to be public housing.

In 1933, I visited a government refugee camp with a group of prominent Republicans. This particular camp was near Acton, south of Bakersfield in the San Joaquin Valley, and I understand it figured in the Steinbeck novel, *The Grapes of Wrath*. We were shown about by the manager; he had had a few houses moved to the site, while other families lived in tents and other temporary housing. On that particular morning, a strike had started in the surrounding cotton fields.

As we walked down the main street of the place, we reached one of the moved-in houses, and on the front porch sat a man in dirty overalls. He had about a week's growth of beard, and was rocking away in a rocking chair. The manager said to me that the man and his family (of ten) had arrived the previous night in their old Model A Ford. They were from Oklahoma or the Texas panhandle. The man's wife was inside cleaning the house while the younger children played nearby; some of the older children had been sent to school. We walked up to speak to him, but he continued to rock, neither speaking nor rising to greet us. After showing us around, the manager said to him, "These gentlemen are mainly well-known Republicans. They want to see what we're doing to take care of the people coming in from the 'Dust Bowl.'"

The man looked us over, then said to me, "Mister, Franklin D. Roosevelt gave me this place; what can you do for me?"

I thought this a striking illustration of the attitude of many people—it was Franklin D. Roosevelt who had taken measures to help them—not the Congress, not the people of the United States, not the Democratic party, but Franklin D. Roosevelt. As for the Republicans, his feeling was that they had neither thought much of these people who had lost their farms and homes, nor done much for them. A little later in our talk, I asked him, "Wouldn't you rather be out working in the fields, earning money?" He replied, "As soon as the strike is over and we get our pay raised, I'll go back to work."

Such was the attitude of the times. Most of these people have long since blended into the community, whether in the San Joaquin Valley or other areas. But, they were almost all great admirers and followers of Hiram Johnson, our fair-minded and honestly progressive Republican senator. This loyalty continued, though he became quite seriously aged before his retirement. He should not, really, have run for his last term. But the people were for him; he felt they needed him, and he was the state's leading progressive Republican.

Part of Hiram Johnson's appeal was all that he stood for. Much of the credit goes to the able politicians like H.L. Carnahan and Frank P. Doherty, who guided him. The reforms he put through were enlarged upon and carried forward in many instances in the programs of Earl Warren and the Republican Party. We think of the Republican Party today as lacking a voter appeal program. They certainly had one then, and a great many humane and progressive things were adopted by initiative and referendum, as well as by direct legislative action. Thus, the party brought in the Australian ballot, the initiative, the referendum, the recall, workman's compensation and others.

H.L. Carnahan, who had been lieutenant governor and also head of the Railroad Commission which became the Public Utilities Commission, was something of a loner, and shortly after the 1936 campaign he asked me to visit him at his office. We had a good visit, and he finally got around to saying to me, "I believe you're the man who could take over for me in politics in California. You could come to my office, and I'd give you some training and background. You can practice law with me, and take over for me politically."

After my talk with Carnahan, I went back and discussed the matter with my associates in the office, and with my family. We all agreed that it was not my desire to be a political lawyer. I went back to Carnahan and thanked him for his offer, but turned it down. It saddened me to learn, some three weeks later, that he had shot and killed himself. He had not told me that he was a cancer victim, and knew he was in a terminal condition.

His group, I'm sorry to say, rather fell apart after his death. But there were many able men among them who continued to be active.

Although Los Angeles was then, as now, the biggest city in the state, the San Francisco people knew their politics, and by controlling the legislature and appointments, had the real control of both Republican and Democratic parties in the state. Among them were such people as Marshall Hale, a big department store man; Jared Sullivan with the Anglo California Bank; Robert Dollar of the steamship family; George Cameron of the *San Francisco Chronicle*; and J.R. Knowland who ran the *Oakland Tribune* on the other side of the Bay. There were also some other prominent San Francisco industrialists who were nominally Democrats, but worked for San Franciscan control of California politics and business. Here was the power.

The Merchants and Manufacturers Association of Los Angeles had always been a strong and financially able group, active in the interchange of ideas and the protection of their interests, at times, in the legislature. One of the difficulties I had with them from 1936 to 1952 was their continuing effort to put a "Right to Work" constitutional amendment on the California ballot. Perhaps they might have done it before 1936, but it was obvious to me that they could not succeed at this time. I was opposed to putting such propositions on the ballot when we were a minority party. We had to get a lot of Democratic votes, and our candidates would be handicapped by having to take a stand on such issues as the right to work, which I considered a non-partisan issue. We had, after all, a lot of strong blue-collar voters–union members. If brought up, it would quickly become a partisan issue, regardless of whether it really was or not. This situation continued until about 1954, after I went on the bench. It was in 1956 when Knowland was going to run for governor that he agreed to support such an issue. It was put on the ballot as a constitutional amendment, and the proposition was defeated. If there was to be such a constitutional amendment, it should have been at a special election.

In 1938, George Newell, a young real estate man from Ventura, was elected president of the California Republican Assembly. The meeting was in San Francisco, and I was named vice president.

There was a deficit of some $16,000 hanging over from the campaign. It had to be met, and we were anxious to find places to get this money. The San Francisco group assured us that they had the sources, and would raise the money—no matter who was elected. Elections were held, and George Newell went in as president of the California Assembly for two years. As vice president, I would presumably be the next president in the election year of 1940. We went our separate ways, and left George with the job. He worked hard at it, and we appreciated what he did. After a few months he came to me and said, "Mac, I'm sick; my blood pressure is over 210, and the doctor says that I must rest. I'm going up to Lake Arrowhead for a month, because otherwise I just can't continue."

So, I took over the actual work as acting president. The first thing to do was try to raise the rest of the money to pay our debts. I got in touch with Preston Hotchkis, a member of the assembly and of the finance committee for the Republican Party in Southern California. He agreed that the money must be raised, and said that he would take over the job. At that time George had whittled it down to about $9,400, all of which was way past due. After a very short time he accomplished the job. I was astonished when Preston came to me with the money which he had gotten from unimpeachable sources. I took the check, put it in the bank and immediately started paying the debts. Two or three days later, I wrote to George Newell at the lake telling him the good news. My letter didn't reach him in time; he had died a day or two before it arrived.

We held a special convention in Sacramento. San Francisco again took the position that they should have the presidency, but the group was not happy with their failure to meet the previous commitment they had made. I stayed in my room, and did not go down for the convention. They came up to tell me that I was president of the California Republican Assembly. So, I served less than two years, finishing out the term of George Newell.

Shortly thereafter, it became time for the convention of the Republican state central committee of California. Strong support came to me for the state chairmanship, but I said I would not take it, since I could not give it the necessary time. I had to do something with my law business, whereas a state chairman properly should give a great deal of time to his work, travel about the state visiting with voters, help with the problems of the people and so forth. He should unite the party in a well-planned program of Republican work. I thought the office of state chairman was deteriorating. The one Republican in constitutional office at the time was Earl Warren, and he was not partisan-minded and never would be. It was about this time that I was busy with the Economy Block. I thought I had a deal worked out with the Merchants and Manufacturers Association. Their head man came to me and offered that he and "his group" would finance a vice chairman or executive secretary, who would go about the state. I felt this would work out, and talked to the man they suggested, Senator John Phillips of Banning. He agreed to take the job, but they failed to come through with the money; I saw nothing but an empty promise, so I refused to be state Republican chairman. My nominee, John Phillips, went on to become a member of the United States Congress.

The large papers of California seem to have some strange way of communicating with each other, which I never attempted to fathom. George Cameron of the *San Francisco Chronicle* always lunched at the Pacific Union Club. Sometimes there would be others present, and he always picked up the check. The men of San Francisco knew, when contacted by a member of the group I have mentioned, that it was time to reach for the checkbook. The men would call in Dick Barrett and say, "Time to get started; here's a room and a lot of telephones, and here's a list of givers." Dick would get on the phone with lists of "A," "B," and "C" givers, and the collection would begin. San Francisco was way ahead of everybody else, and could actually take the state leadership.

Let me give an illustration of how the "San Francisco First" idea sometimes worked. There was a fine young fellow in the Junior Chamber of Commerce in Imperial Valley. I knew him in the Republican Assembly. He wanted to go to the legislature; he was certainly qualified and able, and would represent the community well. The young man came to Los Angeles and went to the Chamber of

Commerce and some of our businessmen and said, in effect, "I have made a survey, and I know I can be elected to the legislature; I've sounded out my county of Imperial. The problem is, I don't have enough money. I need $10,000 more to run for the office. If you can help me by raising campaign funds, I'll be another strong conservative Republican in the legislature." Los Angeles said this would not be a thing for them to undertake. Los Angeles never learned the value of getting together early and planning for legislation beneficial to the area. At that time, and as long as I was in politics, their financial committees were organized largely during actual campaigns; there was no organization that would "commit."

This young man then went to San Francisco seeking campaign funds, and after a short time, the word got to Dick Barrett. Soon, Dick, or "they," looked up the young man, and it wasn't long before they sent him word, "We're not asking anything of you at all, but we think you would be a good man in the legislature. We're sending you $5,000, and we'll send an additional $5,000 if you need it before election day." The young man was elected to the legislature.

On the last day of legislative session, there is always a plethora of bills to be acted upon; they "stop the clock" and finish voting. One of these bills during the first such session of the young man's tenure, was a bill for an appropriation to dredge a portion of San Francisco harbor. It was a legitimate bill; the harbor did need to be dredged, and it was a proper expenditure. At the same time, Los Angeles was also importuning the legislature for funds, also for legitimate projects. Much to the surprise of the Los Angeles people, the young man voted for the San Francisco harbor dredging bill, and against any "pork" for Los Angeles.

Was I surprised? Of course not! If he can help his friends and those who helped him, where it is proper, a legislator will always do so, even though others also need money. So, San Francisco continued to operate in this far-sighted manner.

Finally, times did change. The growth of population in the south entered into voting membership. Also, the new voters largely came from "Dust Bowl" areas, where distressed people looked to the federal government; most of these were, or became, Democrats. The tremendous personality of Roosevelt and the national concern for people out of work or in need of funds also contributed to the end of our period or cycle. I believe in cycles in politics. All these things contributed to movement of primary control of the legislature out of San Francisco. It happened in 1938 when Culbert Olson was elected governor and had a group in the assembly favorable to him. The whole political climate changed in a couple of years.

Olson had Eastern ideas of politics through party patronage down through the whole party structure. In the first place, this system didn't suit the lobbyists, who worked very well with the system in place prior to Olson. This group, along with others, decided that the situation was intolerable. The people Olson was appointing to office were neither qualified nor able, with, we thought, one exception. This was Edmund G. Pauley. Ed became the Democratic state committee fund raiser, and raised money to pay off back bills. He later became Democratic national finance chairman and did a great job at that.

In any case, the first I knew of the plan to gain conservative control in the legislature was when I received a call from Charles Blythe, the Republican finance chairman in the north. He told me that he and his group wanted to raise money to support an "Economy Block" in the north, and wanted us in the south to raise a like amount for the Block's work. I asked what they wanted to do; he said they planned to have a paid secretary for the Economy Block, who would have his office in Sacramento. He could write speeches for the Block, and could have a place where they could gather. He thought the group should meet for supper every week or two and consider whether or not to support a matter. He said they should make speeches and get statewide coverage. They needed money for these things. I took the matter to Asa V. Call, and he and the group considered it. They reported back to me that they wouldn't put up half, but would raise forty percent if the north would raise sixty.

Understandably, the south wanted first of all to know who would be the man in Sacramento, running things. This was discussed, and finally Ross Marshall, political editor of the *Los Angeles Herald*, was agreed upon. He was given a year's leave of absence by the Hearst newspaper people; this was later extended by a year or more. Ross Marshall was a good conservative Democrat, as I remember him, and a good politician. He knew many legislators, and he could write. Moreover, he knew how to handle legislation, so he was a good choice. He went to Sacramento and got two rooms at the Hotel Sacramento; these, for years, served as headquarters for the Economy Block. I took charge of financing the dinners for Southern California.

When, for example, the assemblyman from the 53rd Congressional District, Val Latham at the time, was to give the dinner, I would go out and collect the money for it. There would be at the dinner not only the assemblyman, but state senators and other visitors. If a county central committeeman wished, and paid, he could have one or more guests. Thus, givers were happy about what was going on. For awhile I had no difficulty raising funds from the county general committee members, and I did some of this in the north, too. However, before long they began to lose interest; things were going along all right, and the novelty had worn off. So, I had to start raising funds from other places.

The Economy Block in the legislature was nonpartisan in its leadership, but in the Senate the acknowledged leader was Gordon Garland, a fine conservative Democrat from the San Joaquin Valley. I used to attend sessions and visit with legislatures quite often, because of my connections with the Republican Party, and sometimes in connection with nonpartisan legislation. I never engaged in anything that brought me financial return by reason of going to the legislature, and for this reason I was accepted. I did get the law changed with respect to some matters of legal procedure, such as the hearings in probate matters and the like.

I should, perhaps, clarify my statement regarding the great things accomplished under Republican control, such as the Australian ballot, the initiative referendum and recall, protection for women in industry, and the like. We have to remember that many of the business interests and newspapers were not technically Republican; in fact, as I recall, the Hearst papers were generally and technically Democratic. But they were more conservative, even in those days, than the *Los Angeles Times*. The *Times* of today, in my view, is not at all conservative. Then, during the Great Depression, the Black people stayed with the Democrats; it is only natural that they did, and for the most part still do. The business people didn't seem to understand the problems, and did not work with, or for, these people.

For years our office represented the Los Angeles Housing Authority. This legal chore was not brought in by me, nor was I particularly in favor of it. However, it was a civic-minded thing to do, and was brought in and handled through David, then later through Charles McDowell. I was accused one day, on the floor of the Los Angeles City Council, of being a "Communist" because I

represented, as its lawyer, the Housing Authority. These well-fed
ladies hissed and booed me; they chose not to believe there was, and
is, poverty and squalor such as fine ladies of their type never see. I
may say that I had no objection to supporting temporary help
through public housing. I did, and do, object strongly to several
things about the way it was operated. Also, I thought the construction of these structures was inexcusably poor. They would not last,
and would soon become slums. As a matter of fact, that is precisely
what happened after our office no longer had to do with their management and upkeep.

David, I believe, had been asked to take this assignment by Harry
Chandler and Manchester Boddy, publishers, respectively, of a
Republican and a Democratic newspaper, and both prominent in
business. They felt it was a controversial field, and should have a
conservative as the advising attorney. After David died, Mayor
Fletcher Bowron appointed Charles McDowell, later my partner. We
kept one lawyer down there at the housing authority all day, every
day, as a rule.

The connection opened the door for me to get Republicans down
to the authority properties, and to obtain entrance for candidates to
go and meet voters. People would turn out and listen, but how many
votes we got, I couldn't say.

I recall one city councilman, a conservative Democrat. He was very
much against public housing and said so frequently. He proceeded
one time to attack me quite viciously on one of Reverend Fifield's
Sunday evening broadcasts. Fifield was the minister of the First
Congregational Church, and a powerful man in Los Angeles. He
couldn't keep from getting into politics, and I often wished he would
be better informed before taking stands on matters, such as public
housing. This council member, on the air, claimed that I had "prosti-
tuted" my position as Republican national committeeman by taking
the job as attorney for the housing authority. This, of course, was
nonsense, since our office had had the appointment since 1938, and I
did not become national committeeman until 1946 or 1947. I had not
even been a member of the firm when it took the appointment.

The charge made headlines and was very harmful. I complained to
the Federal Communications Commission. I was then authorized to
practice before this and some other commissions. The FCC advised
me, after looking into the matter, that it was prepared to take away

Dr. Fifield's broadcast license if I so requested. Such a move was quite within their power at the time. The FCC's licensing power was sovereign, and their regulations had the force of law. Among those regulations were very stringent rules as to what a licensee might allow to be put on the air.

I did not feel that to take away the radio outlet of a church organization was the thing to do. I therefore refused to request, insist on or recommend drastic action. They did, however, require Dr. Fifield's station to apologize to me over the air. Of course, the apology couldn't and didn't undo the damage. And as I recall, the apology got no media coverage at all. News is news only when it happens; after the broadcast is over, or the newspapers hit the street, there is no going back to the status quo ante, so to speak. The sensational radio of the day, like the sensational television of our time, was quite good at starting shock waves, but not at calming them once started.

I recall making a survey of the homes in Maravilla Park near Monterey Park. This area was largely Mexican-American, and the average income was quite low. The survey showed me that scarcely one home in ten took a daily newspaper. But all received "throwaway" newspapers, of which there were many. These people, in large part, read these throwaways, and a good many of them read the editorials. I found that they were an excellent way to reach these people. We put in ads with respect to candidates, showing their value in matters affecting the readers, and we also tried to get favorable editorials; we even wrote some of them in our effort to get votes.

We had some fine ladies in our women's groups, many of whom liked to go to the various neighborhoods to campaign and leave literature. Unfortunately, they seemed to prefer going at a time when these Mexican-American housewives were busy with children or housework. Moreover, the expensive car was parked around the corner, and the children soon had told the whole neighborhood about it. I finally had to restrain some of these volunteers because this was decidedly not the way to "win friends and influence people." Said one of the women to a friend of mine, "You don't understand our problems, and anyway, why do you only come around at election time?"

As I've indicated, I started in politics at the very bottom of the Depression, at which time the Mexican-American vote was solidly Democratic. In my attempt to get votes for the Republicans, I had a talk with a Mr. Adams who lived in South Pasadena. He had been in the hardware business, but at this time, 1932, he managed many properties. He and his group owned a lot of properties on the east side of Los Angeles, the Mexican area. He had a number of store buildings, and he would allow use of an empty one. He started a number of clubs; I think there were nine at one time. On a number of occasions I went around with him to meetings. I bought doughnuts and coffee or tortillas, beans and coffee, and we got some fairly good crowds. I was trying to do a little missionary work for the party and its candidates. Sometimes I brought a speaker. Mr. Adams told me—as the Mexican-American lady mentioned before had said—that you can't get their votes by having parties and speakers shortly before elections. They like going to meetings and having something to eat; they are invariably courteous to the speakers and candidates. But what they are saying to themselves is, "He's a nice fellow, but unless he shows some interest in me other than just at election time, I'll know that he is only interested in my vote."

The situation has modified since then because of television, and great effort has been made to get the Mexican-American vote. But most of the success in this effort has been on the Democratic side.

We had, and still have, a number of very fine and capable Mexican-Americans in the Republican Party, but they seem badly split up among themselves. The fact that I had connections with Plaza de Los Angeles and El Pueblo de Los Angeles did not do our Republican efforts any harm. Nevertheless, it was not a decisive factor; it gave us entry, but that was about all. Another illustration of the fact, so necessary for a minority party to keep in mind, is that elections are not won; they are lost. They are lost between elections; the vote at the polls is merely the confirmation.

A political campaign is not unlike a war in many of its aspects, except that you must smile and make friends. How I disliked, and still dislike, the speeches made by too many of our top Republicans who get red in the face and shout the old and totally inapplicable cliches. "We've got to get down to the grass roots! We've got to get in there and fight! Get in there and fight, because 'you can win, Winsocki, if you'll only buckle down.'"

It is certain that you have to work and turn out your vote; this means you have to "make friends and influence people." You must go after the conservative Democratic vote, the nonregistered and nonpartisan. This is not done by "fighting." You do not make the donkey love you by hitting him over the head with a railroad tie.

So, how do I think it should be done? Well, perhaps I'm wrong, but I may say that we learned to take care of a strongly Democratic electorate in California and, except for the election of Culbert Olson (from whom control was taken for two years by the Economy Block), we were in office in the state of California from the time I got started in 1932 until I left at the end of 1952, and we still had control when I left. Nor did we do badly on national matters; we had a majority in the lower house of Congress for most of my active time, and we had Senators Knowland, Nixon and Kuchel, and of course, President Eisenhower whose election brought an end to my political activities.

The Republican Party was organized by concerned people whose backgrounds were varied: Whigs, Know-nothings, Mugwumps and the like, who met many years ago in Ripon, Wisconsin. Some say elsewhere, but I think the Ripon meeting—about 1854—was the first group of what were then considered liberals. It was decided to found and unite in a Republican Party, and in 1856 it was decided that these founders were to go back to their respective states and organize a Republican Party there. The party was to be made up of people whose ideals, principles and determination were similar to those of the founders. Eventually, delegates from all these states met and chose General John C. Fremont as a presidential candidate. In the minds of some of us, myself included, this wasn't a very good choice; he did not seem to have been a very stable man. Four years later, Lincoln was the candidate.

The founders decided that they would meet again with interested leaders from each state, particularly with the delegates from those states. A national committeeman was to be chosen; each group was to return home, elect a national committeeman and set up a headquarters. This was done, thus establishing a pattern of control, but all had in mind that there must be "give and take," especially in a new party. One great leader and teacher in this connection was Abraham Lincoln.

We think of Lincoln as a statesman, and certainly this is proper, as he may have been the greatest statesman the United States has produced. Yet, though it is known to very few, Abraham Lincoln was one of the most astute practical politicians of his time. He had great political organizational ability, and when the 1860 convention took place, it was found that Lincoln somehow had representatives in all the state groups. When they came together, he was the "standout." Though he headed a new and not very experienced party organization, he was the past master at setting up delegations the way he thought they should be.

A presidential candidate, and finally the presidential nominee, has a free hand in the choice of his running mate; this is a matter of general agreement, and is no doubt as it should be. He must try to choose someone from another state. If he is a congressman or senator, he probably, though not necessarily, will choose a governor. Courtesy allows the nominee his choice.

In the last minutes of a convention at closing time, the national chairman for the next campaign is chosen. The president has his say on this, and he may not do so until later. Also, the national committeeman and national committeewoman for each state is selected, approved and seated for the next four years. Sometimes the national committeeman chosen by a state delegation may not be the best man to carry the campaign for the candidate for president. That is why this seating is left to the very last thing in the convention. Some of these national committeemen are strong personalities, and they may have tried very hard to put in another nominee. Take the example of California when I was three times the Republican national committeeman. On each of those three occasions, Earl Warren was our state candidate, and I was his choice. On the last two I believe Knowland was senior senator with Nixon as junior, and as always I was supporting Warren. At the 1952 campaign Eisenhower was nominated. Most people feel that Earl Warren had no chance, and I think the chance could have occurred only if the choice of a candidate had gone to more than three ballots. I had word directly from a labor representative that the 103 Taft delegates would have swung to Warren if Taft had not carried by the end of the third ballot. Of course it was decided on the first ballot, but Eisenhower okayed me.

It was common knowledge, and the subject of much gossip, that Taft wanted Knowland as his running mate. In the California situation, at the time, Eisenhower was not tied in with Knowland, but more and more with Nixon. The California delegation, many of whom wanted to vote for Eisenhower, voted for Warren on the first ballot, as promised. It was intended to caucus again after the first ballot results were in.

In the Phyllis Schlafly book, *A Choice, Not an Echo*, she makes some very odd statements in connection with convention politics, some of which are simply untrue. There was no pre-convention deal, as she contends, between Warren and Eisenhower. Moreover, there was no deal with respect to Taft. I can go into this with assurance, because I was the one on the ground for two weeks before the convention in the hotel used for committee meetings and for the national committee. I talked at considerable length with the representatives of every candidate. It was I who carried the message to Knowland from the Taft forces; Taft spoke through Congressman Clarence Brown of Ohio. They wanted to know when Knowland was coming, and asked me to get him to talk with them because Taft wanted Knowland as his vice presidential candidate. This was not just a political ploy; Taft and Knowland were good friends and worked well together in the Senate.

I spoke to Knowland by telephone, and he said to tell them there was no such possibility. He had given his word to Warren, as we all had, and he would stand behind Warren. I also know first hand about Eisenhower's choice of Nixon as running mate. Henry Cabot Lodge was the chairman of Eisenhower's committee of five for the purpose of choosing a vice presidential candidate to run with him. I was with Nixon when Lodge advised him that he was the committee's choice for vice president.

Ms. Schlafly said that there was a deal to the effect that, in return for California's support, Warren would be named chief justice, or at least justice of the Supreme Court. This is simply not true; Warren's appointment was worked out long afterward, and in the working out, I was one of those consulted by Herb Brownell. We get a lot of startling ideas from people who are, perhaps, better writers than researchers, or possibly, simply write what they would like to believe.

Theodore White in *Breach of Faith,* an excellent book on the Watergate affair, writes that the most able and professional group then in California was Whitaker and Baxter of San Francisco, and that their firm ran the Republican campaigns here. This is somewhat less than accurate. I knew Clem Whitaker before he married Leona Baxter, and I worked with both on many occasions. They did not really get into national politics until after Nixon became vice president. They had no real power at the time I was national committeeman through 1952. They did have some power and were used to a considerable extent in San Francisco. They were an expensive group and put out reams and reams of so-called "news" which they tried to get printed in the newspapers. This is a growing phenomenon, the matter of professional people who turn out large quantities of publicity and mile after mile of television and radio scripts. We put out some publicity and got our people on radio and television, but it has now become a professional game, no longer under the control of the party chairmen or groups.

The people in the campaign "business" are invariably good salesmen for themselves, but often don't seem to understand the political thinking of the average voter, or how to give proper advertising to a national candidate.

It is necessary to exercise judgment and tact to keep excellent campaign workers from going to pieces under the pressure or leaving. Murray Choitner was a hard driver, and he drove himself harder than others, but it took him awhile to develop judgment in the driving of others. I recall one time during my control of activities at a statewide meeting in Fresno that Murray was representing Nixon, and there were plenty of other candidates. All of a sudden someone pointed out to me that Murray was out on the platform telling others what to do and where the chairs for Nixon were to be. Seating is a matter of real seriousness with all candidates and all public dignitaries; no one candidate can get away with fixing this to suit himself, nor can any candidate's representative. Such matters often leave scars. Murray was a paid manager, and the meeting was not his to arrange, so I had to step in.

Speakers who come from the East—I think of Dewey and Eisenhower—do not know regional problems, and they seem particularly uninformed on the common problem of water. They know nothing, usually, of the Colorado River controversy with Arizona and Nevada, and they should step very carefully in connection with such matters. So, we would brief these speakers, especially candidates, in advance of any news conference. We would send someone to meet with Eisenhower, Dewey, or whoever ahead of his arrival, and try to fill him in. They did not know of the big fires, the earthquakes, the irrigation projects or the droughts. Water will always be a California problem. It made real problems in trying to elect Republican candidates in the Sacramento and San Joaquin Valleys.

Every candidate had to be briefed on this. Likewise, when he went into the Santa Clara Valley, he had to know something about wine, prunes and the like.

So, right after the candidate is chosen, or even before, an advance man was sent into each of the areas to learn the local problems and talk to the local radio, television and newspaper people, especially the local newspapers; they were our strong point. All this local information and thinking was gathered into our files, and we used the information in state campaigns, of course, but particularly with national candidates. Speakers must know the booby traps and be able to speak plainly and strongly on points of concern to a particular district.

It is necessary to know your enemy. This means being prepared, not only for what he *might* or *should* do, but what he *can* do. You must know or learn about what today are called "dirty tricks," and how to deal with them or avoid them. By and large, I still think it is best not to play any. In my days in politics, we ran into many, but as far as I know, we played none, really, unless it was a dirty trick to arrange to have the contents of the wastebaskets of the other side delivered to a particular place. Then, somehow, we got hold of them and could look over the carbons, incomplete papers and so forth. This was something both sides did, and all knew it. We had to anticipate what we could and make plans accordingly. We found the other side doing one thing: somehow our bank statements, as to financial condition, were getting into the enemy's hands. Bank statements are not really confidential documents, but are they for campaigns?

Dirty tricks can take many forms. During the presidential campaign, we set up a meeting in the Hollywood Bowl where Dewey was to speak. It was widely publicized for a considerable time in advance. I had arranged for the use of the Hollywood Bowl, and had a contract with the Association. It was a standard contract, and provided in the small print that the person or organization having the Bowl for a given night had the right to use the Bowl the night before in order to rehearse, set the stage, lighting and other technical details, arrange for security or arrange seating for certain dignitaries and groups; all of which would have to be done to put on an event in good style the following night. All this was, and probably still is, a normal thing in any contract. All this and many other preparatory things were necessary for the type of event we planned.

All of a sudden about a week before the event after all the publicity out of a clear sky, the team around Harry Truman decided that he should make a trip to Los Angeles, and that he should speak in Los Angeles the night before Dewey's speech. Is that a dirty trick? We thought it was, and none of us liked it, but it is politics. Frankly, it disturbed me considerably that the president had apparently been a party to the trick of coming to speak the night before Dewey, but I had no idea that he actually intended to speak in the Hollywood Bowl. This was undercutting Dewey with a vengeance!

Then I got a telephone call from someone I had never heard of. The call ran something like this: "Aha, I've been trying to find out who had the Hollywood Bowl and is trying to keep the president of our country from speaking in the Bowl. So, it's you! You bought up the night before Dewey is to speak, just to keep the president out of the Bowl!" That was, of course, totally untrue, and I said, "Just a minute. This is the first I've known that the president wanted to speak in the Bowl on that date. I got the Bowl some weeks before the president decided to make this trip, or at least before it was announced. I knew nothing of his wanting to use the Bowl until I heard you speak to me. I have the standard form of contract, and you must know that it always gives the Bowl for the night before one uses it. Now, I'm only the representative of the committee. I'll be meeting with them tomorrow in San Francisco; that meeting is already scheduled, and not because of your call. I'll see, if the president so desires, whether we can release the Bowl. There is still a week before the president arrives, so you will have plenty of time if our committee decides to release the Bowl, which they probably will." I was certainly upset by his attitude, but agreed that I would telephone him from San Francisco with the committee's decision. I asked that he send me a letter advising me of what difficulties he had had in getting the Bowl, and covering our conversation. I never received any letter, nor any apology of any sort.

At eleven o'clock the following morning, I called the man and advised him that we had given the word to the Bowl management to release the Bowl the night before Dewey's speech. This was 2:00 p.m. Eastern time, so he had plenty of time to put out the news that afternoon. Nevertheless, that same evening, Fulton Lewis, Jr., a conservative Democratic columnist, came on the air with a story that the Republican party in California, headed by McIntyre Faries, had tried to prevent the president from having the Hollywood Bowl to speak the night before Dewey. Newspapers picked it up and headlined the story.

I immediately tried to reach Fulton Lewis by telephone, but could not do so, so I sent him a wire, explaining the situation. I learned that neither Lewis' legman nor Lewis himself made any attempt to check the veracity of what some paid Democrat staffer had told them before putting it on the air. Moreover, Lewis had gone so far as to castigate the Republican Party, and me in particular, for trying to keep the president out of the Bowl—a barefaced lie, as a little checking could have disclosed. He, did, however, read my telegram over the air the next night. So much for dirty tricks, though I could relate a few more.

We always believed, or tried to believe, "Be sure your sins will find you out," as the Good Book tells us. We also believed that, if you are honest, you can "Look the whole world in the face, for you owe not any man," to paraphrase Mr. Longfellow. In 1940 and a time or two thereafter, every single check that was paid in connection with the campaign went out over my signature. Each check had a voucher, signed by our certified public accountant, before it came to me. He put on the voucher the fund on which the check was drawn, how much was in that fund and also what the budget was. In this way I would know how near exhaustion the budget had come at the time, along with other necessary information. The finance committee required my actual signature, so I did see and go over each check. In the 1940 campaign, I think it was $538,000 that went through my hands. This was a considerable amount of money for the Southern California headquarters, bearing in mind that some of the headquarters had their funds, too. Their funds did not always come through my hands, but all this was over my signature.

It was a good campaign, though a losing one. Willkie was a great man, and deserves credit for trying, but he could not prevail against the grip Franklin Roosevelt had on the hearts of the people. This was the one campaign that we ended with a real surplus—at least, the only one I know of.

While the campaign was in progress, I found that reports of our campaign funds, in and out, were being passed on to the Democrats by the local Bank of America. This was denied by the bank, and I don't know what individuals were responsible, but the word leaked regularly with respect to what came into and went out of our bank account. In any case, I was satisfied with the proof and switched to the Farmers and Merchants Bank.

Whether the switch had any bearing or not, shortly after the campaign was over I got a call from a cashier or one of the officers of the bank. He advised me that a representative of the Department of Internal Revenue was there wanting to look at the party account and my own bank account, including the firm's. He asked if I wanted the bank to oblige the IRS man to get a subpoena; they could require this at the time. The IRS did not have the absolute powers they now enjoy. I said, "Of course not, let them look."

Soon afterward, I began receiving telephone calls from the Internal Revenue Service in Los Angeles, and I also had a letter from them. Finally, one of them said to me on the telephone, "Why don't you come up and see me?" I agreed and asked when I should do so. He said, "Well, any time you like." I told him in that case, I'd be there immediately.

Arriving, I was ushered into a small inner office cubicle whose walls did not reach the ceiling; obviously anything said could be heard over the walls, though we could not be seen. I did not know whether anyone was eavesdropping or whether there was a listening device concealed somewhere, but I had nothing to hide.

There was a small table and two chairs: one of them was occupied by a rather handsome young fellow who pretended not to know what it was all about. He began asking me questions across the table; I answered immediately, one after another. After a few questions, he would get up and go out; soon, he'd return and ask more questions. It seemed apparent that he was getting instructions from someone. Finally, he came back from one of those trips and said, "Oh, the boss says he knows you, and he knows that none of that money stuck to your fingers. Go on home and forget about it."

That was, in fact, the last I heard of the matter. It wasn't until this last conversation that I realized they had doubts about me individually. I can see why they would feel that they must investigate the handling of so much money including a trust fund or two. So much money distributed over my signature, and apparently with no one's supervision, was something to question.

I had something to use, if necessary, to get back at the IRS or the Democrats, if needed. I knew that an appeal for funds had gone out to contractors who had government contracts under that Democratic administration. Further, I knew that these solicitations were typed on the typewriter of a government-paid executive in the local Department of Internal Revenue. We had the typewriter checked out by an expert. On the night that the letter went out, we knew that the list of names to which it was sent contained many, many persons who held federal government contracts.

We never used this information, and never told the Democrats that we had it. Yes, I think such solicitation by them was in the nature of a "dirty trick" and undoubtedly illegal, besides being unethical. We were saving that information to use if it became really necessary. We did not know which, if any, of these persons had contributed in response to this letter, but we could easily find out, and would have done so had it ever become necessary to use our facts.

I was checked at each campaign by the IRS. Then, when I went on the bench, thirteen years later, I asked that all my records be checked: political, law office and personal. I was sitting as a judge one day when a messenger came in to tell me that some city was on the line for me. I excused myself and took the call in my chambers. The conversation went like this: "This is so-and-so, assistant attorney general from Washington, but at present in (wherever). It has been my job for years to monitor the political monies spent by you. You are cleared and will never hear from us again. Also, your personal income tax and other matters are completely checked and okay. Your partner asked that we do this, and it is now complete." I said that I knew this, since I had asked my partner to make the request. He repeated that everything had been checked for the last so many years (I forget the number). I was clear and clean and would never hear from them again, and I have not.

If, right after Eisenhower went into office I, the Republican national committeeman, had been checked and they claimed that they found something requiring further checking or special audit or even indictment—then think of the chance Earl Warren had taken in making me California national committeeman three times! All politicians take this chance, particularly governors when appointing a person to be a judge of the Superior Court.

It will be apparent that a great love of the game is a prerequisite for the person who seeks the national committeeman post. There is much to do that must be done much to learn that must be learned. It is essential to success that these things be mastered. Half measures are no help and can be of great harm to the party and its candidates.

# Chapter 15
# Politicians

The Republican National Committee had a meeting in Seattle, Washington, at the invitation of Governor Landis. I was in a subcommittee meeting until rather late, five or so one evening, and as I came out the door I saw Mrs. Faries seated with a rather stocky, pleasant-looking young man. They rose at the sight of me, and Lois said, "This is Walter Hickel of Anchorage, Alaska. We've been sitting here waiting for you; Walter would like to talk to you, and he'd like to get to talk to the people at the meeting." Well, our meeting was just over, and I invited him to have dinner with us. He accepted, and a good friendship began. This, as I recall it, is the story of his early life. It reads like the Rover Boys.

Walter Hickel's father was a sharecropper, or tenant farmer, in Kansas. There were, I believe, ten children in the family, Walter being the oldest. When he graduated from high school at seventeen, valedictorian of his class, and with honors in debating, he knew it was time for him to move on; there just wasn't room for him in the family home. So, he went to work in the grain harvests, gradually working his way west. He became friends with an English boy who had decided he would go to Australia. He persuaded Walter to go along and grow up with the country, but Walter was only seventeen, so he needed his father's signature to get a passport. His father refused. They followed the harvest until they got to Oregon, and that is where Walter went to work in the orchards of State Senator Jones, in the Willamette Valley. Walter was a good worker, and the senator tried to get him to stay, offering him the job of foreman, but Walter had decided to go to a new area, and fixed on Alaska. He borrowed twenty-five dollars from Senator Jones and, with another young fellow, took ship to work his way to Alaska.

They landed in the city of Valdez and went north to Anchorage—then, and still, Alaska's largest city. It was October, and the ground was frozen. Walter pawned his watch for five dollars which was enough for them to get breakfast on the day they arrived. Soon they got a job stringing wire. The boy with him couldn't take the weather, and died of exposure. Walter had borrowed some money, a "grubstake" so to speak, from a local merchant, and in two weeks paid him back.

Walter felt the city had a great future, and he began borrowing money to build houses. He sent for a boyhood friend from Kansas, who became his foreman. He sent for two of his younger brothers, who came and worked for him. Soon he had a project of a hundred houses, but instead of selling, he rented them. He built and rented another hundred houses, and then another hundred.

When I met Walter in Seattle, he had two things on his mind. First, he wanted to borrow half a million dollars from a Seattle insurance company to build more houses. Secondly, he was very much disturbed at the way the "ins" (who happened to be Democrats) were exploiting the development of Alaska, gaining concessions rather than planning in the interests of the area or its citizens. He decided he would try to get Herbert Hoover to go up to Alaska and look over the problem, perhaps make a speech or two. So, to assist him, I had a talk with Governor Landis, and introduced Walter to him. He and the governor talked, but he had to settle for a new senator from Idaho for a speaker. Hickel sold tickets for the dinner which was held in the Elk's Club lodge in Anchorage. People pooh-poohed the idea, but he had a full house for the dinner, and he came out with about seventy dollars profit. People came to respect Walter, and because of his efforts, Anchorage had a new post office and better mail delivery. He became Republican national committeeman and then governor of Alaska. After Nixon's election he was soon named Secretary of the Interior.

I talked with Walter in Los Angeles shortly after the inauguration of President Nixon, and at that time I outlined my thoughts on a joint "Friendship Park" above and below the Mexican border. Unfortunately, the Mexican government would not go along with our plans at the time. There was a great deal of correspondence with

Washington on the ramifications, including development of a thermodynamic power plant to the east of the Salton Sea. More recently, a great many things have been done to preserve our desert area and the proposed park area, including taking care of the fish and game. President Ford signed a bill declaring a great portion of this land a wilderness area. So, perhaps, my initial work with Hickel, and his efforts, have accomplished something.

• • •

As the 1942 state campaign neared, which is to say at the end of 1941, I felt that Earl Warren had done a great job as attorney general of California. I think most people agreed. His office had handled well the routine civil work, and excellent criminal work had been done in connection with appeals. He had successfully prosecuted the perpetrators of the East Bay Ship Murder incident. Also, he had succeeded in stopping the activities of the gambling ships operating three miles off the coast of California, in the Los Angeles area. Shore boats would take people out every night to gamble on these ships; they felt they were doing nothing illegal on the theory that the ships, were three miles offshore and not in the state's jurisdiction. Warren raided these ships and brought the gamblers into court. Much to the surprise of nearly everybody, the courts held that the three-mile limit extended from point to point—not from the nearest distance to shore.

I had obtained an agreement from the finance committee, or the Los Angeles budget committee, to put up some of the money left from the 1940 campaign for the purpose of taking a public opinion poll. I had also talked with Charles Blythe, head of the finance committee in San Francisco. I felt it essential that we find out what people thought about the Democrats in office, and seeking office, as well as about the Republican candidates in the 1942 campaign. Bear in mind, this was a state campaign, not national.

Thus, late in 1941, I got in touch with Charlie Blythe. I asked him to get his people to raise 60 percent, while we would raise 40. While he agreed with the idea, he was unwilling to raise 60 percent; so we agreed on a fifty-fifty effort, which I thought would probably work out. I went back to Asa V. Call and the group that constituted the budget finance group of the Republicans in Southern California, who still had money left from the 1940 Willkie campaign. They agreed to supply the funds.

We got hold of John Knight, a pollster by profession, and also a member of the legislature. We worked out a public opinion poll which was not conducted in the name of the Republican party; in fact, we thought it very wise to cover up our political identity. So the poll was done in the name of some mortuary group. There were a lot of questions in the poll, which was not written, but conducted by personal interviews, ala Gallup and others. One question was, "Do you know the following persons?" A list followed containing several names including Olson, Warren and other political and business figures. Then we asked, "If you know them, are you for or against them?" We got a lot of answers, most of them categorical in their nature. We went on to ask, "If you are for _____ , why are you for him? If you are against him, why do you oppose him?" Other questions, buried among the nonpolitical ones, were: "If you were to vote for a governor, which would you vote for among the following persons? If necessary, would you cross over from your party to vote for one of the other party; if so, which one would you favor?"

Again, bear in mind that this was a door-to-door verbal poll, not a written one. We, of course, had to have a say in the choice of persons to be interviewed the groups chosen—political, financial, religious, labor, ethnic and so forth, also the geographical areas of the state chosen. It was quite scientific, at least for its time, and very interesting. When it was compiled and tabulated, Charlie Blythe gave a copy to Earl Warren. He took it home to study; the following morning he told us, "I will run for governor." So we knew we had our candidate.

During the period of the Olson administration, a year or two before the poll, I was in Sacramento on some business; I recall it was in connection with the Economy Block. I got a call asking me to go to San Francisco to the office of Jared Sullivan at the Anglo Crocker Bank. I did so, and found quite a number of prominent Republicans, money men, on hand. Sullivan was not there, but was represented by his right-hand man, Dolan. In addition to the San Francisco men there were only two from other areas: J.R. Knowland of the *Oakland Tribune* and yours truly from Southern California. Another, from the Oakland Shipyard group, had been invited, but did not attend. I soon learned that I had been invited to discuss with these men the idea of raising some money to publicize Earl Warren with the idea of running him for governor in 1942. The San Francisco group was willing to put up $15,000, and wanted the finance people in the south to raise a like amount for the purpose.

I agreed to discuss it with the proper people, and came home and talked with Asa Call and others of the local Republican finance committee. I left them to discuss it without my presence. I believe they did raise the money and provide it for the stated purpose: to build Warren up to run. I am sure some of them were not too happy about the expenditure, but a Republican victory at the time was most important.

Warren ran and was, as always, a loner. He took the position that it was not the thing to do to endorse openly with some exceptions, other party candidates or propositions. He did endorse one or two propositions. He told me of one he had promised to support long before he ran for office. It was a commitment to some labor leaders. This made little difference since the propositions he supported were going to win anyway.

Warren took a lot of "flack" from Republican finance leaders and from other people because he did not build himself up and work with other Republicans who ran for office. There was much unhappiness in women's organizations. On the other hand he never bucked any Republican who ran for office, and was in some instances, covertly helpful. This was particularly so, I happen to know, around Oakland and Alameda where he was friendly with the Knowland family. I believe this same attitude of not working with other Republicans was a problem in later campaigns when he was a candidate for vice president. Yet, he generally followed it, except for Bill Knowland. The friendship with the Knowlands, both father and son, was real and deep.

Earl never made any real money for himself, though he was the keenest of the trio—smarter even, I think, than old J.R. Knowland, and certainly far more astute than Bill. I remember an election night when I tried to find Warren; I finally tracked him down at Bill's home, watching the returns there. I recall being at dinner once at Bill's house; we were using some very unimpressive silverware. Helen laughed and said, "Earl has the silver and china; he's using them at a party at the governor's mansion." Also, I recall sitting in Knowland's Washington office on more than one occasion at around 6:30 p.m. when a call would come through from Warren in California. Bill and Earl would discuss legislation and matters of interest to California. There was friendly and excellent cooperation between Governor Earl and Senator Bill.

Many have called Earl Warren a fence-sitter; they've said he was wishy-washy, even made cartoons about it. I, who knew him, was amused by this; it was so untrue. Earl was a Scandinavian hardhead conceived in Iowa and born in a poor little house in a poor district of Los Angeles, the old Ann Street School District. The house is gone now, though Bill Campbell tried to get hold of it and preserve it for its historical interest. Warren's father was a Republican, but he had the Scandinavian idea that the state should care for the ill. He was affected by what he had seen. Warren himself, when ill for about ten weeks during his term as attorney general, thought, "What if I had no salary or income?" Hence, in his mind, insurance against catastrophic illness was very important. He felt that families should not be destroyed or their future mortgaged by bills when there was a no-fault catastrophe. So, he brought up his famous proposal for catastrophic illness insurance.

The medical profession was instantly up in arms; they hired Clem Whittaker and Leone Baxter to head their fight. They spent tremendous amounts of money to defeat Warren's plan. What Warren sought at the time was mainly catastrophic insurance, not to cover all ordinary health problems. It was not a terribly radical position.

While Warren was still a boy, in 1901, the Llewellyn and Baker Ironworks went out on strike. Warren's father was among those who went out. Those were bad days for labor. I recall, in 1907, riding on the Highland Park streetcar in Los Angeles, and seeing the police disperse some strikers from around the Baker Ironworks. The police were mounted and used both their horses and their clubs. In 1901 the railroads, among others, blackballed strikers, so when the strike was over, Earl's father had no job. He moved up to Bakersfield, a strong union town, and got a job as a car builder. He worked hard and started buying up old houses, which he fixed up and sold or rented. I've talked with J.R. Knowland about that period of Earl Warren's life, and I know that Earl carried papers in that tough town. He also had a job as a "call boy" going around the roundhouse in the early morning with a lantern and waking the workers due to come on a shift.

A little later he started to learn to play the clarinet; according to him he played a very bad clarinet. He started with a high school band and became a union musician. He later went to the University of California where he worked his way through, largely by playing the clarinet. He once showed me his gold Musicians Union card, of which he was very proud.

So, we have some of the background which caused him to become more and more like his father in his thinking, both as governor, and on the Supreme Court bench. He had a number of union people in his governmental advisory set-up, but their thinking did not especially pervade his governorship; he did go along with a lot of liberal proposals in the legislature whether or not he had anything to do with their being there.

During the last days of the depression and into World War II, there were great numbers of rabble-rousers. There were also numbers of communist sympathizers, that is to say non-communist party members who thought communism, or at least collectivism, offered a panacea to our form of government. As was only natural, most of these people centered their efforts on the aged, the needy and the unemployed. There were a number of differing elderly and unemployed groups that could be tied together from a voting standpoint. For example, there was Dr. Francis E. Townsend and the Townsend plan. Townsend was a fine old gentleman, originally Republican, but nonpartisan after he formulated his plan. He originally organized in the Midwest. His plan was to grant to each oldster $200 a month— good money in those days. They would be required to spend it all the same month, so that amount of money would be in circulation and help the economy. I don't think there was a medical plan included. Dr. Townsend had a large following though his plan, as far as I know, was never tried anywhere. I talked with him on a number of occasions. He made some very good suggestions to me in a backhanded way that I appreciated.

Also, there were the "Ham and Eggers" who were local to California. They had their main work in Southern California which even then, had more needy old people than most places. This group was headed by a couple of brothers named Allen. They were trying to get a constitutional amendment through in California, which would enable them to do something which would provide the needy with ham and eggs, or rather, the money to buy them. There was no Social Security or much of anything else at the time.

Then came the greatest organizer of them all, at least locally. His name was George McLain, and he continued until the Nixon days. He was disliked and mistrusted by most of the legislators, perhaps with cause. He built his group well. He had a magazine, *The Pensioner*, and he spent hundreds of thousands of dollars on systems, such as Addressograph, to make copies of the voter's registration for his correspondence. In the Los Angeles area he had a complete, up-to-date daily copy of the great register of voters. He knew when the registrations were changed, when new people were given the right to vote—he got it all. This, and the machines to do it, cost a great deal of money which he got, mainly, from pensioners. However, he also sold his mailing lists. Politicians and businessmen bought them.

All these people were busy about the time Warren was in office. There was another one, whose name I don't recall, who was a real organizer. He staged a "jalopy" march on Sacramento which started in Los Angeles and rapidly grew on the way to Sacramento. He stirred up a lot of publicity and loudly proclaimed that our callous government was not making any real effort to provide food or jobs for the needy. He demanded a meeting with the governor to make his charges, and Warren agreed to meet with him.

Now, Warren was always a very good listener, and on this occasion he outdid himself. He listened for about thirty minutes to the tirade of this man who repeatedly proclaimed that nothing—his word, "nothing"—was being done, that those in office did not care about those out of work and so on. Finally, Warren, who did have a temper, had one of his rare outbursts. He replied to the man along these lines:

"I have listened for half an hour to your ranting and complaining that nothing is being done. I was really hoping that you came here to offer something of concrete value, some suggestions as to what more we might do. Instead, you do nothing but castigate all the good citizens who are working, planning, paying taxes and trying to make jobs. You apparently only want to make enemies of everyone in business or public office. Now, just where do you think I got all these gray hairs? I'll tell you: it was from lying awake at night trying to think of more things that might improve conditions in California, so there would be jobs, work and money to support the poor; so there would be more new highway programs to make jobs; so there could be opening, widening and lighting of streets, making of subdivisions, building of houses and factories, building of new hospitals, water projects, sewer projects, building of new schools, new shopping centers—anything and everything that might create employment and help support our citizens. These are the things that create value and jobs for the people of the state. You come here and do nothing but accuse us of not being interested in providing for our people. Now, suppose you just take five minutes and give us some of the concrete things you are going to do to create jobs and help support the poor."

Warren stood, thanked the people for coming and walked out. The man had no reply, and Warren went over very big with the press and public. Though I did not always agree with either his legal or political decisions, Warren always struck me as a superior man.

Warren's family and his wife Nina's family were strongly religious. The guidance of the Bible remained a part of their lives, but he never traded upon religion. That was between him and his God, just as Masonry was his credo. I have never heard anything but good about the living standards and habits of our grand master of Masons in California.

Warren had a temper, as I have mentioned, but he could and did forgive those who aroused it. I incurred his wrath by criticizing in good faith some ways his campaign leaders were handling his primary campaign. It was not his handling, but that of some of the people he had put in to "front" for him—fine young people who, nevertheless, didn't know what a campaign was all about. I tried, with no intent to criticize, to suggest some things that should be done and had to be done in the final campaign. Warren wanted no permanent political structures; he was like Hiram Johnson in this respect. But, his anger against me cooled, and he supported me for Republican national committeeman from California. I recall on one occasion telephoning Governor Warren because I sensed that Senator Knowland was "on the wrong side" of some legislation, that his position seemed inimical to California's interest. Warren listened, as he always did, and I suggested that he might telephone Knowland. Warren thought awhile and said, "Oh, when the time comes, Bill's conscience will tell him how to vote, and he'll vote right." And Bill did. I suspect, though, that Warren did talk to Bill about our conversation.

Although Earl Warren and likewise William Knowland have figured very largely in my account of the political wars, it will be no surprise to the reader that I, likewise, include them among those who have been of influence on my thinking and my life, at least to the extent of a couple of anecdotes or observations. One such about Warren is amusing: He was a most courteous man and, when governor, always made it a practice to telephone prospective judges prior to the actual appointment. One morning, Landy Rhoades, then of the municipal court, answered the telephone about 6:30 in the morning. A voice said, "This is Governor Warren. I would like very much to have you move up to the Los Angeles County Superior Court. In my estimation you would make an excellent judge of the Superior Court. Will you accept the appointment?" Now, Landy Rhoades was a humorous sort of fellow, and didn't know Warren well. He jumped to the conclusion that the call was from someone playing a joke. So he said, "Well, if you're the governor, and you are making me a Superior Court judge, you just come right down here and tell me so."

Now, unknown to Rhoades, Warren was at that time staying at the home of his friend, Joseph Musgrove. Joe's house was near Santa Monica in the "Uplifters' Club" area of the canyon. Not many minutes after Judge Rhoades hung up the phone and, no doubt chuckled at how he had stopped the joker, his doorbell rang. There stood Governor Warren!

Warren was very proud of his appointments, and he made a great number of them. I think in the ten years he was governor, he made 46 appointments to our Los Angeles Superior Court. I recall a time, I think in 1947, when Ed Shattuck, Bernard Brennan and I were talking casually with Warren. It was just before he made a number of Superior Court appointments to Los Angeles; the legislature had just created some additional places on the Superior Court here. I think it was Ed who asked, "Governor, how is it done? What do you do when you get all these hundreds of names of people who want to be appointed judge?"

Warren replied, "I keep a separate file on each person desiring to be a judge with a master list. I have a short biographical sketch made concerning each one. When the time comes for me to make appointments, I sometimes consult with several people, particularly when there are a lot of appointments to be made. I didn't always consult the same persons, because I don't want anyone to be considered my spokesman. I don't have a spokesman. Then I take the list of names and run through it, picking out those I think should be considered. I call not only for their biographical sketches, but their entire file, their letters of support, the histories of what they have done, and so forth. From this I develop a smaller list for final consideration; I may consult again with persons whose opinions I value, and then I make a decision."

He went on, "This time, for instance, I have 872 people to consider: lawyers applying to be, or suggested to be, Superior Court judges in Los Angeles County. Now, many of them are fine people, but would not necessarily make good judges, in my opinion. And, by the time I've gotten through the list, there will no doubt be additions to it."

Warren reflected for a moment; then went on. "A man who wants to be a judge, if he is smart, will apply, or have someone apply for him; he'll send in one letter from a community leader telling of his value to his community, and his standing in it; one letter from a presiding or other top judge telling me what an excellent trial lawyer, or drawer of pleadings he is; a letter from some member of the Appellate Court telling how well he handles an appeal, and how well he writes a brief; and perhaps one or two letters attesting to his good character and neighborhood value, or any special point he wants to make. If he's passed over once, surely something will happen to enable his sponsoring friend to write and tell what a wonderful job he did, perhaps on such-and-such a case in which the decision was in his favor. And that's where he should stop."

I think that is a good summation of Warren's description of how he made appointments. This, by the way, was not an official meeting—simply a conversation in the lobby of the Biltmore Hotel in Los Angeles.

A lot of talk went on for years about a Warren-Eisenhower entente. It's all bunk as far as I'm concerned. Taft wanted to get Warren and Knowland on his bandwagon. But, it was after the nomination and during the presidential campaign, I believe, that Eisenhower first learned of Warren's desire to be on the Supreme Court. Bill Knowland spent considerable time as coordinator on Eisenhower's special train, and I have told how close Bill and Warren were. Bill told me that it was on the train that he talked to Eisenhower about Warren's Supreme Court ambitions. Knowland brought up the subject. Bill said Eisenhower agreed that, if everything worked out right, Warren would be put on the Supreme Court.

There were no vacancies at the time, but shortly after Eisenhower became President, a vacancy arose by reason of the death of Chief Justice Vinson. Vinson's death was sudden and unexpected. At that time Bill Knowland was in Chung King visiting or doing some business with Chiang Kai-Shek. I got a call from J.R. Knowland, Bill's father, and he said, "Earl is just walking up and down all night long, wearing a path in the rug." I asked what Earl was worrying about. J.R. said, "Well, he's so anxious to get that chief justice job on the Supreme Court. He was not promised the chief justiceship, only sort of promised a judgeship, but he's just crazy to be chief justice."

I said, "Where's Bill, and what's he doing?"

"Bill's on his way back from Chung King. He'll be in Cairo tomorrow, and from there he'll telephone Eisenhower for an appointment."

The next day I was having lunch with a friend at the California Club when the political editor of the *Times* came over. This well-known conservative Democrat wanted to bet me that Warren would not get the chief justiceship. The bet he had in mind was a hundred dollars. I certainly did not intend to tell him anything, and I did not care to bet on what I thought was extremely close to a sure thing. I told him I didn't do much betting, but I'd bet him ten with my friend as witness.

Bill came back and talked to Eisenhower. The next thing I knew, U.S. Attorney General Herb Brownell phoned me from Sacramento where he had gone to talk with Warren. He wanted to talk with me and came to Los Angeles. At the time neither of us seemed to have an idea that Earl Warren might be considered too liberal. His association with the conservative Knowlands had always been close, and though he had made some labor appointments, they were good labor people, not members of radical groups. They were good, capable people with good reasons for their appointment. Anyway, as part of my job, and because of my knowledge of the facts, I gave Warren a clean bill of health as far as any radical thinking on his part was concerned. We cleared him, and the appointment was made.

I continued in contact with Earl Warren after he became chief justice, though of necessity my actual visits with him were few. No one, least of all Dwight Eisenhower, had any idea what a stormy petrel Warren would turn out to be as chief justice; time has given us a better perspective of his work. The 1954 case of *Brown vs. Topeka* in which Warren wrote the decision was the real beginning of the breakdown of racial segregation in this country. It should be remembered that the decision was concurred by all eight other Supreme Court justices. It was a remarkable feat.

There was great astonishment and much anger at the time among many conservative people. Then the muttering of "impeach Earl Warren" began to be heard. There were many people in that movement; they simply did not think the way Warren did, and their first idea was to impeach him. All in all, things were very warm everywhere for awhile.

The Los Angeles County Board of Supervisors faced a dilemma; it is, or was, common practice in major public buildings to hang a picture of the person who had dedicated that building. The Los Angeles County Civil Courthouse, the big main courthouse, had been completed, and the supervisors were very proud of it. But, Earl Warren had turned the first shovelful of earth of that building while he was governor. The supervisors named a committee to commission a painting of Warren, and they had chosen Emil Kosa, Jr. But, because of all the furor, they did not feel it was a time to be honoring Earl Warren in such a public manner.

Some years later, I became presiding judge of the Superior Court. Someone then on the Board of Supervisors said, "Now, it can be done; the presiding judge is a friend of Earl Warren and he's willing to take on the duty of seeing to it that the picture is satisfactory to Warren. Then it can be hung, and there can be a proper ceremony." I was consulted, and agreed to go back and consult with Warren. My wife, Lois, went with me, as did Emil Kosa, Jr., the artist, and his wife. Well, Earl Warren did not like the way his hands were done, and Emil did them over. Actually, I don't believe he particularly liked the picture.

Warren and his lovely wife, Nina, invited us and the Kosas to dinner, and we had a relaxing time.

Warren was always wary of talking about his decisions, and I knew better than to bring them up. But he did say, "You know, we receive many letters from people in the penitentiaries and their families. We have much evidence of discrimination and unfairness, particularly in the South. I know there always has been, but it is continuing. For instance, here is a quote from a trial judge in a southern state court. It's in the record, so there's no question about it: 'An hour and a half is plenty of time to try any jury case where a nigger is charged with murder.'"

We all expressed our revulsion at this, and Warren went on, "The situation is so bad we just have to do something about it. I don't know yet just what it will be, but we're going to do something. It will probably be something that is unnecessary as far as people like you are concerned, and as far as most courts are concerned. You and they don't need such rules as we probably have to adopt, but a lot of people and a lot of places do need them. There will have to be mandatory changes in procedure, and we have to decide how to work them out." Well, we all know what was worked out; "Miranda" and other such cases came about as a result of this determination by him and the majority of the Supreme Court Justices.

I wrote to him occasionally, and I was always able to see him when in Washington. I did not and do not consider him either a radical or a leftist. He was a humanitarian and in my opinion the great defender of the individual against big government. It seemed to concern him greatly that the little fellow was at the mercy of "big government," especially if that "little fellow" was of a minority racial background. Years later, after he had his heart attack, I wrote to him as a fellow member of the "coronary club." I got a fine letter back in which he told me of his plans for the future. He was especially interested in the "World Organization of Lawyers for Peace and International Law." After he died, I wrote to his wife, Nina, and got a good note back from her. She seemed to like my feeling, and agreed with me that he was a representative of the little fellow against big government.

• • •

When Truman was president, he decided to supply Korea with only a tiny amount of aid, which the Republicans thought exceedingly unwise. It became necessary, in the view of the United Nations, that we, along with Australia and a few others, go in and stop the "revolution." We thought we were getting into a small "police action," to use the Truman term, and very few of our troops wanted to go back. We let a lot of draftees go home, and among the groups that were in any way outfitted or ready for battle, was the California National Guard. They were among the first to be sent, and the spearhead group was from the Los Angeles area, mainly Mexican and Black American boys from Watts, Compton and the surrounding area. Off they went, though they were really not properly trained, equipped or led for such an action as they faced.

I was a trustee or director of the Los Angeles County Church Federation which had within it the great bulk of the Protestant churches of this area. Dr. Forrest Weir was the head paid employee. He telephoned me saying that there was to be a meeting in Watts of the Protestant church pastors of the area and that he couldn't be there; would I go and represent the Church Federation? I felt that I had not done much of value during my term as trustee, so, though it was raining heavily, I said I would go, and did. The water, when I got there, was over the curbs, but I found a place to park near the door of the Methodist church where the meeting was to take place. There were only a few people there around a potbellied stove. It was warm around the stove, and we sat and talked. The pastor, a nice man, was a former Pancho Villa bandit who had been converted.

I was terribly disturbed by one thing he had to say: "You know, six hundred of the young men from my parish area were in that National Guard unit that went to Korea. Of that six hundred, four hundred are dead."

I said, "You mean wounded, casualties?" "No," he said, "four hundred are dead." This shocked us all. He went on, "You see, those boys had joined the National Guard because it gave them a little money, they had companionship in the evening and they were doing something for their people. They enjoyed being into things, and this was a good way to do that. But, the North Koreans had to be stopped, and they were the people who were sent to stop them."

Next day, I told Bill Knowland this story. He was very much against the way the Truman administration was handling the so-called Korean War, and we agreed on the proper approach to the Mexican and Black American group. So, Bill went up and down the state with his big stride and thundering voice saying how badly the war was being handled and how wrongly these people had been treated. Perhaps not all of these people understood just what it was all about, or whether Bill's fine points were right or wrong, but they did understand that something was wrong. They also knew that Bill had been drafted, had risen through the ranks and had become a Major. He was attacking the Truman administration, and they had voted for him. Thus, we carried areas which were normally 90% Democratic. We carried the state by over a million people in the primary, getting the Democratic as well as the Republican nomination. One of the biggest factors, in my estimation, was the handling of the Korean mess and the treatment accorded minority citizens by their military and their country.

There is still some discussion as to why Bill Knowland resigned his senate seat and returned to California where he ran for governor. I think two situations, along with other considerations, gave him little choice. The first of these was the fact that he was badly needed in the affairs of the family business. J.R. Knowland, Bill's father, was very old. Bill's brother was running the paper, or attempting to, and he was not considered capable of the job. There was also the fact that he opposed Goodwin Knight. Bill had said to me, "Goody Knight must not be governor of California; he's too close to the Teamsters, and they're too close to some others." This should not be construed to mean that Knowland was anti-union. His family's paper, the *Oakland Tribune*, was a union paper; the paper and the union worked together very well, but Bill had no use for the Teamster leadership. He considered them a sinister group. This opinion was shared by many including the McClellan group.

Bill attended some of the McClellan hearings in Washington, and Helen, his wife, attended nearly all of the meetings. I was in Washington, and my wife, Lois, attended one of the meetings with Helen. There were no seats for them, so with the assistance of Knowland's office, they were given seats right down in front. The questioning was being conducted by Robert Kennedy, and a number of union people and lawyers were sitting at his table. Seated behind the table, Mrs. Faries saw Kennedy pass a note to the union leaders which she was able to read. It said something like, "How am I doing?" This certainly shocked her; obviously he was working with the Democrat union leaders against the leaders of the Teamsters.

There was a recess, and Lois went out to talk to the attorney for the Kohler interests, whose group was apparently being questioned. Some will recall that there was a strike at the Kohler plant in Wisconsin during which terrible things were being done; it was a very bad situation. Bob Kennedy was apparently trying to keep these things out, to have only good things said about all unions other than the Teamsters. Kohler's lawyer said, "This is the kind of thing we've been getting all along; he's for other unions and against the Teamsters; so, we can't get our evidence presented."

Mrs. Faries called me and asked about speaking with Fulton Lewis, Jr., the columnist. He had called and asked to talk with her, and she had put him off. I told her not to talk to him. She had already mentioned the matter to the other ladies who were at the hearing with her, and I said she should tell the story to Senator Goldwater who was inclined to give the matter immediate publicity. I felt, however, that this was not the time to use this information; the time for that would be in the campaign. So, the passing of the note or its contents was not used; Goldwater was to hold it for the next political season.

Knowland felt that Goody Knight was undoubtedly tied in with the Teamsters, and he wanted to save California from what might result from this. He consulted only with his conscience. Helen told me that he came home one evening and went to his room for a time. He came out and said, "Helen, I'm going to run for governor of California." Although she was a very able woman, politically wise and experienced, he did not even consult her. His conscience told him to do this thing, and he felt he must.

I think had Bill consulted as he normally would, it would have been easy. Given a chance, we might well have been able to convince Virginia and Goody Knight that he should have a career as a United States senator. He was a good speaker, and she would have loved being a senator's wife; it should have been very easy at that time. But Bill's letter to me, written the week before he announced, was mailed with an ordinary stamp and did not reach me for five or six days. By the time I received it, he had announced. I'm afraid I might have broken my resolve to have nothing to do with politics while a judge; I probably would have phoned him immediately and suggested to others how to straighten things out before any announcement. Seeing the announcement in the paper, I telephoned California's then Republican national committeeman, Ron Button, who was very close to Knight, and was state treasurer. I asked him if he had been consulted; he had not. Had he been consulted, had I talked to him, and he in turn to Bill and Knight before the announcement, I'm sure things would have been different. Or would they? I take with several grains of salt the talk about the *Los Angeles Times* being consulted.

• • •

In 1946 Bill Knowland was to run for U.S. senator, both to fill the remaining term of the deceased Hiram Johnson, and for the following six-year term. It was necessary to file and run for each; we referred to these as short and long term. We thought that he would be the only candidate and that our Republican finance committee would immediately rally behind him. Much to our surprise, another person, a complete unknown, filed as a Republican for the senatorial job. His name, oddly enough, was Hiram Johnson! Perhaps he and his backers thought this would guarantee his winning, but he didn't get very far. He had never been really active in politics, and some harbored the suspicion that he was planted to keep the finance committee from putting money into Knowland's campaign. It was then the unwritten rule that, where there were two valid Republican candidates in the primaries, the Republican finance committee would support neither of them. This man filed for both the long and short terms, so the finance committee was bound to refuse to be of assistance to Knowland's campaign. We had, therefore, to get into the business of raising money necessary to publicize Bill Knowland.

I was fortunate in obtaining for treasurer a terse, solid and conservative Republican, Joseph Crail, Jr. Joe and I personally went on a note at one of the banks, and at one time we owed it over $26,000. We were personally liable for its repayment. I didn't have a lot of money, but we did get it whittled down by the end of the primaries to about $16,000. Joe and I had to raise the full amount, so we got some professional help.

When the primaries were over, Knowland had the Republican nomination. We had cross-filed, but the Democratic nomination had gone to Will Rogers, Jr. In fact, counting the overall vote of both parties in the 1946 primaries, Will Rogers, Jr. and the Democrats were ahead by over three hundred thousand votes.

Also, Joe and I had to pay back the bank. We divided the remaining debt, and I think at the end of the election we each had to pay back $1,365. It didn't break either of us, and I was happy to get away with such a small amount.

• • •

The "Red" issue was the recognized issue of the 1946 campaign. But we handled it somewhat differently from the method of Nixon and his campaigners. By the time of the final election, Knowland was impressively leading all the candidates. He had proved himself a top campaigner and a powerful type of man. People were convinced of two things: first, his candidacy was not just a sop thrown to his father who had sponsored Earl Warren; and second, he was a better candidate. By election time most people had caught on to the fact that Will Rogers, Jr. was not, and would never be, a man of the stature of his famous father.

While I was working with the general finance committee, we were doing our best to support all Republican candidates including Nixon. I objected to the strength Nixon was putting into his efforts on the Red issue, particularly in connection with his San Gabriel speech, his last one; but my objections were overruled. Though the Red issue was unquestionably a "gut issue," I felt that Nixon's personalized treatment of Voorhis was self-defeating. Nixon, I thought, had the election won by this time, and it was time to win friends for the Republican Party. Although there were disagreements, there was certainly no break of any kind.

Did time prove Nixon right? Actually, I think it did. Remember the campaign for senator against Helen Gahagan Douglas, the Pumpkin Papers, Alger Hiss, et al. It was a good issue, a gut issue, and I felt and feel that Nixon was honest about it; but I thought he was a bit of the boy debater and a little cold. It seemed to me that it could have been handled better. Knowland, as I indicated, had shown himself to be a man of great strength, courage and ability. He went up and down the state with about three speeches. He was a slow starter as a speaker, but always went over well in the end. In my evaluation there are two main types of political speakers. One is the type represented by "Goody" Knight—judge, lieutenant governor and finally governor of California. Goody was a humorous speaker, very well-liked, and said some excellent things. But when he finished, you'd turn to your neighbor and say, "That was a great speech, wasn't it? What did he say?" Which is to say, Goody did not make a final impression on you with his point. Somehow his points got lost, and the listener would end up with a good general impression of the speech rather than of specific points. One did not go home thinking that he and the speaker were together on a particular line of thought or program. One didn't think, "Here is our champion!"

Knowland, on the other hand, was not a humorist. He was quite serious and really a bit dogmatic. Now and then he'd manage a little joke that got a laugh. It took his listeners a little time to follow him, but when he reached the end of his speech, people were thinking along with him. He would wind up with his customary ending, and the audience would stand up to cheer.

Knowland was never considered a great speaker. He used the same message over and over, but it worked. In the final election of 1946 he won by some 400,000 for the short and long term. In his second election in 1952 he retained his Senate seat by, perhaps, a million votes. He was a real friend to me and a good man to work with.

Many people don't know that Taft voted with California on the Colorado River legislation. During my service as Republican national

*McIntyre Faries and Senator William "Bill" Knowland*

committeeman, about 1948, Preston Hotchkis, president of the Colorado River Association asked me to go to Washington to lobby for the Colorado River water legislation in favor of California. I thought there was, and still is, great equity in this. It was California that put up the millions and millions of dollars in connection with the Hoover Dam, the All-American canal, the business of the Imperial and Coachella Valleys, electric power and so forth. Without California there would be no worthwhile development in the Colorado River basin. We have, to an extent, lost our hold, and we must still develop more. We were successful in our efforts when I was Republican national committeeman, and I was glad to go at Preston's request to talk to our congressional delegation and with some of the senators.

I let the association pay my way to Washington, but took no pay for myself. I walked into the minority leader's office first. This was Joseph Attleboro of Massachusetts. I said, "I came back here because our people in California are disturbed about the Colorado River legislation. They're afraid that they're going to lose out on the vote, and that water is absolutely necessary for California." Joe wanted to know why the Californians felt that they might lose out. I said, "For one thing, because sitting in your office most of the time is a friend of yours and mine. I'm talking about the national committeeman from Arizona, Clarence Buddington Kelland. We know he controls the *Arizona Republic* newspaper in Phoenix." Joe leaned back and laughed. "What kind of a politician do you think I am?" I asked what he meant, and he went on, "Since World War II you Californians have given me nineteen very solid California Republicans in Congress. That's the majority of our delegation. I'll never let them down. Bud Kelland is very helpful publicity-wise, but he can't carry the Colorado River water legislation for Arizona. California is going to have the water and power that it needs, and that it has paid for. It should have it."

I then went to see Robert Taft who was floor leader for the Republicans in the Senate. The Republicans didn't have a majority at the time, but everyone thought the world of Bob Taft, and he was very powerful. After a nice little visit I said, "Bob, I was looking at the newspapers on my way here, and I see that every state has its own boondoggle. You know that results in lots of trading back and forth, the old 'pork barrel' business. Now Southern California has put all this money into the Colorado River; we developed power, we developed water, and we developed land that needs this water, especially the Imperial and Coachella Valleys. We built the dam, we levelled and tilled our land, we guided water down there; people have moved there and invested their savings. We've spent millions and millions. Now along comes Arizona which we admit is dry. They want to compete with our valleys; they want to get the water we've spent so much to develop and move onto their dry land. There just isn't enough water to take care of them and us."

Taft replied, "I don't pay attention to that sort of thing. I have many things I'm supposed to be concerned with, and I give my thoughts to those things. Such matters as you're talking about, I turn the decisions on those over to someone I trust from the general area." I asked, "Well, who are you trusting in connection with that area?" He replied that he was trusting Senator Milliken of Colorado. I said, "Well, Senator Milliken is one of the group on which Arizona counts for a vote. They trade back and forth on projects, whether the area in question is Republican or Democratic. If you follow Senator Milliken, you'll vote for the water to go to Arizona." Taft said, "I have indicated that I think a project must be able to stand on its own feet; it must pay out in the long run."

I may not have stated my case too well because I was caught a little off guard, but Taft did vote for California on the two occasions concerning the Colorado River.

• • •

After putting Knowland in the Senate and Nixon in the House, the next great spurt of effort came in 1948, the year of Dewey's defeat in the presidential election. As is often the case after a lost election, there were those who sought a scapegoat, and in this case there was an outcry against the chairman of the Republican national committee—at this time, Senator Hugh Scott of Pennsylvania.

The cry to make him the scapegoat for Dewey's defeat arose particularly from some very conservative Republicans who normally find a majority on the committee. The newspapers naturally played up all of this, and I thought it a travesty to try to make a scapegoat out of this fine, liberal Republican senator. The national committee, not one chosen by the nominee, had run the campaign.

The full committee shortly called a meeting to be held in a hotel in Omaha, Nebraska. The debate started on the subject of whether we should have a new national chairman for the national committee. I had an official position in the Scott group, but having talked the situation over with Knowland and Warren, I remained aloof and went unfettered to the meeting. I thought it wrong and unfair to eliminate Scott, though at the time I didn't know him very well. The debate continued ad infinitum. I counted noses and thought we had about a four-to-six majority for retaining Scott; but, as the debate dragged on, people began leaving to confer in the halls, or for any reason at all. I felt we were being talked to death, and if the restlessness increased, we might lose. Warren and Knowland left the decision to me, so I moved the previous question, shutting off the debate. Scott was retained. People got a great kick out of my staging this maneuver, and I was talked about as Scott's manager.

I persuaded Senator Scott to come to California where we had a luncheon for him. At the speaker's table I sat next to Harry Chandler who by that time had retired from the *Times*, but kept up his interest in the welfare of the Republican party. As the meeting was going on, he turned to me and said, "You know, in the last analysis, what we pay for in life is good judgment." I agreed with him, but I never knew just why he said that to me at that particular time.

• • •

Tom Dewey was comparatively young, trim-looking, always meticulously dressed and wore a carefully trimmed little moustache. I shall always remember the remark made about him by Alice Roosevelt Longworth, daughter of Theodore Roosevelt and doyenne of Washington and Long Island society. She spoke of him as "the little man on the wedding cake," which did a good deal of harm to him and his campaign.

Dewey was an excellent speaker though sometimes less than shrewd with regard to his subject matter. He was a courteous and able man. I got to know him fairly well and liked him personally, but as a candidate, he was just about the worst possible. Though he was born in Michigan, he never came to understand the people west of the Alleghenies. He had to be advised by his secretary, a most capable man, on almost everything he should do from a political standpoint. His New York friends thought he knew how to campaign, but neither he nor they knew how to campaign nationally. He and the group around him seemed incapable of following suggestions as to how people from the other parts of the United States thought, felt and reacted. The common story was that at every railway stop, he would get off and buy newspapers from every district, then go back and read them on the train. He thought that he could understand from their reports and comments what was going on and if things were going well.

Now, I don't want to downgrade the importance of newspapers, particularly in those days; they were of importance. But this is not the way to keep your fingers on the pulse of a campaign. Other things are far more indicative, and one of those is to watch the size and temper of the crowd. Are they enthusiastic? Do they seem dissatisfied with the answers to questions regarding things of their interest? I made it a constant practice to canvas the people at the edge of the crowd, gain intelligence on local issues and pass the word on to the candidates I was with. This I regard as essential.

People everywhere are interested in jobs, very much so, both in a personal sense and with regard to community prosperity. Our constant awareness of this fact is one of the main reasons for our long success in carrying California. They wanted orders for the airplane factories and other factories. Californians are interested in their agricultural problems, their roads, the care of the sick, aged and poor, in the whole economy of the state. Of course, in times of crisis their interest extends to national and foreign affairs. One simply must know, when campaigning, whether an area is happy or disgruntled, and why.

Dewey was expected to carry California, but lost by about 22,000 votes. He need not have lost, if certain situations were handled better. Note, if you will, that all the things I cite are little things, but these were fundamental errors that should have been avoided. They could have easily been avoided if he and his group, particularly Dewey himself, conferred with his western advisors and with local leaders. I recall the state chairman of Iowa saying to me, "How can any candidate expect to carry the state of Iowa when he comes here wearing a Homburg hat?"

Considerably before Dewey became the nominee, he came out to California at the suggestion of Bill Campbell's brother. Bill's brother was at the time the office manager or administrator for Senator Borah of Iowa. Bill gave a dinner for Dewey in a room at the Jonathan Club. All of the guests at that dinner were important Republican political people. The room had been thoroughly worked over for "bugs" (listening devices) ahead of time. The dinner was a very quiet affair, not publicized at all, and as I say, we had very carefully checked security. But when Dewey arrived, late of course, he had three guards with him. These proceeded, without a by-your-leave, to make a sort of Keystone Kops search of the room—turning sofas upside down, looking behind pictures, doing all sorts of silly things. Needless to say, these important guests were offended at this totally uncalled-for and high-handed behavior. It made a very bad impression. All eventually sat down, and we had a nice and courteous dinner. Even though we had tried to appear unconcerned, as Queen Victoria was wont to remark, "We were not amused."

At the time of the campaign the 160-acre water limit for one owner was a great issue, particularly for the San Joaquin and Sacramento valleys. There it was really vital. The main newspapers of the area were the "Bee" papers, owned by the McClatchy interests. They were Democratic papers, and were the leading papers in Sacramento, Stockton and Fresno. These papers with the *Bakersfield Californian* blanketed the valleys and were outspoken political leaders. Radio and television had less power politically then. These papers, though Democratic, supported Earl Warren and occasionally other Republicans. We thought that we had persuaded them to support Dewey; they were willing, but with the proviso that he gave them a satisfactory answer on the 160-acre water limit. He did not have to come out against it, but merely to say that he was unfamiliar with the legislation (true enough) and would study it, after which he would come out on the matter. At any rate, that was our plan.

Kyle Palmer, political editor of the *Times* and a man who knew political situations, was put on a plane to Arizona where he met the Dewey train. It was his mission to tell Dewey about local problems and local situations, the matters of importance on which he should touch, particularly the 160-acre water limit question. Kyle went, with Harry Chandler's blessing and proper credentials. He was allowed on the train, but was completely walled off from Dewey—not permitted to talk with him. Later, when riding through the San Joaquin and Sacramento valleys, Kyle did get to mention the problem to Dewey, but was ignored. Riding through the very place where this issue was crucial, Dewey paid no attention.

To no one's surprise, this stupidity caused the loss of support of the crucial newspapers, and Dewey's defeat in California.

When Dewey's train arrived in Barstow, a big wild west affair was in progress. This, I think, was coincidental to the Dewey presence, simply a local celebration with people from all parts of the state. When the train stopped, horsemen gathered at the rear end of the last car. One horseman held aloft a little girl bearing a big Mexican hat which she was to present to Dewey. I was on the rear platform when Dewey came out. He took the hat from the little girl, merely nodding thanks. Any politician, no matter how inept, should have realized and taken advantage of the opportunity this presented for "politicking" by taking the little girl in his arms, giving her a hug for the photographers, putting on the hat for pictures and the like. Dewey did none of these obvious things; he merely laid the hat down and walked back inside. The horsemen gathered around the platform and clearly expected him to say a few words, perhaps comment on the beauty of the horses and their outfits or surely shake a few hands. Nope! There were a lot of newsmen who were disappointed to see the affair fall so terribly flat. The flop was widely published all over California and elsewhere—another good way to lose a campaign. Next, the train pulled into San Bernardino where the station had a large space for gatherings of this sort. Dewey did not have his picture taken with any of the Republican candidates from the district; he didn't talk properly to the mayor, the board of supervisors or the press. So again, he went wrong with the newspaper people who were gathered to report on the arrival of the Dewey entourage. The people of the great San Bernardino valley were hurt and alienated to an unknowable degree.

At that time Dewey gave out copies of the speech he intended to make in Los Angeles. We had arranged for him to speak in the Coliseum, and we had it pretty well filled except for the east end which was blocked off. Well, Dewey gave out advance copies of his speech, and it wasn't bad. For one reason or another, perhaps his being told that we had a lot of elderly people here in Los Angeles, he decided to give a different speech. The speech he gave had been seen by none of us, and it was decidedly not the right speech for this area. He had no idea what California was doing, or what organizations here represented old people and other interests. The speech revealed that ignorance; it was an unwise speech for the Coliseum or Los Angeles.

On another occasion Dewey spoke at the Hollywood Bowl. The affair was well handled by the Hollywood people who conducted it, notably the Screen Writers Guild. There were in attendance, to meet Dewey, a great many motion picture people—writers, producers, managers, actors and others. There was a room at the side at the back of the stage where he was to greet the dignitaries. After his speech there was to be a reception in that room; people would have an opportunity to shake the hand of the presidential candidate. Everything was going according to schedule; there was plenty of time, and Dewey went with his little bodyguard into the room and began greeting people. The movie cameras were grinding, stills were being snapped, and Dewey was being introduced to people who had much to do with publicity, not only in California but also across the country.

Murray Choitner had made arrangements for Dewey to be photographed with the motorcycle officers guarding his entourage. This was a common thing for a candidate to do, a thing Earl Warren always handled well. This motorcycle group was a fine body of men, very clever riders who demonstrated their skill in the aisles of the Hollywood Bowl. Well, the greetings were in full swing, and even though there were the inevitable few trying to crowd in who didn't belong, the situation was quite under control. While there was still about an hour left of the time assigned to the greeting of the people, Dewey's little bodyguard suddenly decided that this was enough. Having no idea of the importance of this event to the whole campaign, the bodyguard insisted to Dewey that it was time to leave. Dewey should not have left early, and particularly he should not have left without conferring with any of us who were in charge of the affair. The bodyguard took Dewey by the arm, practically forcing him out the door and into his car. There were no good-byes, no apologies, nothing; he just left. The guard, having virtually shoved Dewey into the car, slammed the door right on the hand of the secretary of the Hollywood group who had arranged the affair! The hand was badly hurt, and to say there were "boos" is to put it mildly. This inexcusable boorishness, leaving with neither thanks nor apologies, left many people who would have been for Dewey very angry. The whole deplorable incident was reported not only throughout the Hollywood community but also in the national press. This Hollywood Bowl incident by itself was enough to make the difference between winning and losing, and so were several other such mishaps.

• • •

There is much to say about Richard Nixon, and I stress at the out-
set that I feel no need and have no intent to add, subtract, attack,
defend, castigate, laud or evaluate Nixon for posterity. These are personal memoirs intended to illuminate my times, my part in them and
my dealings with the men who molded them. Nixon was certainly
one of those molders.

I must say that I have read many books about Nixon including two
by himself. Most of those written after Watergate were written
hastily, some out of burning hatred for Nixon, others with the idea of
making some quick money by capitalizing on the public feeling
aroused by the events and the hearings. Some were vituperative; one
or two were friendly but guarded; very few were of any value as
comparative history, as time has already shown. In my judgment
for what it is worth, the one written by Theodore White is probably
the best.

While I could perhaps be called a "Knowland man," I served a
party and my country in my political life, not any particular man or
interest. Thus, when Nixon was the party's choice for any office, I
served his candidacy to the best of my ability. I never had "Potomac
fever," or any desire to live in Washington, so while I was on several
occasions a Nixon supporter, I was not a "hot" supporter. Still, as
events would have it, I was one of the earlier and more important
Nixon supporters.

About two years before Watergate I received a personal letter on
presidential stationery, signed by Richard Nixon—his name, not his
usual "RN." I have several letters from him signed with the "RN."
The letter says as I recall, "Dear Mac, twenty-five years ago I met
with your committee, and the die was cast that I should enter politics
by running for Congress. You and the other five at that university
club meeting have remained my close friends. I want you to know
that I feel and will always treasure that friendship. I am now and will
always be grateful to you as a friend." Sincerely, Dick."

It was a beautiful thing for him to do, and I have no doubt of the
sincerity of his affection for the original seven of us. On November
14, 1971, I was the victim of a cardiac infraction. Jerry, that loveliest of
ladies, my new wife, insisted on rushing me to Good Samaritan
Hospital where I went into a coma and was clinically dead for three
minutes. I wanted to get strong enough to be home for Christmas,
and the doctors told Jerry that I could go home on the 23rd, but

would probably have to come back, since I had not been through all the tests they wanted, nor was I very strong. I went home on a gurney and was put on a hospital bed in our living room. On Christmas Eve, the telephone rang, and Jerry answered it. I was close enough to hear both sides of the conversation. It went something like this: "The president (or, possibly, the White House) is calling Judge McIntyre Faries." Jerry said, "Who?"

"The president of the United States."

I was too overcome to speak with him, even if it was the president. Jerry, for her part, thought it was a joker and said, "Put him on."

He came on saying, "Jerry, I've just heard that Mac is extremely and seriously ill, and I wanted to wish him a Merry Christmas." Jerry thanked him and told him I was too ill to talk (in fact, I was too choked up), but I signalled her and she extended my wish for a Merry Christmas to him and his family. She told him his call meant much to me which of course it did. His call probably had a great deal to do with my successful return to health. It was an extremely thoughtful and kind thing for him to do, especially since he was in Washington at 9:30 on Christmas Eve. Unquestionably, he had his family around him and had many calls to make to relatives and notables.

I have no idea how the information reached him. The call came out of a clear sky as far as I was concerned, and my wife swore she had not let the word out to him; but as I say, I am sure the incident contributed to my full recovery.

I would like to think back to 1946 when I lived in the 12th Congressional District, the district was represented at the time by Democrat Jerry Voorhis. While in college, Jerry had been a socialist. He was a very fine-grained man, comparatively young, our congressman and a true politician.

The 12th Congressional District was Democratic, but not heavily so. We Republicans remained in power and were able to carry it, except for Congress. We in the district set out to get a new Republican congressional candidate. Fred Houser had been the candidate several times, but he could not stand up to Jerry Voorhis who could wear a slouch hat and beat-up shoes, carry or smoke a pipe when he was in an area where that made an impression and then dress up with his tie straight when making an address at some formal affair.

Now, Jerry was not a communist. He did espouse some collectivist ideas, and when he left Congress, he became head of some collectivist institution or enterprise in Chicago. I have great respect for him, and have talked with him on a few occasions. Some people called him a communist; it is a fact, though a regrettable one, that many average Americans equated any form or degree of collectivism with communism. They immediately labeled many persons and ideas "communist," as sort of a knee-jerk reaction. George Bernard Shaw had some rather trenchant comments on this.

At the time Nixon came on the scene, close to the time of the 1946 elections, communism was, as our polls and conferences disclosed, the great issue of the election in California. No doubt the same was true elsewhere, but our concern was California. This held true all through the campaign, and I personally took cognizance of it for the Knowland campaign.

Roy Crocker, with whom I served on the high school board of South Pasadena and San Marino, arranged a meeting of a "nonpartisan" group of seven of us. There was already a loose confederation of individuals from the various towns making the 12th Congressional District which was nonpartisan. Their purpose was to find a good man to run for Congress against Jerry Voorhis. There were a lot of these towns and a lot of small newspapers. I think it was the two from Whittier who came up with the name of Richard Nixon. They were Rex Kennedy, publisher of the *Whittier News* and Ben Perry of the Whittier branch of Bank of America. Nixon was from Whittier, had gone to Whittier College and, shortly before World War II, had been in the office of Thomas Bewley, Whittier's city attorney. Though Nixon had practiced law for only a short time, he had been "noticed" as a good speaker and a man of promise. He had been in some local theatrical events and had met "Pat" Ryan after his return from Duke University.

Nixon spent some time in Washington as a civilian government employee before going into the Navy. His military record was excellent; he had risen to the command of a landing craft. At the time of his discharge he was a lieutenant-commander (reserve). So, while Nixon was getting out of the military, these two men got in touch with Roy Crocker and perhaps also with Roy Day, Los Angeles County Republican chairman at the time. They proposed the name of Richard Nixon and wanted to have him "looked over."

The war was over, or nearly so, and Nixon was scheduled to pass through Los Angeles on his way back to Washington where he stayed for several weeks before he was discharged. He was still in uniform when he passed through Los Angeles. The meeting was set up for the seven of us including Nixon. There was Nixon, Crocker, Perry, Kennedy, Bernard Brennan, Roy Day and myself. We sat around in a small room at the University Club and discussed the situation in our district. Finally, Nixon said, "I'm in your hands. If you want me to run, I will." Thus began Nixon's candidacy for Congress.

It was an easy matter, I may say, to sell him to the rest of our people. We checked him out rather thoroughly before talking to him and after. I don't believe we actually made any commitment on that day but we set up a dinner and invited the representatives, chiefly the owners, of all the small newspapers of the district; there we "sprang the news." Most of these men were Republicans, and most of them had the respect of the district. There was no commitment at the dinner, but all of us knew that it would be Nixon. The financial and news leaders were ready to go. They were headed by Carl Miller, who was the man of the area for the *Wall Street Journal* and also controlled the *San Gabriel Valley Tribune*, and Richardson of the *Pomono Progress*. Then, and so far as I know, not until then, was the Los Angeles County central committee brought into the campaign. The entire arrangement was made before the membership of the county central committee really knew about it. This was my understanding then, and is still my belief, though some have written that the whole credit was due the committee. Of course, Roy Day knew about it, and he was on that committee, but I believe he was properly instructed to keep the committee out of it until after the nonpartisan meetings of people all over the district—Republican and Democrat alike—could be accomplished. We knew at the time that the Republican county central committee was not capable of handling the campaign of a minority party. To be blunt, I have never known a time when a county central committee in California could justly be termed a capable body.

Yet, in fairness, I must qualify that. There is a possibility that, unknown to me, it was in fact Roy Day, the county chairman, who was in this case the unseen hand. I can't say categorically that it was not he who thought up the plan of the nonpartisan "grassroots" groups from each town to choose candidates, acted as go-between and arranged the publishers' meeting and dinner; in short, he was at least in some degree the brains of it all. It is certainly true that almost all such committee men and women try hard and faithfully. I know, I was one for ten years.

Well, Nixon moved in and took the anti-communist line. It was, I'm sure, in accordance with his beliefs, and I've already said it was the biggest, hottest issue of the time. Even the Catholic Church fathers agreed that this was so. Communism was the matter voters seemed to get around to in the question and answer periods that followed the debates. Soon it became an important issue in the debates themselves.

Nixon had been a college debater and a debater of note in law school. He was much more personal in his debating than some of us would have wished, but he was wonderful. He early showed himself a man of comprehensive and incisive mind. He would outline his four points at the start of a debate and then proceed to make those points. At the end of his twenty-seven minutes, or whatever his allotted time might be, Nixon was through; he had made his points, covered his subject and had his audience with him. I did not criticize his campaigning except, perhaps, for the last debate in San Gabriel which was the most heated, and also the most important one. I rather felt that he was bearing down too heavily on the communist issue, and didn't hesitate to so indicate. I was convinced that there were other issues that people were interested in. At the time I am compelled to say that he appeared to be right and not unfair in forcing the issue. Certainly he carried the area very strongly.

Murray Choitner, I think, believed way back in Nixon's first campaign for Congress that this man was presidential material. By 1948, many others had the same idea. It was, I seem to recall, Bernard Brennan, one of the original group of seven, who was responsible for an unauthorized letter which went out to twenty well-known businessmen. These were not the usual finance group with whom most of us worked, but twenty businessmen who were particularly good backers and financiers. The letter said that each of the twenty was urged to give an amount; I don't recall with certainty whether it was one or five thousand dollars into a fund to be used in supporting Nixon for an eventual presidency.

Several of these men told me about it; the fund was raised, and they had a meeting with Nixon afterward. I did not think it wise in any way to get into the situation, that is the setting up of the fund. Whether this money went through proper channels or not, I do not know. I definitely do not believe that Nixon was ever less than honest about this or any money. But he, and Murray, wanted to control things, as did some of the others, and it showed. I am convinced that none of the money found its way into any of their pockets. The point is that, while campaigning for Nixon for Congress and later for the Senate, all of them were pulling for him to be president.

I think few people know as much about Murray Choitner's campaign work as I. There were those who called Murray "Nixon's hatchet man." This I do not consider fair or accurate. He was close to Nixon when the latter was vice president and afterward when he was president. I know Nixon discussed appointments with him, such as the appointment of the Federal Communications Commission, and had the duty of informing unsuccessful applicants that their desire to be appointed this or that would not work out and why. I was in his office on one such occasion while he was talking by telephone to a very important man who wanted the chairmanship of a particular commission. The man later became head of a very important commission, but not the one he was then seeking. I heard Murray tell him that it would not work out; that particular job, in the president's estimation, should be filled by General Lucius Clay. Clay, in fact, did get the appointment.

To go back to Nixon's campaigns for congressman, and later for senator and vice president, I was the man he consulted in Southern California on matters having to do with national Republican politics. I often had to turn down Nixon, or more accurately the members of his group, on things he wanted. He and his group always sought the maximum funds for Nixon. This gives rise to one of the peculiar little problems a man in the position I then held is required to handle.

Often friends of a particular candidate are able to give, and do give, substantial funds, such as a member of the Doheny group or the Seavers who were big givers. They lived near William Campbell who wanted to run for Congress. Now, there wasn't a chance in the world to get Bill elected in that district, but nevertheless we had to pay some attention to these people who gave thousands of dollars with the impression that they were contributing to Camprell's campaign. I had to cut in and see to it that their money did not all go to Nixon and to others whom we felt had a good chance to win.

Throughout these days there still remained a strong vestige of the old Hiram Johnson group. There were others who were close to

Governor Merriam, others who were close to Warren, and still others who favored Knowland and sought to have all their money put there. We, to the best of our ability, put together a group which comprised elements of each of these political leanings. The finance group had to make a lot of hard decisions. I recall a time when we had about $40,000 and were striving to decide how to spread it around keeping in mind that some of it was from the Seavers, the Dohenys and like people. The Nixon group made a real drive to get all or practically all of that forty thousand dollars.

They didn't succeed, and I suppose some blamed me on this and other occasions. But let me record in fairness, if for no other reason, that I never had any trouble with Nixon himself on these matters. He was a fair-minded man; he was also smart enough never to bring up the matter of his funds personally or directly with me or the group. Also, he was unfailingly courteous while accepting and at least appearing thankful for what he got. He was, though some may find the statement unpalatable, a smarter man than some cared to think, and smarter than a number of his advisors and supporters.

Just as an instance, let us go back to his congressional days and the handling of the money raised by Dana Smith and others to build Nixon for president. They solicited, and successfully raised, a fund which went to an individual trust fund. This money was not to go through the national finance committee, or the state finance committee, or any regular organization. Had they consulted us, some of us could have told them how such a matter should be handled. And, had any of them consulted us, the fund could have been handled for Nixon's benefit without any need for the "Checkers" speech. We would not have had to endure the spectacle of Nixon crying on the shoulder of Bill Knowland, his senior in the Senate.

My friendship with Nixon continued, I think unimpaired, though I did not immediately write or wire him that I thought he was fine, and thought he should continue to be our candidate for vice president. As California's national committeeman and vice chairman of the national executive committee, I was constrained to await Bill Knowland's opinion and that of the committee president, as to whether Eisenhower was going to keep him on the ticket.

After Nixon returned to California following his unsuccessful bid for the presidency in 1960, he decided to run for governor. I suspect, actually, that the idea arose from his group who saw it as a stepping stone to the presidency. By that time I was on the bench and out of politics. Had I been consulted, I would have advised him not to run for governor at all. Had he insisted, I would certainly have advised him not to go about things the way he and his group did; they certainly didn't do a very good campaign job.

I would have advised him to return to Whittier and live there, saying when he got settled, "Here I am. I want to help my home state which has been good to me. What can I do to help?" Instead of this he moved into Truesdale Estates, a wealthy, exclusive section of Los Angeles. He then proceeded to put his children in Marlboro School, politically a very poor choice. The school is a private, very select girl's school, no doubt a very good school. But it was then thought by many people to be anti-Jewish, particularly the Jews themselves. Thus, he made the same political mistake Eisenhower had made when he went to stay with Paul Helms, Paul Hoffman and some others at Smoke Tree Ranch in Palm Springs, anathema to the Jewish people. So, these two moves by Nixon were not the wise thing for a defeated politician to do. There was speculation as to what sort of deal had been made in connection with the property in the Truesdale Estates. It may well have been, and I have no reason to believe it wasn't, entirely proper. The point is that this was the worst possible time for Nixon to give rise to any questions.

He started running for governor. Nixon was a member of a small, but very fine, law firm which had its offices on the same floor as those of Asa V. Call. Asa called upon Nixon, as did the others, when Nixon's office celebrated his return. As it happened, Nixon had to pass Asa's office each morning as he came to work. Bear in mind that Asa was the top financial chairman in connection with Republican politics. Yet, Nixon never returned the courtesy of Asa's call or consulted him while running for governor.

Asa Call was a pretty tough man and not small of mind about things of this sort. Like a number of us, he thought he knew a number of things that Nixon should know and give weight to in his campaign. However, Nixon had his own particular group which didn't help at all with Asa or the group he knew. I was not active politically, nor had I ever been a member of that group but I knew most of them, and had long worked closely with Asa. Asa told me later, in no uncertain terms, what he thought about Nixon and his campaign for governor.

Another of the group, and one close to Asa, was Frank P. Doherty. Frank was, I felt, probably the most "savvy" person in Los Angeles. His very able son was assistant city attorney and represented the City Council for many years. Frank could cut through to the point more speedily, when a cutting was needed, than anyone I knew. He had been Hiram Johnson's campaign manager in Hiram's last two campaigns for the Senate. They could, and did, get the migrant vote in the valley, though these people were virtually all Democrats. Frank was a political brain and a man of great presence as well as ability. Nixon did not consult Frank either, nor did any of Nixon's group. This was incredibly short-sighted and foolish. Not only did Nixon lose badly in the gubernatorial campaign; he also offended people who could have been of great use to him later.

On the day MacArthur returned at Truman's orders from Korea, the Republican national committee's executives met in Tulsa. I was senior officer present and was interviewed by a man from *Time* magazine who had a prepared list of about seventeen questions. His first question was, "Will the Republican national committee support MacArthur for president?" I replied, "The national committee will support and try to elect the party's nominee when named by the convention. It will support no one until then." There were numerous other questions. In the next issue of *Time*, the entire interview was reported in one small paragraph. The sentence ending that paragraph read: "When McIntyre Faries, vice chairman of the Republican national committee, was asked if that committee would support MacArthur, he said, 'No.'"

Now, this was a complete distortion of both the letter and the spirit of my reply to his question. The crisply written story was the thing, in *Time's* estimation; fact or truth was secondary. Perhaps I should have explained in terms suitable to that reporter's apparently limited grasp that our committee had no support function until told by the party convention whom to support. In this article both what I said and its importance were subordinated to what was considered crisp writing. I can recall as far back as with Governor Merriam seeing this sort of misinformation being printed.

I was furious and wanted to take action about it, but we all decided it would be unwise. It was the first time this had happened to me personally, and I was livid, but I didn't even ask for a correction. I felt we had to get along with *Time* and its controlling group. I had learned, and the lessons were repeated, that while one can demand and get an apology for something garbled or misquoted, the press has a chance against you every day of every week. If the media gets "down" on a person or group—and being made up of fallible human beings, they do—there are many ways that they can make you and your associates suffer including ignoring what you want reported as well as misreporting.

I certainly have nothing against *Time* magazine or its publishers then. As it happens, I knew Henry Luce and his wife, Claire Booth Luce, though not as well as my older brothers. They went to school with Harry Luce, as we called him in Che Foo, when we lived in China. Luce seemed quite fond of David, and he came to our office to visit him a few times. I worked with Claire Booth Luce in the Willkie campaign in 1940. So, the personal situation was not strained, but I was terribly cut up for a moment in Tulsa.

It was now time for us Warren supporters to work with him in choosing the delegates to support him at the 1952 convention.

Bernard Brennan was secretary of our little committee, and had the list of political backgrounds and histories of those being considered for delegates. All of us discussed just what the qualifications should be and how each rated. I pointed out to Warren that some of these people were, indeed, the strongest Republicans and best workers in their district, but I was not sure whether they were for him, Taft, Eisenhower or someone else. What were his thoughts?

He said, "I'm primarily interested in clean Republican leaders who their areas feel are representative. If each signs a statement to support me, that's all I'll ask; I'm going to trust them."

I went to Chicago two weeks ahead of the delegation which travelled by special train. Earl Warren also had to go early. As a loyal Warren man, I kept Bill Knowland, our chief delegate, informed about the arrival of the train, Nixon's late night and early morning meetings, their attempted reception coup and the like. But for Knowland's loyalty, California might easily have divided between Warren, Eisenhower and Taft with perhaps the majority going along with Nixon and supporting Eisenhower. What would the nominee situation have been then, if there were a convention deadlock? I knew, for example, from Lloyd Washburn that the 103 Taft labor delegates were ready to switch to Warren on the third ballot.

Some of Nixon's people, such as Murray Chotiner and Brennan, along with others, planned a big reception for him. Word of this was carried to my wife, Lois, who in turn looked me up at the convention hall and told me. The ladies and I rushed back to the Knickerbocker Hotel. Sure enough, the hotel people said that Choitner, Brennan and others had "taken" the big hall which would hold about four hundred people. They were to hold a reception that night for Richard Nixon. I said, "For what? He's only a senator and junior to Knowland at that. Anyway, we're pledged to Warren."

The hotel representative replied that he knew nothing of all this; he had simply followed orders. I immediately got hold of Knowland and Warren, and we insisted to the Nixon people that this must be a reception for the delegation as a whole. We said we must have Earl and Mrs. Warren, Bill and Helen Knowland, and Nixon and Mrs. Nixon in proper order in the reception line. Well, they were "caught" and had to go along. The reception was duly changed around, and it turned out to be a beautiful affair.

There was something else I had to find out about and pass the word. It was obvious that Nixon was shooting for the vice presidency, but how? I found out that very night about one o'clock or two o'clock in the morning, actually. Meetings for Nixon were being held on the top floor of the Knickerbocker. Charles Thomas, our delegation treasurer, was active. I believe he had his eye on the post of Secretary of the Navy. It looked as though the delegation might break up, and many delegates might bolt. We were aware of these meetings although the participants didn't know we knew. The result was that we called a caucus of our entire group on the night before the first voting. It was agreed that we would vote unanimously for Earl Warren; Chairman Knowland would cast the ballot in accord with the agreement signed by each delegate before leaving California. However, after the first ballot, we would probably caucus again if there was time.

There never was a second ballot. These things and more are related in the excellent book, *The Judge Who Changed America*. But, if Warren was as bitter against Nixon as Pollock says in that book, he never showed it, so far as I know. I had more of an inkling about it when the Bancroft Library at the University of California wanted to get an oral history from me of matters concerning Warren. I agreed, but soon learned that they were primarily interested in the Warren-Nixon "feuding," and I stayed generally away from that in my answers to the questions of Ms. Amelia Fry. There are about 150 to 180 pages of mine there in the Bancroft Library or the library in Boalt Hall partly on the matters just related. My successor, A. Ronald Button, "could not be located" for an interview.

After Eisenhower's nomination on the first ballot at that 1952 Republican convention, the delegation honored me by selecting me as a member of the committee to advise the nominee that he was the party's candidate for the presidency. As if he didn't know! The committee was representative.

Well, I was named to the committee; I'm sure it was because I was the ranking representative of the large California delegation following Senators Knowland and Nixon, and I had been a member of and vice chairman of the executive committee of the Republican national committee. So, we solemnly proceeded to Eisenhower's headquarters at the Blackstone Hotel, and there stated our mission to the man in charge. This was Herbert Brownell, my old friend who later became attorney general. We were invited in and seated in a semicircle to await Eisenhower's entrance.

His arrival was punctual as usual. He accepted our news and proceeded to ask each of us for an appraisal of his respective area. As I listened, I was filled with consternation. Why? Because it was obvious to me that these other committee members simply did not know their states or the greater areas surrounding their states—the areas, in short, that they presumably represented. Oh, they knew the thinking of the money groups, but the thinking of their voters and the facts of politics appeared completely foreign to them. It appeared that the group was made up largely of representatives of the "Fat Cats." They were the people who knew where the financial bones were buried, but little or nothing of the thinking of the common man who does the voting.

I had, of course, my own thoughts as to how the California campaign should be conducted. Since the first days of Roosevelt, in 1932, California had been carried and held by the Republican minority party, with the sole exception of Culbert L. Olson's election to governor in 1938. As briefly as possible, I expressed my firm belief that California could be carried. Herb Brownell spoke briefly of my background, and I assured everyone of my support.

I felt I should make my support a matter of record from the beginning, because I had voted for Governor Warren to whom I had been pledged along with the entire delegation. Also, I was known not only as a Warren man, but a Knowland man, not primarily a Nixon man. This was because I had chaired Knowland's campaign, but not Nixon's. I might say here that I did not always agree with both or either of them, but I did in a general way. Both Warren and Knowland had named me to the national committee, and I had, as I say, chaired Knowland's campaign for Southern California in this as well as in the previous election. But, I was the Republican national committeeman, had headed a successful campaign and was kept on by Eisenhower.

Arthur Summerfield of Michigan, later Eisenhower's postmaster general, was Republican national committee chairman. When the national committee was considering the seating of contested delegations, I was amused to note that Arthur kept his attorney beside him for advice through these sessions. He was very careful in his votes. On the whole his voting was very favorable to Eisenhower. I believe mine was also. Before going into these sessions, I had talked by phone to both Senator Knowland and Governor Warren, California's candidate. Both advised me to use my own judgment, and they would back me up. I felt that some questionable work had been done by those representing the Taft forces, particularly in connection with the seating of delegates from Louisiana and some other of the southern states, including the Texas delegation. This was where the fireworks started prior to the convention, and Dewey and some others did Taft a lot of harm and Eisenhower a lot of good in this connection.

The National Committee was technically in charge of the campaign, but Eisenhower did something unusual for the time; he formed an Eisenhower campaign committee. This committee was what he really relied on to plan and carry out his campaign activities. The committee was headed by Leonard Hall, a congressman from Oyster Bay, New York. Leonard had a great personality and was tremendously popular in Congress. He was a very pleasant fellow and a good campaigner on his home ground, but he knew nothing about the West. He thought this was one great United States, which of course it is, but the campaigning out here is quite different from that of New York or Boston.

I think Eisenhower did well to have the committee, but at times it made for mix-ups. As an example, I got word, as was proper, from Arthur Summerfield, some two or three weeks before Eisenhower was to visit Los Angeles. This was in the form of a telephone call, giving us dates and making suggestions. One of the instructions was that, while Mrs. Eisenhower would be on the train the morning of Ike's arrival, he would fly into the Los Alamitos airport at Long Beach and be brought up by open car through the main industrial districts of Los Angeles. I demurred to this, saying it was an awful task with which to burden the candidate. He would be standing in the open car for more than twenty miles, waving, receiving cheers and flashing his famous "V" for victory sign while smiling to the people. Eisenhower was great at this kind of thing, but it seemed to me too much of a good thing. But Summerfield said this was the plan, and I was overruled.

I also feared a security problem; I felt Ike should probably come to Los Angeles International Airport and then to the hotel. The Ambassador Hotel had been agreed on by the Secret Service and everyone else, as the place Eisenhower should stay. I made plans accordingly, and the advance men came here. I made arrangements with the hotel, getting a whole floor along with additional accommodations. We were able, through the advance man, to get the number of rooms needed for the candidate's party the press, the Secret Service and others. We were advised as to the kind of suite the Eisenhowers wanted and where they wanted the various members of their party placed, including their guards and the newsmen with them. We provided a good-sized room for their meetings, a place to file and phone their dispatches, and a host of other things which had to be provided for. Not least of these were arrangements for baggage, typewriters, directions, cars and the like.

This is always a tremendous logistics exercise which has to be carefully worked out. Minor auditoriums have to be found and provided, and there must be places for various party locals and state and national bigwigs to stay, and places for them to confer at need. The bigwigs were largely lodged in the bungalows outside the hotel building; this included not only those from Washington, but some of our own California officials to whom attention must be paid. Nixon wasn't there, but there was a place for Senator Knowland. These things are very interesting, and the check charts provided by the advance man were a help.

Then, of course, I had the problem of how to work all this out with the state central committee of California, with the county central committee, and some other Republican organizations, such as the Federation of Republican Women which was the biggest organization of them all. Then came the Republican assembly and a host of unofficial groups. One of the things that must be figured carefully in every campaign is how to find a place for everyone who thinks he is somebody, then for those who really are somebody, then for other active Republicans. And, there's the other group to be taken care of: the Democrats, particularly those with big names who have "crossed the line" and come to support the Republican candidate. These people are highly important, since both then and now, Democratic votes have to be obtained for our minority Republican party to win.

It is essential to find places for all these people in connection with the automobiles and the parade headed up by the presidential candidates, but even more so at the big public meeting that is always arranged. Now at this time of year, it is not safe to arrange anything at the Hollywood Bowl, and it was not thought advisable to stage, as we had for Wilkie, an event at the Coliseum. So, the next best place was the Pan-Pacific Auditorium.

I called in Laughlin Waters, state chairman and former head of the Young Republicans. I also called in John Krehbiel who was Los Angeles County central committee chairman. Murray Choitner was on our payroll as manager of the campaign here. He was very important, and like Krehbiel, he was a tie to Senator Nixon. I worked well with these people; we had no personality or arrangement difficulties. I was the connection with Senator Knowland and the national committee and locally in charge of the arrangements for the presidential candidate. The persons mentioned were the contacts with the local people here. I believe I was able to be of great help to them in explaining routing, the policing arrangements we had with the sheriff's office and the Los Angeles police and the Long Beach police. In addition I was acquainted with the arrangements of those who would furnish the cars, primarily members of the Auto Club staff and of the motor car dealers association.

As for television, it was still in its infancy and of no great consideration. The broadcast people of that time were not so outspoken as were the newspaper people. They seemed, then, particularly anxious to stay out of politics, but were eager to know everything and to cover all that was happening. Not so easy was dealing with the newspaper people, particularly those from the small publications, even the throwaways and ethnic press. All these people had to be taken into consideration and provided for in various ways.

There were several preparatory meetings that once swept in that very able lady, Jacqueline Cochran, famous aviatrix, who had been an early Eisenhower supporter. She lived in Palm Springs and had a capable group of people, mostly New York and Palm Springs women, willing to spend money. They looked as though they had decided to take over. So, I set up a meeting for them with the well-organized group we had for planning events. This group was presided over by Laughlin Waters. Loc was a fellow with a big smile and a hearty laugh, but he was plenty tough. Jackie and her group said at the meeting, "We're going to do this, and we're going to do that," and on and on.... It was apparent that Southern California organizations meant nothing to them; they intended to take over.

After she had finished, Loc Waters leaned back and smiled. "Well, Mrs. Cochran," he said, "that's an awfully good plan. But I'm afraid you're too late. You've come in from outside after we've put on a campaign and arranged the reception for Eisenhower. Now we're going ahead with it as it's arranged." Mrs. Cochran was astonished that we were not going to take advantage of their plan. "No, we're not," said Loc. "This affair is being put on by the Republicans of the area, and their allied Democrats, and the arrangements we've made will stand. But, we'll certainly see that you have places to sit, and we'll arrange for you to meet General Eisenhower if that's what you want." Mrs. Cochran was visibly quite unhappy and left, though to do her justice, she was not unpleasant about it.

I don't really remember the weather through all of Eisenhower's time here. I do remember that it became stormy on the evening he spoke, but it was not bad for his trip into town from Long Beach.

Mrs. Faries; Mrs. Kenyon, head of the California Republican Women; and Mrs. O'Donnell, who was next, were to meet Mrs. Eisenhower at the train and take charge. They were at the hotel for hours. Mrs. Eisenhower insisted on going over all the arrangements; she made one or two minor changes in room assignments. She said it was absolutely essential that her husband have a rest every afternoon of at least forty-five minutes. Given the chance, newsmen and self-important strangers who could not get to him would do so at any and all times despite all orders. They must be kept far enough away, and she arranged to have Secret Service people between Ike's rooms and the press. Of course we had local police as well. The arrangement was that the sheriff's office and the Los Angeles Police Department would alternate in taking primary responsibility for policing when a distinguished visitor came to town.

The ladies took good care of Mrs. Eisenhower and became friends with her. In fact, when she left, she took Mrs. Faries' face in both hands and said, "Oh, that we could have a Mrs. Faries and a Mrs. O'Donnell in every city! You people have made me the most at home of any city I've been in."

So, Eisenhower came in from Los Alamitos airport. There were good and respectful crowds, even through the industrial district. There were a few heckles, but most of the remarks were friendly. Ike was superb at recognizing people and catching the things they shouted at him. He stood in the car the entire trip, waving his "V" sign and shouting at people.

When he arrived, Len Hall and his group had the idea that they were going to change everything around. They got in touch with our command post by phone; I recall that DeeDee Bennet was on the phone at the command post. Len Hall proceeded to tell her all the changes he wanted made, so-and-so of the Secret Service to such-and-such a place, such-and-such a newspaper man to a different place, and on and on. DeeDee "yessed" him throughout all this and took it all down. When he finished, he said, "All right?"

DeeDee said, "No, Mr. Hall, it's not all right. We have no authority to change anything, and I'm sorry, but I can't do it." Hall appeared to come near exploding, though he remained courteous. He asked by what authority she refused his instructions. She said, "The authority of Mrs. Eisenhower, the advance man and the national committeeman. Mrs. Eisenhower dictated the room arrangements for her, her husband and the staff; the advance man made the other arrangements, and they've been approved by the police and the campaign management. I can't change them."

Then Len Hall got me on the phone and wanted to know why Eisenhower had been put through the ordeal of coming all the way up from Long Beach airport; I replied that this had been done on the instructions of national chairman, Arthur Summerfield, and over my strongly voiced objections. I reminded him that this had all been done by the advance men who were under his management, that we had merely arranged it as per their instructions. Hall said nothing further by way of criticism.

Eisenhower was a little late in getting to the hotel, but had his rest period as prescribed by Mrs. Eisenhower. He then met with a few press people and dignitaries. A lot of people were on hand, and they were largely kept out of mischief in the big auditorium on the hotel grounds. There were lots of things happening that most of them enjoyed, such as introductions of actors and other celebrities. It was a well-arranged event, and went well though there were a few minor problems at the Pan-Pacific Auditorium. A few people had managed to get backstage who shouldn't have, and one or two of them tried to make trouble. For the public and press, everything went well; the people were enthusiastic and seemed to enjoy the event. The auditorium was more than packed, every possible space being filled. It was an excellent place for the event with a tremendous parking area which was handled by experts. There were a lot of busses, but as usual in California, most came by car.

Ike's visit was good, his speech was good though hardly outstanding and all went well. Some of us, well-screened, went out to the airport afterward because Ike was leaving that night. This was the original airport; Los Angeles International Airport terminals had not been built. We had a room with a bar, and it was a real problem deciding who should be admitted. Murray Choitner was in command of the door, and he did pretty well. I spent most of my time at the door because everybody wanted in. They could think of some reason why they should come in. Everyone wanted their picture taken with the presidential candidate. The room could not accommodate them all, and a great many were disturbed because they couldn't get in. You would be surprised at some of the reasons people gave.

Ike was very pleasant with everyone, but when the time came, we managed to smuggle him out a side door and get him to the plane. I tried, as always, to look over the crowd to spot the things that should be done rather than inflict myself unnecessarily on the candidate.

I felt it was a well-handled event, and I believe that all down the line, the members of the committee felt the same. It is so essential in matters of this sort that everyone winds up feeling he has been recognized and the top brass knows what he did.

Yes, Ike carried the state.

At the time of the election of Eisenhower to the White House and

Nixon to the vice-presidency, delight reigned among Republicans. You would scarcely believe, unless you have been involved in politics, some of the claims made by individuals after the election as to their part in it. Many of these were made in the hope of prominence, recognition, letters and the like. Many were made in the hope of political favors, such as appointments to positions they coveted. There were always lots of people, after an election, who laid claim to rewards for their activities. Many were not rewarded who should have been. Quite seriously, it is the little fellow who does the door-to-door work who should be rewarded, and generally is not; the story of the widow's mite is an apt one. So, there was always the problem of and for many people at the end of a campaign. There was also the problem of financial and other records that had to be prepared and saved. I learned as early as 1934, that people in small areas who felt themselves to be political leaders, liked to retain their lists of names and addresses, so they would be called upon to take part in the next election.

Very soon after the 1952 election, I had on my desk the problems, plans, ceremonies and pleasures of the upcoming inauguration. Nixon's group was deliriously happy, and requested that they be allowed to "take care of themselves." I confess it took me some time to learn what they meant by taking care of themselves; they wanted to take care of themselves, but they wanted us to help them do it.

Thus, for example, they would not look to us for tickets for the inaugural. I was told by John Krehbiel (later ambassador to Finland) that Nixon would take care of them. This was not quite correct; they wanted a lot more tickets. On the other hand, they didn't want many of the duties of preparation for the inauguration, like securing guest accommodations for other than their group, etc.

There were about six inaugural balls, and the Nixon group was always after more tickets. Of course, there weren't enough to go around for any location. They particularly wanted reservations for the armory which was the number one spot. It was only there, and possibly in one other location, that the president and Nixon, would actually make a speech. So, I was roundly criticized for not having bought a larger box for the California delegation in the armory. Even the state chairman made a number of caustic remarks about me to various people. He did so, as it happened, not realizing that I had bought the box out of my own pocket; it was never charged to the

Republican party. These boxes were hard to get, but his criticism continued even though I let him sit there along with a number of his group. Now, he could have bought a box for his group, or had me buy one for the state central committee. But he told me, in no uncertain terms, that I wasn't on the job. He did learn later that there was nothing to stop him from buying a box, and moreover, that the box he was invited to occupy had been paid for by me. He did have the courtesy to apologize.

Immediately after the election, the matter came up of California's participation in the Washington parade and the inaugural. This included the problem of housing the many Californians who would go to Washington at that time. This would include many people who had worked in the campaign, had been delegates to the convention, or were to be included in the Washington affairs as entertainers, technicians, motion picture people and many others. We had not one, but two horsemen's groups; a group of Palamino riders from Long Beach and the sheriff's posse from Contra Costa County. We thought it advisable to have one from the North and one from the South. We also had a float and a marching band. Now, the participants were all fine, thoughtful people who arranged to take care of their own finances. But where in the city of Washington, D.C. would we put up one hundred horses? Not to mention the fact that there would inevitably be horses from other states, too. Fortunately, through the good offices of Bill Knowland's administrative assistant, George Wilson, we found places for the horses in Silver Springs and another place.

I remember that Monty Montana, a Western personality and expert roper, was to be there with his family on horseback. He wanted to rope President Eisenhower while riding past him. All this had to be cleared with the Secret Service. I didn't personally do this, but did give my permission, and told him who to see. There were innumerable such details, some of them very costly. We took three floors of a large hotel, and again I had to dig into my own pocket to the tune of thousands of dollars. I am happy to say this was all repaid, but the books had to be kept on all these matters.

Tickets were a constant problem. A certain number of them were given to the campaign treasurer to give to large contributors. They got the number they at first asked for, but later needed a lot more. In addition the Nixon group came back and wanted more tickets. To my great pleasure we were able to get some through Joe Martin, Republican leader of the House of Representatives, and some from other sources.

The Washington group was very helpful, but they had sent out big lists of invitations to come to Washington for the inauguration. Many people made the mistake of interpreting this as an invitation to the balls and other events, whereas it merely invited them to come to town. They learned that they had to purchase tickets to balls, dinners and other events; this made much trouble for us. Our congressmen were all very helpful in getting tickets, mostly from Democrats. Some of these were given to us, but we often had to pay for them. They had their friends, too!

We had a California register at the hotel, and it was signed by 1936 Californians who had come for the event. Doubtless, there were many more who did not sign the register. Other than all the problems mentioned, and many more, I had to raise money to cover expenses in advance of lots of arrangements; we had thought this might prove difficult, but it was comparatively easy. Someone suggested we call the Los Angeles Bank Clearing House, and I did so. A couple of men there gave me a great deal of help.

There was a continual round of dinners and parties; one affair was given by the San Joaquin "Turkey King" and some of his friends who put on a party in the great ballroom of the hotel. They did this at their own expense, and it was free to the Californians.

All the entertainment during the inauguration was arranged by motion picture star George Murphy. He had been president of the Screen Actors Guild, and was active in Republican politics; he later became a U.S. senator from California. George got fine entertainers and celebrities who worked very hard at the balls and parties.

It was a revelation to me how many Californians were there and how many things they needed. In addition to those for whom arrangements had been made in advance, there were many who "just came." I particularly recall two very serene old ladies whom my wife and I encountered in the hotel lobby. They said they had come to attend the inauguration. We asked them about their tickets, rooms and so forth; they said they hadn't heard anything about tickets. They were American citizens who had voted for Eisenhower, and they'd come to his inauguration. Of course, all we could say was that we'd do what we could. Well, these nice old ladies said that they'd just be there hoping something could be worked out. They were good Republicans, and they just must see the inauguration. So they were content to "leave it to God and us." Well, God is a great helper of such persons, and in this case He had a great helper in Lois Faries. The two old ladies did get to go to the inauguration and one or two of the parties.

The bookkeeping was a terrible chore. Mrs. Faries kept very detailed books, not only on finances but also my other activities. These were required by the law. I offered these books to the Los Angeles central committee, and to the state central committee some years later after the time had expired that the law required me to keep them. They didn't seem to care about them, so I turned them over to the Republican associates who did want them.

I hold to certain principles, and I think most of those who have been successful in politics have the same idea. The first is that campaigns, as I have said before, are generally lost, not won. The second is that the most important thing in politics is to discover all you can learn. Knowland, as an instance, lost California by not consulting. Nixon lost the governorship of California by not consulting or refusing to consult. Early in my time, Merriam lost to the Democrats by failing to consult; Goodwin Knight lost out in California because of a Teamster influence and by not consulting with the right people. Proper consultation could have avoided all these pitfalls.

I would like to make a couple more observations. According to my way of thinking, politics is "the science of getting things done in government." I think I got that definition from Professor Werner of UCLA in the 1930s, and I never heard it improved upon. Politics is not, or should not be, groups seeking their own interests at the expense of others or the body politic. Pressure groups have always existed in our national politics: slavery supporters, abolitionists, prohibition advocates, senior groups, gay groups, various "rights" groups, ethnic groups—the list is endless. Certainly each group has a right to pursue its interests and goals. But this is a big nation with many people. It stretches over many kinds of country: rain belts, dry areas, cold country and subtropics, agricultural areas, many manufacturing areas and cities, etc. A political party must consider representation of each and all of these groups, these areas, their problems and needs. Above all, a national party must embrace the credo that "we are all together." A whole people, and indeed a party, must do what is best for the entire body of the United States, not any particular area, financial level, or any other part or parts of the whole. All interests must be harmonized; a very difficult thing to do, but the only way the country can prosper.

I have talked with at least two of our Republican national committeemen on the subject. I've suggested that in the "slow" time, between elections or campaigns, conferences should be called by the party. These should be with labor interests, manufacturing interests, agricultural interests, even religious groups, and should be the basis of an attempt to harmonize the various kinds of thinking long before the Republican national convention. It would be a gargantuan undertaking, but think of the possible benefit to the Party and the country!

I brought this thought up to Senator Robert Taft between elections. I said I was surprised that the Republican party had no coherent plan for the operation of the country, no legislation to immediately introduce in the event of a political or a financial disaster or other emergency. Taft—Mr. Republican, as he has often been called—said, indulgently, "Just leave it to the senators and congressmen. We can take care of what is needed when it is needed." I remember looking at him in amazement.

The position of the national committeemen to whom I talked was the same. So, the party has remained undecided as to how to meet problems, and consequently, is impotent. It is the position of those in Washington that when any need arises, they can solve the problem by passing a bill. Of course, this is much too late from a political standpoint. Moreover, such legislation has a long period of gestation.

I try not to be a pessimist, but to me this bodes ill for the hope of accomplishing things through the Republican national committee.

In any case, with this chapter I close the story of my twenty years of involvement in the political fortunes of my state and my country. It was a hard, though good time, and in many ways very costly, not only to me but also to my loving and ever-supporting family. They have my gratitude and my love.

# Chapter 16
## New Directions

So, after twenty years it had happened! The duration of my political activities had been much greater than I had originally intended. Now, we had elected a Republican president, and vice president, and had a majority in both houses of Congress! I had enjoyed the political life, particularly the friendships with so many of the leaders. But, it had been selfish of me. My wife and daughters had not had the good life they should have had; my income had been less, and I had not accumulated much for the years to come. My years for business life had dwindled, but I still had confidence in my ability to practice law successfully and happily. This, I was determined, would be without trading on political friendship or experience.

For twenty years I had put up to seventy percent of my time in those matters, and I was now the head man of our law office. David had died in 1944, and Charles McDowell in 1950. The other lawyers were capable and reliable, but all looked to me to bring in the new business without which no law firm can grow or survive for long. I had consistently refused, insofar as I could identify it, to take political business; this meant I had lost the business of some friends and not gotten business of many others. Friends would say, as this actual example illustrates, "I wanted you to organize my new automobile agency, but I thought with all the politics, you'd be too busy." I had turned down two Washington law office partnerships. I had also turned down some large fees and retainers, some of which would have run over long periods of time.

Businessmen of whom I had heard, or were likely clients, would send in some innocuous piece of business and then, after some time and maybe another small piece of business or two, would come in to say something like this: "We have a lot of idle equipment, and we hear the government is going to spend millions of dollars in Laos (or some other country). We could use the business, and would perform it well. It occurs to us that you know your way around Washington, and we don't. Why not come in with us on a retainer, and let's go ahead and try to get some of this government contract business?"

Perhaps I should have gone in on such business opportunities. Certainly from a financial standpoint I should have, but I chose not to do so, even though completely legal. I remember one group who came to me. I had done some small legal business for them. They said to me, "Out by Los Alamos (where the atomic bomb was completed) in New Mexico there is going to be a lot of housing created by the government. We want you to put in a bid for us to get in on it. We don't know how to go about getting this type of work, whereas you know about these things and the people involved." Another instance where I refused a large and long retainer. Perhaps I missed the boat, but I felt then and now that I can live better without using political position to obtain this type of business. The old bromide to the effect that "opportunity knocks but once" isn't true, at least as I have found life.

It was several months after the election, and choices for important federal offices had almost all been made. Financial reports were complete. I had not intended to get into politics in the first place. I had done so as a favor to a friend, but there is no denying that I loved it.

Now I was growing older, too old to continue with the things I had been doing. My finances were such that I could live comfortably, but I owed it to my partners to build up the business again. I had to raise our hourly rates of charge and encourage my associates. Also, I wanted to do better for my family and have more time with them.

I was reflecting, thus, on a weekend in my office. As was usual on Saturdays, and sometimes Sundays, I'd gone down to make my preparations for the coming week. I laid out my work, looked over my records, and planned how I would distribute my attention to various matters. Just about this time, Bill Knowland walked into the office. After we had visited for awhile, I told him, "Bill, you will have to start looking around for a new Republican national committeeman. It has taken a lot longer to win the presidency than I thought, but I was determined to stay with it until we did. Now, he's in, and we have a Republican Congress. It's time for me to pay attention to my business and, above all, to my family."

He looked hard at me, then said, "You've made up your mind, haven't you?" I assured him that I had. "How about waiting for a vacancy on the federal bench? You can have it." "No," I replied. "I'm not asking for anything."

We visited for awhile longer; then he asked, "If you had the chance, would you go on the Los Angeles County Superior Court?" I thought for a few minutes. The federal court was an unhappy one. Personalities there were a problem, and the work turned out by some was also a problem. But the Los Angeles Superior Court was a happy court, and the judges got along well together. Moreover, I knew many of them. I also knew my California law procedure. The court in Los Angeles County had an excellent reputation, and most of my litigation had been in their courts, though I was also admitted to practice in the federal courts of California, the United States Circuit Court of Appeals for the Ninth District, and the United States Supreme Court. Likewise, I was admitted to practice, and did practice, before the Federal Communications Commission, the Interstate Commerce Commission, and possibly some others.

"If I were asked, and if I felt at the time as I feel today, I would certainly very seriously consider such an appointment. But I will not campaign for it or make any effort to get in." That last phrase had a familiar ring to me. I went on, "I'm dog-tired, and I could probably be influenced by someone who twisted my arm."

About five days later, I was in a conference and had left word that I would take no phone calls. My switchboard operator nevertheless rang in. She apologized for overriding my instructions and said Governor Warren was on the line. I said I'd step out of the conference and take the call elsewhere. Governor Warren, after greetings were exchanged, said, "You know, the legislature is in session and will give Los Angeles County a number of Superior Court judges. I, too, think Los Angeles County needs them. Would you like one of the appointments?"

I said, "Governor, I've been in a lot of battles, as you know, and have a lot of battle scars. I'm a bit afraid people might say it was favoritism. I wouldn't like to embarrass you, and I particularly would hate to let down or embarrass Bill Knowland."

"I have a letter from Bill right here on my desk," said the governor.

I knew then what had happened. He went on, "In that case, the answer is yes?" I said that I certainly would be happy to accept the appointment, and that I felt honored. "Count on it," Warren replied. "You don't have to do a thing more about it." And, I didn't. I sent no letters, I checked with no one; I simply kept quiet. My good wife, Lois, was not too happy about it. She didn't think it would be easy to live on the salary of a judge, about half of what I had been earning. We decided that we would take a little rest, so we went up to the north shore of Lake Tahoe, to a small place where I had been before. After a few days the newspapermen found out about my appointment and got hold of me, so our vacation was cut short.

I cut down my staff after my partner, Charles McDowell, died and then moved into partnership with two lawyers I felt were top men, Wayne Hackett and Ralph B. Hubbard. I told them immediately of the plan to go on the bench and asked them to start thinking of what they would do if my appointment should come through. I also thought it fair to tell the others in the office of the probable appointment, so that they could start thinking. I asked that they say nothing because first, it might not happen, and second, it would be very bad politics; I might lose the appointment if anyone talked. They agreed, and all kept commendably silent.

As I said, I don't think Mrs. Faries was very happy about the prospect. She felt that now I was recognized as an important lawyer and a community-minded person, and also that my friendships with the better-known people of the city, county and state had a value application to business. I had turned down the judicial appointment some fifteen years earlier, under Governor Merriam, but this time I was determined. I felt I would like to round out my career in law as a judge. I knew I would enjoy doing the work and having that standing. Also, I truly felt the appointment was not primarily political. I was known to be a good lawyer, operating an excellent office and recognized as a cog in the wheel of the community. I had many friends and acquaintances from whom I could get business, but there is always a question when a political person is appointed to a judgeship. I think mine is the only appointment to which anyone can point the finger at Governor Warren for appointing a person in politics. I must say that on a couple of occasions, when he and Knowland had been subpoenaed to appear and testify (a common practice on the part of those who want to gain publicity and get politics into some legal matter), I successfully opposed, in court, their being required to appear.

There was another appointment through Warren at this time of Beach Vasey, his legislative secretary. I asked Beach one time about my appointment to the Superior Court. He said, "I remember your appointment very well. The governor was walking down the hall and stepped into my room, where I was talking with one of the secretaries. He said, 'Give Mac Faries one of those appointments that are coming up soon—the very next time.'" So that is the way my name got put on the list, so far as the mechanics are concerned. The governor knew I was active in matters other than state and national politics from our frequent conversations.

I joined the Superior Court in October 1953, and we appointees drew straws for seniority. Seniority doesn't mean much except in little things, such as the choice of a permanent courtroom. There were eighteen appointees, the largest number ever up to that time. I drew number seventeen. I went home to Mrs. Faries and groused, "How low can a man get? Has my luck run out? Maybe I should have stayed in politics."

The last few years before I went on the bench, I tried very few cases. I did quite a little public utility work because the other lawyers in my office were not familiar with it. However, I made it my business to be in the office as much as possible, because after David died, I was the main source of business. Every prominent businessman who uses lawyers makes it a practice to know a number of them. They are social acquaintances, golf partners, club brothers and so forth. If one does not work out, or is busy with another case, he can call one of the others for future business.

But the "hang" of trial work soon came back to me. I was first used as a vacancy filler; that is, I worked for short periods in different departments. I might be in probate for a period, then in domestic relations for a time. I 'subbed' throughout the year 1953; then, beginning in January of 1954, I was assigned to one court in South Gate. It was a good little city and not really so little, about sixty thousand at the time. Its court also served Downey and some other areas including Norwalk.

I found myself in a one-man court with no courthouse. So, I sat in the chambers of the city council, in the seat of the mayor.

I was very pleased with the people in South Gate, as well as with the lawyers. They had a distinct desire to see justice done.

Locations differ, and lawyers soon learn to shop around and strive to get cases tried where they want. There are certain rules to this, but they weren't really very effective. The big offices were in Los Angeles, and so were the large defense groups. So, larger and longer cases were usually filed in or transferred to the central district.

In Pasadena I was not only presiding judge of a three-judge court, but I had the calling of the calendar handling almost the entire criminal calendar. Long trials, I assigned out; I refer to cases which would take a long period of time. I had the law and motion work and the divorce work. Writs of various sorts and a few civil trials fell to me. The courthouse was only ten minutes from my home in San Marino, and most of the lawyers and many of the jurors were old friends. Every courtesy was extended to us, largely I think, owing to former Pasadena presiding judge, Kenneth Newell. We judges normally ate lunch at the University Club in Pasadena where we paid no dues, though we did pay for our meals. During lunch we would talk over our work, even visit a little, and get back to work in plenty of time. A good part of my noontime was spent, as it was later in Los Angeles, conferring and discussing problems of the law that had arisen.

I have heard it said that there are no interesting cases, and that there are no uninteresting cases. But, to me all cases are and were interesting, and I feel now, as then, that I could learn from every lawsuit I had. First of all, I made it my practice (and when I was presiding judge, made it part of the court) to call the lawyers on each case to be tried into my chambers. There we would talk over the case, and I could see whether I thought they had properly prepared, whether their witnesses were ready, what were the points of law in disagreement, if any, and what problems there were with respect to evidence and to witnesses. This done, I would try, in the absence of objection, to settle the case. This is now standard procedure, but it was not so then.

I found that the flamboyant lawyers are rarely the best ones. It is true there are some flamboyant lawyers who are good; one is Melvin Belli whom I knew when he was a Young Republican. Of the "personality" lawyers of our area he was probably the best, though he had his offices in San Francisco. But, in the trial of most cases, the flamboyant lawyer is not nearly as capable and rarely as successful as the quiet fellow who is well-prepared and who gets you to thinking along the same line with him. He is subtly guiding the trial of the case putting his client's position before you. I have kept no list of cases to support this position, but I think it highly tenable.

The greatest of the flamboyant lawyers was gone before I went on the bench. He was Earl Rogers, who was probably the most sought-after criminal lawyer in Southern California. But he, along with his courtroom histrionics, was an indefatigable worker. It is said that he used to dissect corpses to be able to understand special points.

Jerry Geisler who "broke in" under Rogers was the opposite. He was the "old shoe" type of lawyer who, as we used to say, "climbed up into the box and sat with the jury." I recall one of his best cases which was tried before me in the old Brunswig Building. People of the day looking at him would remark, "Is that the great Jerry Geisler? He's common as an old shoe." He appeared to be; that was part of his charm and served to disguise his very uncommon ability. He did actually seem to become one of the jury. Geisler simply sat in his chair or stood relaxed and calm, and people would like him and unconsciously go along with him. This feeling was almost as true of judges and other lawyers as of the jurors.

I am thinking of a case in which Jerry Geisler represented an unusually beautiful actress. She started out as a child actress; at the time she was in court she was in her twenties. It was a domestic relations matter that received very little, if any, publicity. The young lady had been represented by another attorney who had foolishly allowed a deposition to be taken of a young actor-musician. He stated in the deposition, apparently with a great deal of pride, that he and the young lady had numerous forms of sexual activity. He described how he had accomplished sex in so many ways with the young lady in the Hollywood Hills and elsewhere. I read the deposition before they tried to introduce it; the foundation was properly laid out for its use. I took counsel into chambers and tried to convince him that he should not use it. It was not information necessary to a decision in the case. It was redundant and, since there was no jury, it would not particularly sway my decision. Geisler, now representing the young woman, was anxious to keep this sensational testimony out. He wanted his client as clean as possible and wanted me to suppress the deposition. The deposition before me was highly pornographic, so I kept going with the trial and put off consideration of the deposition. There was a great deal of other evidence, so the deposition was really redundant. But word began to leak out, and soon the media people began to sit continuously in the courtroom instead of the usual practice of coming for short visits. We had to put turnstiles outside the courtroom door along with bailiffs to keep control of the crowds who stood in line to get in.

I finally ruled that I would not receive the deposition. Not too sure of my grounds, I did try to make a record; I held the deposition unnecessary, scandalous, redundant and so forth; holding that it was not evidence except to the character of the young woman, whereas the issue was the fate of the two or three young children she and her husband had. Well, a young fellow from the *Herald Examiner* came into my chambers very worked up. I asked the reason for all this excitement, and he said, "I've been trying for fifteen years to find a case of this kind! Can't you see the headlines? Can't you see what the Supreme Court will have before it? Can't you see what they'll say? They'll say 'First Amendment defied by Superior Court judge! Freedom of the press denied!'"

We talked for quite awhile. I tried to calm him down and suggested that he come back the next morning. In the meantime Nadine Mason, who later became Nadine Bickmore, talked with him. She was at that time the "sob sister" for the *Los Angeles Times*. At that time the *Times* did publish a lot of divorce information and the like. Well, Nadine managed to talk him out of it; I did not invite him to the courtroom again, and he said he would "postpone the matter."

The case wound along. It was obvious that the young woman was sexually active with people other than her husband. The husband, a very clean-cut looking fellow, was a writer for the motion picture industry. While she was working, he would stay home, take care of the children and do his writing there.

There was a group of perhaps twenty young people who occupied the seats in the courtroom. They were clean, normal-looking young people who were there as witnesses to the children's care and the family life of the wife and the husband. Each sought a divorce. Their interest was in the children.

It was a difficult case to decide. There were a number of things not in his favor. I finally had to decide that she was not to have physical custody of the children, but kept the testimony off the record by discussing it with counsel in chambers. I knew that in the interests of all concerned she should not lose her position in her professional career which would certainly have happened if these things had come out.

So, we gave the children to him physically, but did not take joint custody away from her. That is, he had physical custody, but she was not found "legally unfit." I gave each of them a divorce, so she was safe from the stigma.

Well, the crowd left, and I think it was about 3:30 when I announced the decision in open court. I did not leave my chambers until after five o'clock when the bailiffs had all left the area. As I walked out the door, there was a woman standing there. She rushed at me and beat on my chest with her fists, yelling, "Don't you understand a mother's love for her children? How can you be so brutal as to take children away from their mother?" She went on with this including the beating for a considerable period of time. Then I thanked her for expressing her opinions and walked away. This was one of the very last cases tried by Jerry Geisler. He won it because of the psychology he exercised and the determination on my part to keep "dirty talk" out of the courtroom. I wanted to keep it as quiet as possible for these young children and to preserve the young woman's job and position in her world.

A case of an entirely different kind was assigned to me quite early on. By the way, that is the way one got cases; they were assigned by the presiding judge, or the commissioner working for the presiding judge. Today, this is done by an assistant presiding judge. There was a method whereby difficult or highly technical cases which would take a long time could be assigned differently from the regular cases handed out every day. The lawyers on such a case could visit with the presiding judge beforehand to explain the difficulties and ramifications of the case and to seek his approval on the appointment of a group of judges on whom they, the lawyers, could agree. Thus, some four or five judges were selected whom they thought could best try a case of that kind. The lawyers would consult the presiding judge who would sometimes appoint a judge, the first of the approved group whose courtroom "opened up," and the case would be sent to that judge. This is a fairly good and necessary system.

I was fairly new and was surprised to learn that a panel had agreed on me as one of its approved judges; I was assigned the "Greek Orthodox Church Case." I was sitting in the old Brunswig Building, now the location of a number of juvenile courts. The church in question was on the west side of Los Angeles. It was an old Orthodox church where the congregation stood during the entire service. The church had little or no parking space available, and the neighborhood was becoming run down; it was felt unsafe to have social events or evening events of any sort. Because of this, young members were scarce. The church along with other Greek citizens prevailed upon Charles Skouras, head of 20th Century Fox motion picture studio, to head a committee of well-known people including many Greeks to raise money to build a large and beautiful Greek Orthodox cathedral. Skouras was properly authorized by the little church to choose his committee as he saw fit, and to raise money in the name of the church. There was also to be a recreation hall and a priests' dormitory. Skouras, a man of great ability, proceeded to put together his committee. With proper authorization he chose the location on West Pico and Normandie.

The church was apparently "self-governing," though there was a great deal of testimony, both written and oral, on this subject. I believe the church here was technically, in the matter of doctrine, under the bishop from Great Britain, but locally I believe it was a separate organization. It had been getting most of its priests from a Greek Orthodox church seminary in Missouri, but made its own choice as to what might be called the head priest of the church.

As I remember, the land to be used was over two acres. There was adequate parking. This was in 1954 or 1955, and they did build an exceptionally beautiful Greek cathedral. The architecture was outstanding, the interior beautiful and historically correct. The church was equipped with seats; worshippers did not have to stand as in the old orthodox churches, and it was well attended by young people.

Charles Skouras and family gave additional money, I believe, to build a mausoleum on the grounds, so he could be buried there. This contributed to a great deal of friction among the church members and the neighborhood since special licenses and permits had to be obtained. It finally was built, and it is small and not intrusive.

As so often happens when churches move, or new ones are built, there was a rift. Skouras had brought into his committee people who were not old-line orthodox Greeks, but chosen for their ability to get things done. Also, in his fund-raising activities he used methods more of the marketplace than purely spiritual. He was a man of action who had been given a tremendous job to do. He had also been given every proper authorization to do it, but a group of old-timers, headed by a fine old Greek-American who ran a restaurant in Los

Angeles, brought an action in Superior Court to take the construction activities and the raised money out of the hands of the trustees who had been properly appointed with understood and approved duties. The old-timers felt, or contended, that the trustees were not serving the doctrinal best interests of the Greek orthodoxy. The committee felt that its work was not yet complete, which of course it was not. They contended that they had been properly given charge of the raising of the money, the superintending of the construction and so forth. They said that they had made no attempt to interfere with the older group or influence doctrine that should be taught. Such matters are often the subject of considerable bitterness, and a church's problems are always difficult. It is hard to draw the line between finances and the religion taught or promulgated by the church.

In this case, as I recall, the local church itself was the owner of the property. The rift widened, a lawsuit resulted and it was up to me to make a determination; there was no jury. The minutes of the church were kept in Greek, so they had to be interpreted in the courtroom. Also, many of the witnesses had little or no English, so interpreters had to be provided for them. We had representatives of the denomination from other countries, from other parts of the United States, as well as local people interested in the conduct of the church and of the trustees. All this took a great deal more time than anyone had foreseen. I ordered that briefs be filed. As these were capable lawyers, the briefs were excellent.

Skouras was too ill to attend and testify, but I gathered that some of the money raised came from people who were interested in the distribution and showing of motion pictures. I believe, in fact, that most of the money raised came from nonmembers of the church.

I carried the briefs home and studied them, a practice I did not ordinarily follow. I decided that the trustees had been honest, stayed within their authorization and should finish their work. They were still the trustees until there was a new election, had the right to collect money and spend it on the property and the building as they had done.

In writing my opinion, I borrowed strongly from the briefs. It was long, but they seemed to find it interesting; it was well received. I did the best I could to follow the evidence and the applicable law. I tried not to get into rulings on the religious beliefs of the church. I used as my guide, or tried to, "Render unto Caesar the things that are

Caesar's and unto God the things that are God's."

Skouras was delighted with the decision and insisted that it be published in all the Greek papers and publications of the world. I suppose he financed that publication.

I heard that everyone was not so pleased, and they intended to appeal. I also heard that the bishop had stepped in and threatened to excommunicate any who filed an appeal. I don't know if this was the case, but there was no appeal.

It was all very interesting to me, and it certainly was a pleasure to learn the meanings of the various icons and the history of the church. I acquired a high respect for the practices in the Greek Orthodox religion and was very pleased to attend the church on several later occasions.

Another church-related case comes to mind. One of the founders of a Baptist church in the Santa Monica area of the city was a handsome woman, approaching middle age at the time. It seemed that she had been excommunicated from this unaffiliated church—"read out" and told never to come back. She sought court establishment of her right to continue as a member, to attend and to take part in services on constitutional grounds.

She was very much against the minister, and was of the opinion that he should be removed. In the meantime, though, she did a number of things while attending church that were scarcely holy or religious. In fact, they were inimical to the holding of sincere and orderly religious services. As an example, she would sit next to the aisle and occasionally trip someone going by; this was apparently intentional, done to disturb what was going on. She also insisted on wearing large hats that obstructed the view of those behind her. She could sing well, but insisted upon singing off-key and very loud which was very disturbing to those around her.

The church officials had taken the usual formalities of giving her a good talking to; more than once they had tried to settle matters with her, but she was not cooperative. So, they had her up before the church officials, those who were charged with seeing that worship was conducted in accordance with established principles. After being talked to by these officials, she demanded a meeting of the membership. It was duly called, and there was a hearing. Apparently they explained her religious rights to her and took a vote of the entire membership. The lady's cause was very much in the minority. So, they barred her from the church and from attending events there, so she brought this action in court.

After hearing both sides, I finally issued an order that she could not be upon the church grounds from one-half hour before to one-half hour after a religious church service; that she could not slander any church member or member of the board or minister (she had said some pretty bad things); that she could not attend such events there as weddings unless invited. On the other hand, I ruled she could go upon the church grounds and worship alone or with her family or anyone desiring to accompany her, but this must be done when no regular church services were in progress. In short, I did not sever her membership or bar her from the church altogether, but I did recognize that she was committing nuisances and by this adversely affecting the purpose for which the church had been founded, and she had refused to abate such conduct.

As an illustration of how things travel around the world and how distorted they can get in the travelling, see what happened as a result of the routine reporting of this case. I received a clipping by mail with a very strong letter excoriating me for "denying the woman her God-given constitutional right to worship God as she chose." The letter went on to remind me that I had solemnly sworn to uphold the constitution of the United States and that of California which guarantee religious freedom. The letter and clipping came from a little town in Massachusetts of which I had never heard. Nor had I ever heard of the paper which printed the clipping of about four lines to the effect that a Los Angeles judge had denied a charter member of a church the right to worship in that church as granted by the constitution.

Now, I had on my desk at the time some thousands of pages of testimony. I had listened to all the testimony, seen all the witnesses, made copious notes, and remembered everything that had gone on. I had reviewed my notes; I had read the cases cited by counsel. It is a good example of some of the problems judges face.

As I have said, I was appointed in 1953, being sworn in on October 1 of that year. This meant I ran again in 1954, the next general election, and again in 1960 and 1966, as required. I was re-elected each time without opponents. The first time I almost had one—a woman judge from the municipal court, Ida Mae Adams. She had run for Superior Court on other occasions, but never successfully. She did say she was going to run, but finally did not do so.

At one time when I was serving in South Gate, there was a lawyer named Frank Hogan. He called himself Frank "Indispensable" Hogan. When I was named to sit there, he wrote a letter to presiding Judge Philip Richards in which he protested my being assigned to that district. He pointed out that I was a Republican and had been a corporation lawyer. South Gate, he said, was a poor man's district of chiefly Southern people, and that I couldn't possibly give them justice or understand their thinking.

Later there was a divorce case which he was handling. We had divorce cases in those days, not dissolutions; in fact you had to "prove up" even on default divorce cases. Well, in this case, Hogan's client was in default; it was too late for him to appear, though he tried after the default had been entered. So, in came "Indispensable" Hogan to try to set aside the default. He tried to do so by filing affidavits that the client had to spend a great deal of time trying to find the best possible lawyer in the area—that is, South Gate, Huntington Park, Downey, Norwalk and so on. He had finally decided that Hogan was the one man capable of handling this most difficult case (I couldn't see what was so difficult about it). Well, Hogan became too busy, or perhaps had been out of town, but in any case he had not gotten around to setting aside the default of the case. Therefore judgment had been entered against his client and had been allowed to stand for a considerable period of time.

I took the matter under submission, allowing him to submit his affidavits and to support, in any way he could, his motion to set aside the default. I tried to find some way to do so in the interests of justice. But there was no real reason set up in his affidavits except this "cock-and-bull" story as to his being the best and only lawyer in the area who could handle the matter. There were, in fact, a number of excellent lawyers there. I had to refuse the setting aside of the default, but reopened the case for further consideration of the financial problems of the parties. By adjusting finances and property rights a little bit, I saved his face to a degree. Mr. Frank "Indispensable" Hogan wrote another letter to the presiding judge; in this one he said that I was quite a wonderful man. Of course, I was still a Republican and had been a well-known corporate lawyer, but I "had a heart" and was "a good man in seeking out and getting to the important points of a case." Hmmm....

There was a case before me involving mechanics' and material men's liens on a shopping center. This center also involved open spaces for walks, parking, and other needs. Some of the buildings were already occupied while some were still under construction by various contractors for various reasons. There were many companies involved; this project was not under a general contractor. In the course of getting the shopping center built and occupied, some builders went broke, and everything was put in the hands of a receiver or trustee. There were numerous liens which had been filed at various times against all parts of the shopping center.

As would happen, there were numerous lawyers involved in the trying of the consolidated cases. We heard all about the number of nails driven in various walls to put up the siding; the amount of pain endured and financial loss suffered; the percentage of completion of various buildings of one kind and another; the amount of sand and gravel used or committed; the equities involved; the liens that had been filed, some of which were contested; and the percentages each litigant thought he should get of the money still available. These and many other contentions filled the air. I took the matter under submission and instructed the lawyers to file their points and authorities with me. I was sure there would be many recent cases on this subject since shopping centers have become so important, and the problems of multiple contractors impinge daily upon our lives. I read the points and authorities filed with me; there were a great many of them, often running to many pages.

I read the briefs. Then I phoned Glenn Behymer, Esq., son of the great Southern California impresario, L.E. Behymer. Glenn was the foremost authority in the state of California on mechanics' and material men's liens. Moreover, he had drafted nearly all the lien laws of this type for the state legislature, including amendments that had been adopted over the previous twenty years or so. This means that, though his name did not appear in the record books, he was the actual author. I explained the situation I had to Glenn and said, "Seems to me that the courts have gone through a lot of this sort of thing before. Haven't we some decided cases in point?" He said, "Wait a minute, we have been through a good deal of this. Hold on, and I'll look at my notebook." To my joy, he came forth with four decided cases, three of which were almost exactly in point. With this help, I decided the case before me in short order. I wrote a very short memorandum indicating the facts and my determination and citing the cases in support of my position. My decision stuck, which is to say that all the lawyers agreed with it, and agreed that they would not appeal the case which would have been expensive to all concerned. As the earlier cases upon which I had relied were well-decided and had all been appealed, I was applauded by these lawyers who all decided that I knew a great deal about the subject. In fact, I had never had a case on the subject before either on the bench or in my private practice. But I soon had a flood of similar cases set before me. It has been well said that an expert is not necessarily the man who knows the answer, but the one who knows where to find it.

Unknown to me, another judge had a case similar to this one at the same time. He was a very careful and studious judge who always took a great deal of time. He decided to write an opinion on this subject and took off several weeks for this purpose. One of the young secretaries told me that he wrote it by hand and had written and rewritten the decision twelve times which included the typing done by the young ladies who hated it.

Neither of us knew that the other was working on the same sort of matter. I did not publish my decision, but he loved to write decisions and enjoyed having them published. This was all right in itself, but the chief justice of our state Supreme Court, Chief Justice Gibson, had told us all that he preferred we not write decisions, even though the subject matter was interesting and important. He said it delayed our work and pointed out that it seldom kept the courts of appeal from getting the matters in question and having to do the same work all over again. Superior Court judges have these hard cases as "matters of first instance," but they are not just practicing law; they are making decisions. Well, this judge did write his opinion. It was a fine, long-winded decision which was carried in four issues of the *Los Angeles Daily Journal*, the fourth issue requiring many pages of the *Journal*, all of this supposedly for the benefit of lawyers. Now, the case was primarily decided on three of the four cases I had received from Glenn Behymer, and made no new law.

This was the same judge who, upon being appointed, proceeded to tell the then-governor that we would not need any more judges. He said that he could clean up the county civil calendar by himself, if given the opportunity to do so. Judge Burke soon gave him a minor opportunity to do so by putting him in the Law and Motion Department. This is where technical and legal objections to pleadings take place. As it happened, he was, himself, a very technically-minded person, and he soon decided that there should be a written opinion with respect to each of the Superior Court matters of Law and Motion. Now, these amounted even at that time, to more than one hundred per day in the central district! So, what he was thinking of, I don't know. There was at least at that time a practice of assigning a court commissioner to make a note of the decided cases pertinent at the foot of a decision. This served as a sort of memorandum on why the decision was so reached on the particular law and motion matter. It was helpful to counsel in this way. The idea that one man was going to clean up all the backlog in civil cases, when that one man could not keep halfway abreast of the law and motion matters in one of the nine districts, is, on the face of it, a bit ludicrous.

Judge Burke felt, when this judge had been discovered to be several weeks behind in his efforts, that he should not be assigned to any new matters, and should take the time to clean up his back ones. He said he thought three weeks would be plenty of time for this. So, I was assigned to that department, and took care of that Law and Motion calendar. This was supposed to last for three weeks. Three weeks passed, and he was still far from caught up. I don't know if he ever caught up.

This same judge began to get interested in the cases, and without consulting the presiding judge, began to assign himself for total hearing and determination in these matters he had received. This is to say, he assigned them to himself for trial or any further proceedings. He had cases from several years before, among which were some forty-five pending trials. How he got around the rule requiring all matters to be decided within ninety days, I do not know.

He had a school desegregation case; he had it, in fact, for eight years. I may say that he did do a good job on it, but he would do such things as rewrite the clerk's minutes, deciding he didn't like them—not, you understand, the court reporter's record, but the clerk's minutes of the day's proceedings. I recall his rewriting twelve pages of minutes for one day. He finally came down with a decision on the busing situation. He was running for re-election, and I suppose he thought it would be a great thing for him to publish his busing decision. He did so just three days before the final day for anyone to file against him. A comparative unknown filed against him and defeated him. Had he waited just three days more to publish the decision he had taken eight years to arrive at, he would have had no problem. He was, in fact, an excellent judge except for his inability to get his work done.

In the many cases I have tried in my career, I have had very few reversals, and three of those were restored.

There was one case on which I was probably rightfully reversed, although it didn't seem so to me at the time. It may well be that I allowed a little moral indignation to show. This was the case of a man in Hollywood who was on trial for placing misleading ads in the newspapers for girl motion picture or modelling aspirants. He hired a room or two in a hotel or other building to which the girls were to apply. On the pretext of needing to know how they would look in a bathing suit or whatever, he would have the girls parade before him nude. He would then try to induce them to engage with him or others in acts which, to put it euphemistically, they shouldn't have engaged in under any circumstances. He had been tried for this a couple of times previously. I don't know why the other two prosecutions were unsuccessful, but in my court he was tried before a jury, and the jury found him guilty. It went on to the District Court of Appeals, and I was upheld. It then went to the Supreme Court of California. Here my friend, Justice Ray S. Schauer, decided that I had prosecuted. I did not intend to, but perhaps I had. The man had a bad record, and I had thrown the book at him. So, I was eventually reversed. It is said that a man is not a good trial judge until he has been reversed, and I think there may be some truth in that.

I know of three cases in which I was reversed, and higher courts in later opinions came around to my way of thinking. I was quite literal in following the statutes or cases previously decided, and our Supreme Court is now a bit more liberal. I was, in short, the strict constructionist, whereas judges today, particularly in our California Supreme Court, or those in control of it, are often guilty of going beyond the printed pages of the law as made by the legislature or decisions of earlier courts made and upheld in their attempt to do justice. Perhaps this is the wave of the future. But I felt then, and still feel and think, that changes in the law should very seldom, if ever, be made by the courts. Changes should be effected, in and by, the legislative bodies which have been elected by the people.

# Chapter 17
## Presiding Judge

*L*ouis Burke was presiding judge of the Superior Court. We all liked him, and he was a fine judge.

He moved our courts to the new courthouse at the intersections of Olive, Temple and Grand Avenues. On the top floor he made a judges' lounge, and we made arrangements with the public cafeteria to bring down food five days a week; we had our lunch there. One noon, about September I think, about ten of us including Louis Burke and me were sitting at the table getting ready to leave. Louis asked me to remain, so I did. After the others had gone, Louis said to me, "I know that you were a deputy public defender, but that was many years ago, and the same is true of your service in the county council's office when you were attorney for the sheriff's and municipal courts. I think that if you are going to be a candidate for presiding judge, most judges now serving on the Superior Court would think perhaps you were lacking in present criminal experience to be the subject of a favorable vote. Now, I don't know whether you ever want to be presiding judge or not, but if you do, I think it might be a very good idea. I also think it would be good if you would spend some time over on the criminal side. You would do well to go over there. So, if you'd like, I will send you over to the criminal side when there is a vacancy."

I said, "Well, I haven't given it any thought, but maybe, if you'd like to send me over, I would go. You do as you think best." So, shortly after that, one of the Pasadena judges handling criminal work, who lived in Pasadena, said he would like to go over and be a judge in Pasadena. The way was open there for him, and I moved over to the criminal court. I spent three or four months there trying criminal cases. The judges handling the criminal matters in that location were very helpful.

When the year ended, the presiding judge would appoint the new judges to various departments. Judge Burke appointed me to be presiding judge of the criminal departments. I first chose a new judge for my chief of trial departments, and he was a very fine man who had criminal experience.

The day before the cases were to be heard, the clerk's office would send over the cases for the day. It would maybe be approximately 100 cases. Every day that was our calendar. I would look over the cases the night before, and we always looked at them before we went home. I would often stay down until 7:00 or 8:00 o'clock, if necessary, because I thought it best to look over them and make my notes for the following morning.

Sometimes, we would have more cases than we could handle. For instance, all criminal cases are supposed to come to trial within 90 days from the action of the grand jury or the preliminary hearing judge. If the attorney that represented the defendant who was in my courtroom would not waive time, and we were full in all our courts, I would have to ask Louis Burke to lend me an experienced man to hear the case immediately. It worked out quite well; normally, I did not have much difficulty keeping the calendar in shape.

In 1961 the legislature created three new appellate court vacancies for judges. We all worked hard to show the governor how good a man Louis Burke was, and he was appointed as presiding judge of the new division of our appellate courts in the Los Angeles, Ventura, Santa Barbara and San Luis Obispo areas. It was a good appointment, and Louis accepted it. This happened on a Friday, and he called me to come over to his office after three o'clock in the afternoon. We talked for a little more than half an hour. I had been given a lot of difficult cases, and he told me I had done very well except that my judgments were too low; I should give bigger judgments. He told me a few things to look out for and gave me a couple pieces of his philosophy as he gathered up his things. He said the judges had approved, and I was now presiding judge of the Superior Court. Then he was gone.

So, I took over without much background, briefing, study, or organization. He had stressed the importance to him of a larger and better location for the criminal departments. I agreed with him in light of my experience as chief judge of that department.

The board of supervisors at that time was looking with favor at a building that would be too small. It was the old municipal court annex building that had been moved across Broadway and turned around–quite a feat at the time. The building, according to many people, had at one time been a house of assignation. It had been used as an overflow area for the municipal court. It was not very suitable for the purpose for which it was being used, and certainly not suitable at all for criminal trials. For these reasons Burke had been objecting to the board of supervisors' plan to put the new criminal courts building there, and I agreed with him.

Louis Burke was a good administrator. He was very tenacious with his ideas, and he and the board of supervisors clashed on a number of matters. He was usually right, but I can't say I felt that his method of handling the board was the best one. So, when I went into office as presiding judge, I immediately appointed a committee of three of my most politically-minded judges. To head it, I chose a former assemblyman who was quite political, Judge William Rosenthal. This committee was "stacked" with Democrats for the reason that the board of supervisors was in control of the Democrats. Of course, the board is supposedly nonpartisan, but it had a lot to do with politics in the legislature. The then-chairman of the board was, I think, Ernest Debs, who had been in Democratic politics for years.

So, the committee went to work on the board of supervisors. We were finally successful in getting them to agree that the site they had in mind should be used for other purposes or abandoned, and that the new building should be on Poundcake Hill. This was the location of the old courthouse which had been built in the 1880s and rendered unfit for use by the 1933 earthquake. The planning started; they were going to go with a building of eleven stories, but I insisted on thirteen. They finally decided I was right, only I wasn't right enough; it was eventually built to sixteen stories. The whole process required some eight years to complete. Apparently, I was forgotten when they were planning the ceremony and turning the first shovelful of dirt, but at the last moment someone remembered me, and I was hurried over to make my little speech.

The building certainly had its troubles as it neared completion.

There are always structural or finishing aspects that come up and seem not right, but it was finally completed and is now well used by the public defender, the sheriff's office, the district attorney's office, the municipal court preliminary hearings and judges of the Superior Court for criminal court matters. I trust everybody is happy. It was certainly an illustration of just how hard it can be to keep things going in the way of getting criminal courts. It was another of the buildings built with funds, I believe, from the county retirement fund, on a pay-back system. I always questioned the legality of this; I felt it was an evasion of the law. Still, this was the only way the county could get buildings of this kind financed because the people simply would not vote bonds to pay for them.

Besides getting the criminal courts building under way as Louis Burke had exhorted me to do, I felt there were a number of other things deserving of early priority. One of these was my need to get to know the trial bar, as we call it. Many lawyers are never in court, and a great number seldom get to court. But there are those who come into court every day, such as the groups who try the defense cases for insurance companies. They nominally represent the insureds; the insurance companies are generally not named parties to these actions. There also are many plaintiffs' lawyers who made it a business of being in court daily. These defense and plaintiffs' lawyers are the ones who know most about the idiosyncrasies of the judges as well as the trial of cases. I felt it was necessary that I know whether a given firm or lawyer could be trusted or needed to be watched. I perceived that lawyers and clients, as a group, had a suspicion of the courts; that is, they felt as though they were treated by the court as second-class lawyers or citizens. The court was often suspicious of the lawyer and vice versa. I did know that certain court clerks, particularly in criminal cases, suspected certain lawyers; when these lawyers came in, the clerks would cover everything on the desk.

I also knew that there are financial blacklists of lawyers whose checks were not acceptable. Both the sheriff's office and the clerks' office kept our clerks advised of this. It was true that some lawyers were not good at paying their bills, and their checks were apt to bounce. This, though, was only a small group. It was also good to know which lawyers had the reputation of trying to "finesse" or mislead the court. For example, there are lawyers who have too much business. They will phone in, tell the clerk that they are in department

25, and will ask that their case be postponed. At times this turns out not to be the case at all. Maybe their case has already been continued from department 25; anyway, they will not be there. A telephone call to department 25 may disclose that the case has been settled. Some lawyers are not dependable about such matters, and it is necessary that the judges know those who are suspect. This is particularly necessary for judges in department 100, the master calendar of criminal cases, and department 1, the master calendar of civil cases. It is also necessary in the law and motion department, the probate department and others. We judges must get to know these things, and I felt I did not know them well enough when I became presiding judge.

I also had to know which judges were disliked by counsel and why. Counsel has a right to challenge a judge without assigning a cause. Theoretically, there is a cause because they feel they cannot have a fair and impartial trial; that is, either counsel or client feels this to be the case. But, the practice is often used simply to get a continuance which would not otherwise be granted. It is often a wrong thing that a lawyer or his client can take this "one bite" at the judge simply by signing and filing a paper which he knows is not at all true. Judges do get to be known as defense-minded or plaintiff-minded, but this is not generally the case. I know of very few who can rightfully be subjected to such criticism.

These considerations led me to conclude that I should call the civil courts calendar myself in department 1, at least for a time, and thus get to know the lawyers and the various ramifications of practice in the Superior Court. Judge Burke and a couple of his predecessors had assigned a commissioner to call the calendar, hear the motions made before the court when the case was called and assign out the cases. I thought I could carry the load of being presiding judge and still preside almost always over the call of cases in the master calendar department, and I did so. I am sure the lawyers liked this. Not only did it give them a hearing before their clients by a judge rather than a commissioner, but also I tried very hard to see that these lawyers were fully heard in the presence of their clients.

My psychology worked. The lawyers and their clients greatly appreciated what I was doing; and they told me so on many occasions. I was a new man on the job, I was learning with them, and I was courteous. I thought at first I would do it only for a time, until I "learned" the lawyers and the job, but I continued it. Experiments are best done by degrees with a few departments, and I followed this theory. When anything new was to be tried out in connection with law and motion, I tried it out, and then we would discuss it among ourselves.

I appointed two assistant presiding judges; I believe there had been only one before. These assistants were a sort of cabinet; I worked with them, lunched with them and discussed matters, but they were not taken from their regular work to be put on administrative work. Both of these judges were very fine, but I thought it advisable to change them after the first year since neither of them intended to run for judicial office. I thought it best to train at least one man who was likely to become the next presiding judge. Today, assistant presiding judges are elected, I think for two years, and call the calendar in department 1. This gives the presiding judge more time to work on other details of administration.

During my last year as presiding judge, I told the judges that I thought this should be the last year that the then-current system was followed. More and more, new and large branch district courthouses were being opened, and greater effort had to be made for the presiding judge to cover the entire county. I had quite largely left the administrative work of the Long Beach and the Pasadena areas to their presiding judges; but now, with courthouses in Norwalk, Pomona, the San Fernando Valley and other places, the out-of-town contact work was too much for the presiding judge. An assistant would have to take over such matters as the calendar. I knew this was to come, though its time was not yet. We got along very well with the presiding judge and the assistants who could take a given job at any time by virtue of their knowledge of the work and help out in emergencies. There were, needless to say, lots of ramifications.

I certainly felt that judges were entitled to higher pay, as did all the judges. The pay, when I went on the bench in 1953, was around a third of what it is today. We also needed more judges. We decided, as other judges had before us, that it was useless to try to get either more judges or higher pay without the cooperation of the grand jury and the board of supervisors of the county. So, again I gathered some of my ex-legislature friends and, with the cooperation of the grand jury and board of supervisors they descended upon Sacramento and were successful in both objectives. They even got a cost-of-living clause, the first in California!

Before going north, our committee members went to see Jesse Unruh; he was the real kingpin of the state assembly and very powerful in the state senate and elsewhere. He agreed to try to help us. He assigned an assemblyman to carry the legislation through the legislature. This assemblyman was not too anxious to do so, but he was assured by a telephone call from "Big Daddy" Unruh that he was indeed to "carry the bill," which he did successfully. They cut down a bit on the number of judges we wanted, and also on the amount of the pay increases, but we got both plus the cost of living increases. Possibly they were tired of our requests, or perhaps they wanted to experiment; we had in mind that such might well be the case. The laws were passed, and a few days after the governor signed the bills, "Big Daddy" telephoned me and said, "Well, we worked it out for you, didn't we? We were really successful, weren't we?" I said, "You certainly did a grand job for us and the people of California."

It may appear that I increased the cost of operating the judges' department considerably, but this was not the case. There were some raises of salary, but no increase in staff during that period. Very important was the need of a commissioner to work with the presiding judge. Many papers came in which had to be carefully looked over; many people came in the early morning seeking answers to immediate problems. As a rule the judges in the various departments would not be available until nine in the morning, having papers to look over when they came in at eight-thirty. Many problems came to the presiding judge's office at 8:00 to 8:30 in the morning, a high percentage calling for immediate action. Even if not urgent as to action, these had to be studied, affidavits had to be read, law had to be consulted, exhibits considered and so forth. For awhile I had a commissioner, but for most of the time I had Clinton Rodda who had a background which enabled him to work on virtually any sort of problem. Nine times out of ten he gave the correct answer.

I am reminded of a story I made up about a prior presiding judge, though it could be made to fit almost any presiding judge of the Superior Court.

A certain presiding judge was a little late one morning, coming in very shortly before time to call the morning calendar. Several lawyers were anxiously waiting to see him on various matters, and, being a very affable fellow, he stopped to talk with them. Finally, his secretary got his attention and whispered to him, "Don't you remember, Judge, this is the day you're to address the Downtown Rotary Club at noon?" "Oh, yes," said the judge, "I did promise that didn't I, and I haven't even started on it. What was I going to talk about?"

"Well, you've given out that your subject will be the effect of atomic explosions and nuclear weapons on the divorce rate in Southern California."

"Oh, heavens!" exclaimed the judge. "Now I remember, and it's going to take a lot of study. Well, have my commissioner get started on it, and I'll talk to him during the court recess when I leave the bench at ten o'clock."

The commissioner, who was within earshot, spoke up, "Your Honor, you know I have my own calendar, and besides I've already got half a dozen people waiting for me."

"Never mind, never mind," said Hizzoner. "This will have to take precedence. I'm in a bind, and it's up to you to get started on this talk."

The commissioner left, and the judge went on and called his calendar; he came off the bench at about 10:45. As usual, there were urgent phone calls and several people waiting for him. He thought of the talk only as he was about to return for the eleven o'clock calendar. "How is the commissioner getting along with my talk?" he asked the clerk. "He says he has to see you," replied the clerk.

"I have to get back to the bench; you can see I'm already late. He'll have to do the best he can. Tell him I'll see him before twelve o'clock," said the judge, as he hurried back to the bench.

Shortly before noon the judge was able to leave the bench. He hurried to the clerk. "Where's the commissioner?" he asked. "How's he doing? I'll have to read it over on the way and maybe make some additions."

"I'm afraid," replied the clerk, "he didn't have a chance to get it finished." "All right, all right," snapped the judge, "I'll finish it. Just get it and give it to me."

The clerk went for the talk and came back to hand it to the judge who, looking at the clock, was already heading for the steps. Two lawyers whom he knew were just getting into a taxi. They said they were going downtown and would be glad to drop him off, so he got in with them. They had a pleasant trip and interesting visit. They dropped the judge off at the site of the luncheon, a little late.

He took his seat next to the presiding officer and joined the conversation at the table. Matters under discussion were of such engrossing interest that the judge did not look at his speech until suddenly it was time to deliver it.

Introduced, he rose, and, after a few introductory remarks, drew the speech from his pocket and started to deliver it. By halfway through the first page, he realized he had in his hands an excellent piece of work, and he was very pleased to find the commissioner had done so well by him. The speech outlined the four main points to be made and, after a witticism or two which were well received, proceeded to make them very clearly and effectively. By the end of the third page, the judge was so entranced by the quality of the speech, and the enthusiastic reception he was receiving that he thought, in the back of his mind, "I'm going to have to speak to the governor about this commissioner. A man like this should certainly be moved up, at least to the municipal court. Of course, since I belong to the wrong party, the governor probably won't pay any attention, but I really should try."

Then, in his triumphal progress through the speech which he felt was going to substantially increase his reputation as a speaker, he turned the third page. Suddenly, his voice faltered, his face reddened and he began to cough. The presiding officer, sitting next to him, became concerned. "Aren't you feeling well?" he asked solicitously. The judge could only nod. "Would you like some water?" asked the master of ceremonies. The judge nodded again, and water was provided, but he could not continue. The luncheon guests gathered around and rushed him to a waiting cab at his request. The master of ceremonies returned to the luncheon to announce that the judge had taken ill and asked to be sent back to his chambers. Unfortunately, the presiding judge had been so upset that he left the speech lying on the podium. A bright young fellow who is always to be found at these events spotted it. It was still turned to page four.

In large, red-pencilled script in the commissioner's handwriting, page four said, "Now, damn you, IMPROVISE!!"

So, in addition to not making our commissioner sore at us, the moral is that we should, as presiding judges, not try to do too much. Really, we should do the actual writing ourselves, and it was my practice to do so. I never had a commissioner or anyone else ever write a speech for me; look up facts, yes, but not write the speech.

Presiding judges, as do all officeholders, have problems of this sort. It seems that this is particularly evident just after we take office. Whether as presiding judge of Superior Court, chief judge of the juvenile court or whatever; civil, religious, service and other organizations immediately want the new appointee to address their members. He cannot deny all of them, though in most cases he is not yet fully familiar with the work he will be called upon to do. In nearly all cases they want him to outline the plans he had for his particular court or job, and this is a little difficult, too. Even presidents have gotten into a lot of trouble by premature announcing of plans. It might be well for all new appointees or electees to adopt the plan of setting a time later when they will be available for such appearances.

Governor Warren once said to me that he would never speak at any service club. He was fond of many of the persons who headed such clubs, knew many of them personally and would have liked to oblige them. But, as he said, one either makes enemies of all those that he refuses, or he resigns himself to putting in every single noon hour at some service club's luncheon. No responsible executive can so tie up his time; one has to budget, and often fairness demands that he refuse engagements he might like to accept.

Our judges' lounge was on the third floor of the county courthouse. There we could gather at noon, discuss problems, say what we thought of the justices of higher courts and other things. It was a good thing in many ways. "Outside" judges of the court and those from other districts could come in, but no appellate judges were allowed at that time, though I think they are now. The judges' lounge was also equipped with two conference rooms, one large and one small. There were many committees which had to meet periodically, and these rooms were of real value. There was, for example, the committee on rules of which I later became chairman; there was a committee on instructions to the jury in civil matters on which I also served; there was a similar committee for criminal matters. The lounge served many purposes.

While presiding judge, I was able to work out a plan whereby the commissioners could have a place of their own. Some of them were not very happy with this arrangement because all I could do was give them a "judges' chambers" facility. Still, it was more than large enough for a table accommodating twelve or more, a divan or so, and some chairs. I figured, too, that if they wished, they could turn one of the restrooms into a kitchen and have a stove and counter with a refrigerator for food preparation and storage. I arranged for them to get the necessary furniture including some easy chairs. As I say, they were not overly enthusiastic, but I did the best I could within the limitations of the available space and design of the building.

When I served as chairman of the rules committee, one of the members was Judge William Palmer, brother of Harlan Palmer who published the *Hollywood Citizen-News* newspaper. Judge Palmer had been a writer and newspaperman; he published some books and also wrote and published some music. I mention him here because he was the greatest stickler for punctuation and for English usage I ever knew. It is certainly true that in "Rules" one should be particular. There comes a point, though, in my opinion, where precision slides over into pedantry, and he passed that point. It was very difficult to get him away from spending half the meeting on whether a comma or a semicolon should be used at a given point. This was also true in the matter of instructions, both civil and criminal.

One day, as I sat at my desk in chambers, I looked up to see, standing in the doorway, a very large and tall young black man wearing a black turban and a long black gown which came to his shoetops. He flashed a beautiful smile. I got up and went to the door to invite him in. I soon learned that he was a judge of the high court of Nigeria. I found that he was in this country to visit various courts, as an aid in planning the courts of Nigeria. That country had either just received its independence or was about to. We had what I considered a very worthwhile visit, and I trust it seemed so to him. I then invited him to return the next day to lunch in our judges' lounge to talk with other judges. He agreed, and I made up a table of those I thought would be of interest to him or interested in him and his mission. We did discuss many things. It developed that this young judge was a graduate of England's Oxford University, and he told us that Nigeria's courts were run primarily on the British system. One thing we thought was bad, as I recall, was the fact that there was no provision for setting bail during the summer months. A person arrested for a crime during the summer months was kept in jail, according to him a very hot and poor jail, for as much as three or four months, whether guilty or not, until a judge had returned from his summer vacation. I believe that after our visit with this judge, we all had considerably more confidence in the fate of Nigeria's citizens and in the courts of Central Africa.

We were visited by many judges and administrators, particularly in view of the standing accorded the Los Angeles Superior Court among the courts of the nation. Among them was a chief justice of the courts of Indonesia, and with him were two or three other judges. He constantly wore one of the red caps, called a fez, from which dangled a black tassel. I invited this chief justice and his compatriots to lunch with me and two or three other judges at the California Club in Los Angeles. Several people came to our table, some of them asking if my friend was Sukarno. He, as you may recall, was at the time absolute ruler of that country. No, my friend was not Sukarno.

He told us that he received compensation the equivalent of $300 a month in American currency. I asked how he could live on such a sum, and he said he taught law, gave some lectures and wrote legal articles for papers and magazines. I expressed curiosity as to how he could find time for all of this, inasmuch as he had to write all his judicial opinions. "Judicial opinion?" he said, frowning slightly. "Your decision as to why a case is reversed and sent back for trial, or on the contrary, why it should be approved and not sent back down." "Oh," he said with some merriment. "I don't do that. I am chief judge of all the courts—all courts all over the whole of Indonesia—and when I decide a case, that is it. Nothing can be done about it after that; no one can say anything, or should say anything. I just say 'case dismissed' or 'retrial granted' or 'prisoner will serve his sentence'— things like that."

Well, that is certainly one way of getting the job done. I am not altogether sure that we in this country are wise in trying to review each of the higher court decisions in point whenever a case comes up that is appealed; but what we seek is justice, and although the opinions of judges in the past are certainly of great value, they perhaps should not be the decisive factor. However, the problem is that it was justice in that individual case. Is the casebook system the best?

Probably, but the question has been bothering our legal education staffs for many years.

Unfortunately, I had not yet begun to keep a visitor's book, and the name of the Indonesian chief justice escapes me. At any rate, at the close of the luncheon, Judge Emil Gumpert pulled out some cigars and handed one to each of the visiting dignitaries. As luck would have it, the cigars were "Dutch Masters," and this possibly was an untactful thing to do since Indonesia has only recently thrown off the yoke of the Netherlands empire. Of course, the faux pas was entirely unintentional, but one of them did notice; he rolled the cigar around and looked at it carefully, and one could see that this had not set too well with him. Judge Gumpert then very carefully explained that the "Masters" referred to in the cigars' name was the school of great painters in Holland such as Rembrandt of long, long ago. The visiting judges laughed and made light of the incident, but I'm not sure there wasn't a little resentment.

Like all presiding judges, I enjoyed being able to give deserving judges a "leg up" when possible or I felt it to be deserved. One I was happy to help was Judge Joseph Wapner of "People's Court" fame. Wapner was a municipal court judge when I first knew him. He was appointed to the Superior Court by Governor Brown, and it was Mickey who asked me, quite properly, to give him such help as I could. For one thing, I appointed him to head a committee with respect to a daytime release program that was to allow certain prisoners to work at their own jobs during the day and serve their time at night. Such things put a judge in the public eye as well as the eyes of his associates and superiors. They have great bearing on his being moved up if he is good. I also appointed him to work on a program regarding the fixing of bail or O.R. (own recognizance) releases, so as to make it possible for people who, because they had families and jobs, were unlikely to fail to appear for trial. He did very good work and deserved to be moved up. He later became presiding judge, after which he headed the Conference of California Judges and did great work in representing the judges in legislative work and in getting cooperation with the California appellate and Supreme Courts.

Growth and change, the increased impact of man on man, machine on man and the entire dynamic of our burgeoning society had its effect on the courts, as on all other walks of life. One of its manifestations is the constant increase of filings—that is to say, caseload or number of actions brought. We had statistics on each judge and branch, and the total of filings did increase over the entire system at a rate of about five percent a year. Because of the case-setting problems, we had to try to figure in advance the number of judge-days which would be available monthly for trial cases. In addition to the increased filings, a factor in our difficulties was the ideas people have. Judges have ideas, media have ideas, the public has ideas, and heaven knows that lawyers have ideas. The ideas of the latter group are designed to serve their clients, not to delay cases. Nevertheless, such things as continuances, motions for prejudgment based upon pleadings and all sorts of things had to be heard. To work out all of these ideas takes time, and we simply had to somehow get a more efficient way to eat up this five percent additional annual caseload. At the time, we were getting pretty far behind, chiefly because of the earlier failure of the governor to fill judicial vacancies as they occurred.

However, in the last year of my presiding judgeship, we did reduce the civil backlog, the first time this had been done during my time as a trial judge. We decreased by some 1,645 matters in the civil downtown courts without any new judges. We hadn't had any new judges for a couple of years, to my recollection. The number of filings increased as usual, but our judges turned out more work, and perhaps there were more settlements and dismissals. The branch courts did equally well. We started with the idea, then new, of certificates of readiness.

My successor as presiding judge, Judge Chantry, took a very sweeping action, for which he had great hopes. By putting in some new rules, he arbitrarily wiped out the entire backload of cases awaiting trial. In essence, he simply disallowed the certificates of readiness which had been filed in these matters, and required that they be redone and resubmitted. Thus, on paper, the cases he put on calendar for the coming month constituted all the cases to be tried, and the calendar was current. Unfortunately, this did not have the result he had envisioned; his idea was that his action would force many of these matters to be settled or even withdrawn. He only postponed the evil day; the cases were still on file and, when his requirements had been complied with, most of them came back again on the calendar. The courts were worse off than before.

Henry Luce, editor and publisher of *Time*, *Life* and *Fortune* magazines, became interested in the problems of courts in the United States. He was disturbed about their condition and decided to investigate. He put a top writer on researching the subject, learning whether judges were really working, what the problems of the courts were, and what could be done to better them. This writer visited our courts on numerous occasions, most of them before I became presiding judge when Judge Louis Burke was presiding judge. The article he eventually wrote took up almost an entire issue of *Fortune* magazine. Our court, the Superior Court of Los Angeles County, was commented upon in fairly glowing terms while nearly all others were treated less well, some of them severely castigated. Ours was the only court to which the author gave good marks. Let me hasten to add that although the article was actually published during my term as presiding judge, it was researched and written during Burke's term; the credit is his, not mine. Properly, the credit is to be shared among all the judges, past and active, and all the members of the court for doing their job.

Actually, in his final write-up before completing his article, the writer did come to see me; I had been presiding judge for some months. Chief Justice Earl Warren publicly called the Los Angeles Superior Court the finest trial court in the land, and I do feel I had some part in our achieving and holding this stature.

About this time it was my great pleasure to renew my acquaintance with Justice Tom Clark of the Supreme Court of the United States. Tom was a very likeable fellow who grew greatly in stature after his appointment to the Supreme Court. While we liked him, we hadn't thought highly of him when he was a federal prosecutor here. Justice Clark had a very thoughtful habit; when on vacation, he would take time to drop you a few lines of greeting on a postcard. He was chairman of the metropolitan courts committee of the American Bar. I don't know if he started that committee, but whoever did, it was a good idea. Its purpose was to help the courts of larger municipalities, initially those of over a million and a quarter in population. I think later committee membership was opened to somewhat smaller municipalities. The special problems of these large metropolitan districts were brought out and considered at their meetings, which took place several times a year. I was on it from the first, but resigned when I ceased to be presiding judge. Perhaps I should have stayed on and been of value. Judge Chantry, who followed me, took my place on the committee, stayed on and held several offices. He was a great help to its work, and I am sure he enjoyed it. I certainly did during my tenure. We did a lot of work in helping Chicago's courts get started when, by constitutional amendment, the state of Illinois revamped its court setup.

About that time, Judge Emil Gumpert was my assistant presiding judge. He came to me one day and suggested we consider a seminar of our Los Angeles Superior Court, bringing top-notch judges and professors to speak. I thought it a fine idea. There had been seminars of the kind in the East—judges from various states gathering to discuss their problems—but there had never been a seminar of just one court. Our court was so large and varied that it made a good place to start. I made Emil Gumpert chairman of the organizing committee, and no one could have done a better job. He got Tom Clark and other fine judges from several states. We had a three-day seminar, paid for entirely by the judges of our court. As I recall, our attendance was 97 percent of the court.

We also invited judges from our Los Angeles municipal court and our commissioners; the attendance of the commissioners was excellent. We gave one dinner at which Tom Clark was the speaker. We held it in the Blue Ribbon Room of the Music Center.

Professor Van Alstine of UCLA, perhaps the outstanding law professor of the time, gave the final address and was an excellent choice. He did a fine job of winding up the seminar.

All of this was not done under the metropolitan courts committee; it preceded the formation of that committee and was at Emil Gumpert's suggestion. I later went back to Chicago and spent several days with the metropolitan courts committee. The Cook County courts had been combined, and they were putting in a computer which they called the "black monster." Computers were new then, and I watched it work. They put in all the traffic tickets for the day; in twenty minutes it had arranged to copy them all and total them. The computer then immediately put the results at the hand of the proper officials throughout the entire county, such as the police, the sheriff's office, the issuers of drivers' and chauffeurs' licenses, the issuers of automobile licenses and the traffic courts. All this in twenty minutes! Both we and the local judges were sure it would take longer. Thus, when a person applied for a license, to renew an auto license or whatever, the entire record of the applicant and his autos were at hand at the push of a button.

I was very much interested in this and other matters handled by the computer, and I carefully prepared a report for the Los Angeles city attorney's office. We also made additional studies of computer capabilities, or at least I did.

I suggested at the time that our district attorney, public defender, sheriff, Superior Court, metropolitan court and certain others share one big computer which could work for all of us. I can't say that I accomplished in toto what I had in mind, but a start was made. Computerizing of law activities was just getting under way at that time. During this period, I attended a meeting in San Francisco of the State Bar Association where there were demonstrations of various computers and "black monsters." Nearly all government agencies were beginning to install them. Like it or not, it is now an established necessity.

It is not only lawyers who "shop" for judges, nor are the methods used always those set forth in the *Code of Civil Procedure*. I call to mind the story of an incident which, while not without its amusing side, caused a number of unnecessary problems and the unjustified spending of considerable public funds. There was a woman in Los Angeles who, while I was presiding judge, was engaged in putting together and publishing a sort of *Who's Who in Los Angeles County*. This was to be a register of those in this part of California who were in her estimation "important" in the mind of the public. She was having a great deal of trouble with her printer, who had sued her. The printer's claim was for a lot more money than the woman thought she should have to pay. Somehow, she was acquainted with an aunt of my wife, Lois, a dear old lady, but a bit "flighty." This aunt-in-law came to me, thinking she could get a special judge appointed for the trial of this matter, and thus help out her friend, the lady publisher. Of course, I saw through the situation, that inspired her visit. I merely assured her that I would personally see that the matter had one of the "top judges." As it happened, the next civil trial courtroom open for new assignment was that of a very capable and well-thought-of judge. I don't know if he was in the woman's *Who's Who* or not, but I know him to be a first-class man of absolute reliability, Judge Ellsworth Meyer. Well, he tried the case and found against the woman. Whereupon, as birds with feathers ruffled, both the lady publisher and the aunt descended upon me to say what a terrible and unfair judge he was. After they took their leave, I called Judge Meyer and asked him about the case. "There was nothing to it, really," he said. "She seldom got her copy in to the printer on time, but she insisted on getting the proof printing done by a certain date including approval. The printer had to put on extra men and work at night. They submitted their time sheets, work records, hours spent, union pay schedules, and other material. They had in writing the number of times she had come in and changed her orders. I examined the papers and talked with her and with them. The charge was quite proper." The lady publisher proceeded to file affidavits to the effect that I was part and parcel to various heinous crimes, and that Judge Meyer and I were in league with the "Eastern Mafia," whatever that may be, along with other silly and unfounded nonsense. The judge denied her request for a new trial; she took an appeal and lost. Nevertheless, for several years she kept after us. She broadened the attack to include most of the judges on the bench, all of whom she proposed to remove. Among other flights of fancy, she charged that all the judges from the "northeastern part of the country," a rather vague area, were part of a Mafia gambling ring.

As was proper, I advised her on how to make her complaints in the proper manner if she desired to do so. She took her matter to the State Bar and the Judicial Qualifications Commission; this was at the time the name of the body charged with consideration of complaints against judges. It also had charge of disciplining judges where required and of making recommendations for retirement or removal, when indicated, to the Supreme Court of California. This resulted in two separate visits from an investigator by virtue of these charges by the woman, all growing out of the lawsuit she had lost. Of course, nothing came of it because there was never the slightest basis for any of the charges. Even so, we had these things to deal with, and it was, at times a real problem to take the necessary time to do research work or have it done—a frivolous waste of taxpayers' money, but in the circumstances made unavoidable by the vindictive ire of one person who apparently would go to any length to avoid admitting that she had been wrong in the first place.

The retirement of judges is a problem which occasionally arises. Few people, even few judges hear about it. It is always a sad and difficult thing to have to tell a judge that he should retire or step down. I remember, during the early part of my time on the bench, a very admirable old judge who was at the time 83 years old. He had become quite deaf, and could not follow evidence. His wife was in court daily and always tried to "clue him in" to what was going on. Well, this did not really give him the necessary picture. Then, he began to go to sleep while on the bench. The situation became so bad that some lawyers complained, and some even refused to be assigned to him although he was a very capable judge. The time came when Louis Burke decided he had to tell this judge about the situation, and did so. The old judge listened very courteously and carefully until Judge Burke had finished. Then he said very quietly, "Louis, that must have been a very difficult thing for you to do." And he retired forthwith.

While I was still practicing law, I appeared before this judge who was one of two specialists on annulments and the governing laws in other states. Should a parent bring suit to dissolve the marriage of a fifteen or sixteen year old son, for example, the matter would go to him or the other specialist. I brought an annulment action for my client, a doctor. His son was attending a military academy in another state—one of those prestigious military schools to which many people send their sons when the son could not get an appointment to West Point. Near the school was a tavern; the tavern-keeper had a pretty daughter also under age. So, these two underage children proceeded to get themselves married in that state. The two young people probably realized, at least the son did, that it was not a marriage that stood a chance of lasting. Sooner or later they would be unhappy as would both sets of parents. His parents in California asked me to bring an annulment proceeding on the grounds that the required parental consent had not been given, and I did so. The matter came up before this judge, and I called his attention to the fact that the law of the particular state where the marriage had taken place was different from those of Arizona or Nevada, from whence most of our annulment cases came. He took umbrage, shut me up quickly and informed me that he was quite cognizant of the law. He then ruled against me.

I was disturbed. I told my clients that the judge had been wrong, and we were discussing appeal that afternoon. On that afternoon, still the day of the hearing, I received a telephone call from that judge. He apologized profusely. He said that after he left the bench he got to thinking about my saying that the law in that particular state was different from that of the states involved in the great majority of the cases he had tried and in which he was well versed. He said that I had proved right and was entitled to the judgment annulling the marriage. He was both thoughtful and magnanimous in admitting and correcting his mistake.

I once wrote a story about the many things that a presiding judge must do, from the kind of things mentioned to being a father confessor when a judge comes in and cries on the desk about his family troubles. I gave it to a public relations man who said he would print it since he was writing about presiding judges. I never heard from him again and never got my manuscript back.

When I retired (the first time), I made a list of some fifty-two things that I had accomplished as presiding judge. I thought they were of value to the conduct, work and procedures of the court. One such, for example, was a court rule I got adopted. Where the lawyers on a case would agree on a judge to mediate and settle the matter, whether in a criminal, civil, downtown or branch, such judge would be required to arbitrate the case. He might even have to do it mornings before his other work, but he would do it. The judges were very good about this; they would try to settle any matter on request from both sides. This would not mean a formal arbitration with the taking of a lot of testimony, but with proper statements in writing from the parties and such exhibits as the judge stipulated. The judge would then suggest a proper settlement. If the parties did not like it, the case could then go to trial, but a significant number were successfully mediated in this way thus saving a substantial amount of court time.

It has been said, and often is, that there is always a running feud between the board of supervisors and the county Superior Court. Superior Court judges have a statewide mandate; they are judges for the whole state, though elected from a county, and the funds for the courts of a county come through the board of supervisors. Superior Court judges are paid mostly by the state, but part is paid by the county. So, problems can arise, and a serious one existed at the time I was on the court, but it did heal quite well. At the time I first went on the bench, there seemed to be great difficulty in communication between the board of supervisors and the presiding judge. As an instance, during Judge Burke's time as presiding judge, the smoking of marijuana was held to be a serious offense. The board of supervisors along with the greater portion of the public felt that anyone using marijuana should go to the penitentiary. Judge Burke took issue with them on this, feeling that a felony conviction was too harsh a punishment for the offense at least in many cases. His position has since been vindicated, and his view is today generally approved.

This, though, was only one of the things on which he disagreed with the board, and Burke was a very feisty gentleman whose combative nature sometimes raised a bit of bad feeling. He was a marvelous judge, a tiptop presiding judge, who accomplished many worthwhile things. But, at the time I took over the court, there were difficulties between Burke and Supervisor Kenneth Hahn who was chairman of the courts committee of the board of supervisors. Kenneth Hahn had one peculiarity, for wont of a better term, which I believe he never overcame: he felt he had to have a story or two on his work in the newspaper every week, mainly in connection with the courts, as well as stories on other matters wherever possible. I found as presiding judge that a way of getting around the problems this caused was to "feed" to him matters of interest about the courts. He would then put these out in publicity releases over his signature and get credit for them; this worked out very well.

I don't believe I am telling tales out of school when I state that Burke's idea of dealing between the courts and the board should be along military lines. Burke had been an army officer during World War II and thought it wrong for the members of the board of supervisors, who were at the same salary level as the judges, to drive around in chauffeured Cadillacs while the judges had no county cars at all or even recompense for using their own cars on county business. This situation, he thought, was particularly bad with respect to the presiding judge and the chief judge of the juvenile court. Both of these functionaries were required to do a great deal of traveling about the county to speaking engagements and to the various branches. In fact, these two officials could make speeches every noon and every night, if they allowed themselves to be so used.

So, the board of supervisors voted a car—no chauffeur and no guards—to the presiding judge and to the chief judge of the juvenile court. They thereupon proceeded to allot a couple of Fords for the purpose.

This did not go over well with Judge Burke. He strongly felt that as presiding judge he was on a par with any supervisor, and anything less was demeaning; he was convinced that he should have a good, big car and the other perquisites. Finally, they assigned him a new Mercury to drive, and he had to be content with that. The same was done for the juvenile court judge, and both were given marked parking spaces. Judge Burke was not alone in the thought that the procedure followed was indeed demeaning, failing to uphold the dignity of the court.

As I said, Judge Burke's ideas were of a military nature in this respect. He felt, for example, that judges should talk with the supervisors, not with employees or with the county administrative office or other county department heads. He also thought that Ed Gallas, our chief administrative officer, should talk directly and only with the head of the county administrative office. When I became presiding judge, this did not quite suit my fairly easygoing nature. I recognized the value of the military type of setup, but on the other hand, when one knows these people personally, matters can usually be worked out with a telephone discussion. At the time there were problems between Ed Gallas and Hollinger, the county administrative officer. The supervisors thought this was a lot of nonsense and that they were the bosses of all the county including the courts. The attitudes were bad for Hahn and his publicity and for me as presiding judge. But, my practice of feeding stories to Hahn began to help matters.

I suggested that we sit down monthly or every six weeks, have lunch and talk over matters. I invited in Hal Kennedy, the very fine county counsel. I began giving the luncheons myself, and then others took over in rotation; Hahn giving one, and so forth. We made up an agenda and sent it around a few days in advance; we discussed the matters at lunch. We at times got off the subject, but as a rule the agenda matters were covered well. We usually reached some sort of agreement; if not, a matter could be carried over to the next meeting.

The number of cases in the central district and all the other districts continues to grow and grow. Population growth is, of course, one reason, but the fact is that our people become more litigious all the time. Growth is not by simple arithmetical progression. This can be illustrated by calling attention to the corner of First and Hill Streets, where the central district courthouse is located. At the time we located the courthouse there, no traffic lines in the street were necessary; one officer was present during the evening and morning rush hours. Soon, signs had to be put up, "Keep Right," "No Left Turn" and the like. Before long, lane lines had to be painted. More signs and more officers had to be put there with all sorts of lines, lights and directions. The traveling public has an awful time amidst the increased impact of man on man, automobile on automobile and the attendant increase of laws, rules, lanes and frustration. The danger of physical harm increased, not arithmetically, but geometrically; for such reason areas lose their traffic popularity as to use of their streets. Perhaps the traffic pattern at First and Hill is beginning to change, but it is still a tremendous problem. We used to discuss such matters at length with the courthouse committee and other committees of the county, but the options available to alleviate the problem are severely limited.

I well remember discussions with the persons in charge of county parking and similar matters with respect to parking for judges, newspaper people who cover the courts, lawyers and witnesses. It is a real problem every day, greatly complicated by the fact that there are so many employees who should be enabled to park their cars near the courthouse. The cost of lots for parking seems to go up disproportionately to the demand for the spaces. So, as you can see, there are many matters on which the board of supervisors and the county employees have to talk with someone on the courts. The presiding judge cannot do it all, nor can the executive and administrative officers; still, we got along well during my tenure though there were some matters which seemed to be almost in a state of limbo.

Then there was the matter of relations with the press. There seemed to be a continuous problem, particularly with the *Los Angeles Times* and to a lesser degree with the *Examiner* and the *Herald Express*. These latter combined to be the *Herald Examiner*. But the trouble was mainly with the *Times* which seemed to feel it was qualified to pass judgment on the working of the court.

I soon decided that this should not be; there ought to be a way to put a stop to what was often very ill-founded criticism. I considered it incumbent on the presiding judge to see that the misunderstanding did not continue. Of course, we wanted good publicity, and we wanted the public to be properly informed. In turn, we wanted to know what we could do to cooperate, to the extent that a court can cooperate. I could work well with the *Times* representative at the courts. I knew Nadine Mason, a former *Times* courthouse representative, but the *Times* had its policies; it no longer wrote up divorce actions unless they were notable. On some worldnews stories it wrote almost detailed daily transcripts. I could also work well with the *Herald Examiner* representative, Jimmy Crenshaw, a very thoughtful and conscientious fellow. So, I thought I should get in touch with the *Times* editorial group in addition to the man on courthouse assignment. I felt if I could talk to "control," I could get them to understand the thinking and the workings of our court. Soon after I became presiding judge, I invited Otis Chandler to have lunch with me and to bring along any persons he wished. Otis had just become publisher of the *Times*. I agreed to bring some of the specialty judges.

We had quite a number present including most of his editorial staff and some of our top judges. We discussed matters of interest both to the courts and to the *Times*. We did not discuss pending cases or evidence; for that matter, we didn't discuss past cases either. We discussed mechanical problems and the general problems of the community. There was quite open and extensive talk not only the first time but also the second and, I believe, third. I was frankly appalled at the lack of knowledge on the part of Otis Chandler and the rest of his group with the exception of Gene Blake, their courthouse representative. None of them had any idea of the workings of a Superior Court—its duties, organization or responsibilities. Blake himself was an excellent writer and a sensible man, but certainly the *Times* management needed a great deal of education. We didn't get it completely educated, but I thought we did some good.

About a year later, I met Otis Chandler on the street. He called me by name which I thought was fine and said, "What's happened to you people?" "How do you mean?" I asked, puzzled. "Well, you remember those meetings we had. I thought they were very worthwhile." "Yes," I agreed, "they certainly were. I thought we got things pretty well straightened out, so I haven't pushed for any further conferences." "Well," he said somewhat magisterially, "the boys over at city hall, particularly the mayor and city council, came over to consult us. Why don't you people do that?"

At the moment I may have felt some of Judge Blake's explosiveness, but I managed, or tried to, very delicately explain to him that courts do not go to newspapers to learn what the courts or judges should do. Courts make independent decisions based upon evidence placed before them. So, I guess our efforts at education had not in this instance been entirely successful.

Otis was a very able fellow and a good administrator; he learned his job. While he didn't put the same emphasis on things as Harry Chandler or Norman, Otis has certainly done well by the shareholders.

I did not get what I wanted in the way of publicity for the court. I envisioned an article, or articles, describing how the court was set up, organized, staffed, who did what and the like. Well, the public would soon have forgotten anyway; perhaps when one tries to explain too much he only invites a Shakespearean comment.

Every Christmas while I was a judge in the downtown courthouse, I set up a card table at the entrance to my chambers about a week before the holiday. On it, I put a couple of tall Christmas candles, some holly or other Christmas decoration, a fruitcake, candy and coffee. The young ladies in the office served. All the other judges the press, lawyers and clerks were invited to come in. This celebrated the holiday without spending much time and with no use of county funds.

The Los Angeles Bar Association was always an excellent organization though at times there was room for improvement. I can remember the arguments about allowing African-American lawyers to become members of the Los Angeles Bar Association. They had their own organization which was called the Langston Club. Among them were some very fine lawyers. Unfortunately, there were a few who were less well educated, and these were often pointed out. It created an unfortunate situation. I believe that I enjoyed their confidence, and I was in favor of opening membership to them, which was done.

I tend to think that things are working more honorably today than they were when I first became acquainted with the Los Angeles Bar Association. They had a custom of inviting the presiding judge of the Los Angeles Superior Court to sit with them at their noon trustees' meetings paying his own way. They felt that they would benefit from this, and the courts would benefit also; I agreed. I attended regularly; we discussed matters of value, and I trust the work was better on both sides for these discussions.

Different assignments call for differing amounts of off-the-bench work by the assigned judge. In a difficult case the judge will have to do a considerable amount of outside work. This includes not only the reading of briefs, but often the judge must look up the authorities himself. Then there are conferences with counsel and the like. Thus, on such cases and some assignments in specialty departments we used to figure that one hour in the courtroom required two or two and a half hours of a judge's work outside the courtroom. Many laymen, perhaps most of them, feel that judges do not spend sufficient time on the bench daily. Generally, judges work a very full day, not all of which is in the limelight of public view.

The public is made increasingly unhappy by things they see and hear on television. Sometimes these things may be based on fact, but are often distorted. Often, too, such things as a particular court's week may be based not so much on what the judge wants, but on what the attorneys and the jurors want.

I remember a visit from Baxter Ward who later became a supervisor. He was at the time a quite popular television "commentator." Well, Mr. Baxter Ward on a Friday afternoon came into the courthouse with a camera and a crew; this was while I was presiding judge. Now, I understand Baxter Ward had some legal connections; I heard that his father had been a judge. I am sure that what would today be called court-bashing was as popular then as now, and Baxter Ward was on a tear. No doubt this improved his ratings and gratified his ego.

So, into the main downtown courthouse he came with his camera crew. He went up and down the floors looking into courtrooms. He would have a shot taken; maybe he would call out, and no one would answer—all very heady stuff. Then, one of the bailiffs spotted him. It was Judge Louis Drucker's bailiff. He took Baxter to Judge Drucker's chambers where a hearing was in progress. Drucker told Baxter that if he used Drucker's courtroom in his television segment, he would be held in contempt of court. He also insisted that if Ward intended to use such material, he should be told in advance what was to be said and have a right to reply thereto. Baxter Ward did not use Drucker's courtroom or his conversation with Judge Drucker in his television time.

We were, though, somewhat distressed. It seemed to me that, as with the *Times* editorial staff and management, some education was in order. I telephoned Baxter Ward, had him come in and took him to lunch. I did this twice, as I recall. I invited him to come with his camera and crew, and we went through the various departments and the work of the numerous specialty departments which are in the downtown court. I told him to go ahead and take all the film he wanted and to interview anyone he liked. The result was that he was much better advised and came to understand some of the problems of running the court and the work of the various departments. It toned him down to realize what a complex thing the court system is, and also the set of activities and specializations a courthouse contains.

As an example, the law and motion department would never have open court late in the afternoon. This time was set aside for conferences with judges and for working on memos to be made with respect to matters heard or to be heard. Law and motion might well have fifty to a hundred matters a day. It is necessary that the trial judge look over the next day's problems and be ready. Should he fail to do this, should he meet with the lawyer before his thoughts and material are organized, a lot of time will have to be taken. This is a continuing problem. The same is true of the department or departments handling writs and receivers, juveniles, adoptions, settlement calendars and so forth. All this points up that it is really unfair to sound off without knowing the other man's side of the question.

I remember an occasion when a television newsman went on for several days, about having seen a particular judge at a race track one day. He made a great public offense out of this, and it hurt the court while getting publicity unfavorable to the judge, a Superior Court judge. The newsman conveyed the impression that some judges made a habit of haunting the racetrack though he had seen only one on one occasion. What the newsman did not say, and certainly should have, was that the particular judge was at the time on vacation. He loved horse racing and was certainly entitled to visit the track on his vacation. One of the supervisors also saw this judge at the track and sounded off, but later took it up with the judge and learned the facts. Certainly not all of our judges are perfect, but on the whole we had a good and conscientious court with a good spirit.

# Chapter 18
## A Different Life

The time approached when I could retire, but owing to a change in the law at the time, I could also elect to stay on for another year. I reached the age of 70 on April 17, 1966, and by that time life had changed immeasurably.

Lois, my dear wife of forty-two years, passed away in June of 1964. I found I could not bear to remain in the house; I sold it, moved to an apartment in Pasadena and began the process of dismantling in the physical sense at least the structure built up over those years. Most of the things I had acquired, I gave away—first to my two lovely daughters, then to other relatives, to Occidental College, to the School Board of San Marino and finally to the Salvation Army. The latter took away two truckloads of goods from the house and more from the beach house. I gave away five bedrooms full of furniture to various relatives, every stick and rag, down to the pictures on the walls. I gave away several thousand books.

So, the home broke up. Barbara and Marjorie were both married and had their own families. It was the understanding between Mrs. Faries and me that half our assets should go to the girls.

I was contemplating what to do after retirement. The breakup was a hard one for me. It seemed ever more difficult for me to be alone. No doubt this is the reason so many older men remarry, though at the time of Lois' death I had no idea and certainly no desire to remarry. My friend and co-worker, Sally Fonatine, suggested that I read Bunyon's *Pilgrim's Progress*. What a comfort it was to me, particularly the first two-thirds or so. I was able to understand the allegory, and I recommend the work to any who find themselves in grief or

269

*Judge Faries with Earl Warren, chief justice of the United States Supreme Court*

loss. Certainly, no one could have been more thoughtful and helpful than my two dear daughters. I am sorry I did not tell them nearly often enough how kind they were or how much they helped me. I fear I have too often failed to express love. What French writer was it who said, "Anglo-Saxons treat their emotions as they do their desserts. They freeze them and hide them in their bellies."

But self-flagellation is not good, either; the way to make things go right is to break with the past and do better with the future.

I have long loved the northwest country, Washington, Oregon and Northern California. I had more or less decided that upon retirement I would go to that part of the United States or possibly over to the Sierras. I thought I might buy a ranch. I didn't particularly want a ranch as such, but I loved that kind of country and wanted, if possible, to preserve a little of it for my children and their children. I had no desire to create a working ranch, a business venture. I simply wanted to preserve a piece of natural beauty. I kept in mind the lovely country I had seen during my time in Oregon as trustee for Mankind United. One place there greatly appealed to me; it was a ranch, I guess you would call it, on the Applegate River. I knew that river was to be improved by a man-made irrigation district including a lake. I particularly liked the looks of the place and fell in love with it after I had left it——just "rememb'ring."

I drove north on two occasions to visit with friends whom I much loved and admired. These were the Wiemans, Ted and his wife Betty. They understood my problem and were wonderful to me. They drove me down the Oregon coast through those many state parks. I loved that area, too. Then, returning south, I came down through Northern California, and near Eureka I found a ranch that I liked. When I saw this ranch on the Mendocino Coast, I thought that my two ideas might be combined. Perhaps I might give myself something to do as well as preserve a beautiful and financially valuable piece of property for my heirs. The ranch was variegated which is to say that though near the coast, it had lush grasslands upon which were pastured fine-looking cattle; then, going inland on the same ranch one came upon a canyon with a small stream which apparently ran the year 'round. Still on the ranch, there was higher country with coast redwoods and other beautiful trees. I visited the area more than once. It was very attractive, and a few acres could be subdivided with little difficulty, near some trees and a stream. I learned that the property belonged to a man nearing retirement age who also had another ranch which his son operated. His thought was to sell the ranch in which I was interested thus providing himself with a nice nest egg for retirement. He would go live on the other ranch with his son, but plans do change.

Much as I enjoy travel, it has its drawbacks. One of them is the invariable job of dealing with accumulated mail upon return. When I came back, among the things awaiting me was a prospectus and a letter from two fellows I had known years before. When I was in politics, both men had been active Young Republicans, Buzz Forward and William Ryan; they were now engaged in buying and selling land in Northern California.

I decided to see what they had to offer and talked to them on a couple of occasions. They were promoting a number of pieces of property which they thought were excellent buys. I went up to see several pieces. One afternoon, rather late, we were discussing real estate, and as night came on, Bill Ryan said to me, "Let's go out to dinner and make it a celebration. We'll go to the Cave du Roi, and I'll get a beautiful lady to have dinner with us. I call her my adopted mother."

The lady was Geraldine Bergh. She was the widow of the well-known Dr. Arthur Olaf Bergh, pianist, violinist, conductor and composer. Jerry was a woman of stunning appearance, lovely of face and figure with beautiful white hair. It soon became apparent that she had a beautiful character as well and was a most interesting person. We had a delightful evening. I invited her to go with me to the Black and White Ball, an annual event at which many young ladies made their social debuts. It was a recognized social event, including many old Spanish and South American families. In a weak moment, I accepted the task of being master of ceremonies. Jerry accepted and went with me to the ball.

I had, of course, met several ladies since Lois' death, and on occasion had squired one or another to some event. But from this time on, it was Jerry. She seemed to fit and fill all my pictures, and apparently the same was true with her. The gentleman with whom she had been going faded from her life, and soon we began to hear from behind the hands of our acquaintances, a whispered, "There's the man Jerry is finally going to marry." Some kept questioning that I'd marry again, and I had no intention of remarrying. I intended to go north to Oregon, Northern California, or the High Sierras. But times change for us. Too, I was still on the Superior Court.

Around the time we were becoming quite serious, Jerry had been planning a party. I suggested that instead, I host a party at the California Club. It was my thought that I could, in this way, discharge a number of accumulated social obligations, and Jerry agreed to the suggestion. We had a party for some thirty people, as I recall. I enjoyed becoming acquainted, or better acquainted, with many of Jerry's friends.

When the time came to announce our engagement, which was a rather short one, Jerry gave a party at the Beverly Hills Hotel. It was a very successful affair with exceptional decorations, fine music and all the things which go to make a memorable occasion.

I knew that when it was time for me to speak, I would be expected to come up with something novel or memorable, and I tried hard. I'm not sure it was too good, but I trust it went over well enough. I spoke of the Sunday picnic parties of older times when, after church, the people would go to some favored spot in the country and enjoy a special picnic. Then, after luncheon, a couple might take a walk in the woods and perhaps find a big tree. Of course, in those days every young man carried a sharp pocket knife, and there on a tree the man would carve two entwined hearts, and in the hearts, the couple would put their initials and the date.

I said that couples of today could no longer follow this historic and appealing method of plighting their troth. The freeways and the cities have largely taken it from us, and our present customs are different. Nevertheless, the inner feelings are the same today as then, and Jerry and I felt that our two hearts were indeed entwined. Today, I said, we do it by giving and receiving a ring, and with that, I put the ring on her finger, to the surprise of some, and to the delight of all. So, it was official; others had faded from her life and mine.

We were married on December 3, 1965, in the chapel of the San Marino Community Church where I was a member. The Reverend Frederick W. Cropp, my close friend and a delightful pastor, performed the ceremony. The wedding in the late afternoon was a small one with only a few in attendance. It was not feasible to go on a honeymoon at that time; we waited until the following May. However, we did go to Lake Arrowhead for the weekend.

I have always been moved by the concept of "duty"—the word means a great deal to me. You may recall the words of the great USC and professional football player, O.J. Simpson, when asked how he was able to avoid tacklers on the field. He said, "Because I'm a coward." Duty has many times enabled me to overcome natural cowardice, the fear of doing something which involves the threat of danger. Often it is hard to do the thing we know we should do; the concept of duty is an ever-present help.

In May of 1966, my successor as presiding judge, Kenneth M. Chantry, allowed me to take a 21-working-day vacation period which I had accumulated by not taking a vacation the previous year. So, we went on our honeymoon, the first of our several ocean liner trips. We had a going-away party upon leaving at the dock, and many friends were there to see us off. We had a very impressive lanai room on the *President Wilson*. We were leaving for the Orient, to be gone a total of some 45 days.

Before we left, Judge Fildew whom I had known since he was a Young Republican, said to me, "Well, you can't go to Japan without looking up our old friend 'the Greek.'" "I don't know who you mean," I said. "Don't you remember Frank Scolinas?" asked the judge. I did recall a young fellow of that name. He had insisted on running for the California state legislature a couple of years after he passed the bar. Unfortunately, he lived in a district that was about five-to-one Democratic, and he didn't have a chance. I said I recalled Frank, and the judge said, "I'm going to write to Frank and tell him you are coming to Japan."

When we docked in Honolulu, there was a lieutenant of the sheriff's office to take care of us; he had an official car and spent the entire day taking us all over the Island. We got to see some things few tourists see, such as the Chinese markets and the like. He told us he spoke seven languages. He said he had been born in Santa Barbara of partly Hawaiian parentage. We had a wonderful day.

When we arrived at Japan's Yokohama Harbor, there was our Greek friend, Frank Scolinas. I recognized him, though I hadn't seen him for more than twenty years. He had with him his Japanese wife and teenage children.

Frank had been in one of the regiments landing in Japan with General MacArthur. He was then a lieutenant, and, because it was known that he had once worked for the Los Angeles Harbor Commission, he was put in charge of the evacuation of American military prisoners quartered in that part of Japan. He told me that the appearance of these prisoners was the most pitiable thing he had ever seen. He had the ships at harbor, ready to take them aboard. He had hired a Japanese band and taught them to play "Hail, Hail, the Gang's All Here." They learned the tune easily and played it over and over. Frank said the evacuees were laughing and crying at the same time. Their spirit, he said, tore at his heart as they were put aboard. He was successful both from the American and the Japanese standpoint in putting the prisoners on board ship and seeing that they were properly taken care of.

Frank, thereafter, became one of the counsel for those Japanese who were charged with, and tried for, various war crimes. He apparently gained a reputation for being able and fair, and both the Japanese and American military were highly appreciative. As a result, he was one of the few Americans admitted to practice law at the Tokyo Bar, and he proceeded to do so. He was released from the service there and did not come back to the United States. He practiced law continuously in Tokyo and learned Japanese. Speaking Greek, as well as English and Japanese, he became counsel for the Greek Embassy in Tokyo.

While we were in Tokyo, we had a Japanese driver and guide. Our guide was a graduate of the University of Yokohama. He explained to us that entry to the University of Tokyo was very difficult, and he had failed to make it; his grades and his entrance exam scores were not quite adequate. I learned from him, and from judges to whom I talked, that there is a tremendous beginning law class at the University of Tokyo, running into the thousands. But very few graduate, the rest either flunk out or go into other types of work. Of those very few who do graduate, some of the very best are chosen by the faculty to have the honor of going to a very special governmental service law school at the university. From these, the majority go into various types of services. The best ones go into the service of the Japanese government. And from these, the very best are chosen to go into special training for judgeships; they become, in fact, student judges.

When they actually start as judges, their work is like that of our commissioners. They work with and learn from judges, and after a period go generally to three-judge courts. They are then moved up by the chief justice, or he makes a recommendation to the Emperor, and the Emperor follows that recommendation with an appointment. They then become full-time judges and thereafter often try cases alone. From there they may be chosen to go onto the appellate courts.

The chief justice of Japan, along with several Japanese judges who had visited our court when I was presiding judge, gave an afternoon tea for me. The chief justice called in some of the high judges and judges of regular court corresponding to our Superior Court. I think there must have been between fifteen and twenty at the tea. After we had visited awhile, some of them took me to the departments, and I watched a couple of trials in progress. Nobody could have been more courteous and kind than these Japanese people.

We saw, of course, many other sights and then took the train (actually we flew one way and took the train the other) to Osaka and Kyoto. We saw the great statue of Buddha and various temples and other sights in Kyoto and went up to Nara to see and feed the tame deer in the deer park.

I had decided to return, at least for a time, to the practice of law outside the courts. I felt it would be unfair to make any attempt to get my old clientele back from Wayne Hackett and Ralph Hubbard, to whom I had turned over the firm. I have always been glad that I made no such attempt, being very fond of both of them. In spite of this, one or two of my old clients did come back to me, and one of them brought me a lucrative piece of business which was quite different from anything I had done before. It was a merger which required that I work with the Securities and Exchange Commission, the Interstate Commerce Commission and the New York Stock Exchange. There were other counsel involved, some of whom made up for my lack of experience in working with these particular regulatory bodies. I found that in the years intervening since my days in private practice, the law had changed a good deal. A single-handed operator, if I may use that term, usually does not have sufficient knowledge of all these specialties to do a good job for many modern organizations, people and corporations. The law is becoming ever more complicated. For example, there is a new real estate code; federal courts have adopted new and hopefully better procedure systems; there is a new corporation code; moreover, a plethora of new laws emerge from the legislature and the Congress all the time, to the number of five thousand or more annually. We are much more regulated, and it is much harder for a single practitioner to stay abreast of things than it once was. All the general practitioner can do, it seems, is like the internist in medicine—decide which experts to call in and when.

Still, although my background and proclivities leaned more toward work on the bench, I did pretty well. I worked half-days as a rule using office space kindly provided for me by Walter Young &

Associates. I soon decided that I liked the bench work more and was asked to return to the Superior Court.

I was asked this time by Governor Ronald Reagan to serve on the State Parks and Recreation Commission. This was the one commission on which I really wanted to serve. Soon after I began practicing law again, I went on the commission. The commission made its way around the state, travelling every month to a different area. We would stay in a motel and hold our meeting there and go to visit the parks or prospective parks in the area.

It was apparent early that many of these places, those who gave us the red carpet treatment, were notably lacking in altruism; some of them wanted state parks to increase the value of the land they were subdividing. Most wanted to save the money they would have to put out for their own parks and recreation areas. It was simple enough to spot the self-interest that lay behind many of the proposals put before us, even on occasion to accommodate it when the true interests of the state happened to lie in the same direction.

There was a woman from the Big Sur region who was very interested in building up the park system in that vicinity and wherever there were redwoods; another representative from Eureka, was also interested in this area. Santa Barbara was very eager to get us to acquire the Fleischman property. This contained about five hundred acres, and from the financial standpoint, I thought it to be a bargain. But it was apparent that it would be sort of a Santa Barbara city park, rather than a state park. We of the commission were convinced that the city could find the funds if it wished. Since my time the commission has become more city park minded, but at that time, our chief concern was to try to save the lovely mountain and ocean areas and at the same time provide some public recreation facilities.

Thus, we were interested in the dunes of San Luis Obispo and Monterey Counties and very much in the redwoods wherever located. We worked with the "Save the Redwoods League." Jerry and I made a contribution of fifty percent and got the Geraldine and McIntyre Faries Grove into the state park system. I have since added another, *The Grandchildren's Grove* in the wild area near Prairie Creek.

There were also plans for obtaining wildflower areas and red rock canyon areas. We wanted to add more areas near Eureka where the rain forest lies and there are still elk in the wild. It was a problem as to which should be first. We also considered the desirability of putting state parks alongside reservoirs and lakes and the recreation areas being built for the central valley water project, such as Castaic Lake, Hughes Lake, and down by Lake Perris. We acquired the land for the Perris Lake recreation area while I was on the commission.

Our trips up the coast were a great pleasure. I remember going one morning to a small park on the Northern California coast. There were stately elk along the misty edges of the tumbling stream feeding on ferns and leaves. In the other direction were spectacular rocky vistas down to the seacoast. We visited and dedicated a redwood park. The Save the Redwoods League has done great work fund-raising and otherwise helping the state park commission. J.R. Knowland headed the work of the state parks for years and is rightly remembered as the "Father of the California state park system."

I did not stay on the commission long for two reasons: first, I was thinking about going back on the bench, and secondly, I was being importuned to come on the Los Angeles State Historical Monument, now the Los Angeles State Park Commission. I felt I could represent the city of Los Angeles on that commission and not be in violation of the rule that one cannot be on the bench and in the administrative work of the state at the same time.

I think we should all be thankful that the areas were saved and that California did get some beach property plus a few other good areas. It is devoutly hoped that all concerned will continue saving the redwoods and other wilderness areas, so that we and our children can retain some of the glories of the past and beauties of the present.

# Chapter 19
## Back To The Bench

*J*erry died in 1980.

I think I shall say nothing at all about that.

Among my post retirement activities were some tours of duty, so to speak, sitting as judge in the municipal court of Beverly Hills. It was a great pleasure. I "got my hand in" again. I may well have been getting rusty and delighting in being with my friend, Andrew Weisz. Andrew was at the time presiding judge in Beverly Hills; he had been a commissioner when I was on the Superior Court bench. He would have made a valuable addition to either the Superior Court or the Court of Appeals, an opinion many others share with me. He was a very sound judge, with a wonderful memory who handled his court well. Just after I began my time of duty, he went to the Mediterranean, North Africa and Israel on a tour. After his return he invited me back to help out for a month.

This experience has provided some anecdotes which may serve to illustrate yet another aspect of our courts and how they function.

No doubt the most interesting cases are the criminal and burglary cases which are not tried in municipal court. We did, though, have some quite interesting preliminary hearings. A preliminary hearing is held to determine whether a crime was in fact committed and whether the arrested defendant should be held for trial, released on bail or otherwise.

I certainly will speak a good word for the police force of Beverly Hills. It is a comparatively small and wealthy area with enough money to pay the police perhaps a bit better than some other places. They have excellent esprit de corps, and evidently, very good training. I expect, too, that the office of the deputy district attorney who has charge of Beverly Hills is supplied with what it requires as to funds and personnel; I found them pretty well prepared in each of the preliminary hearings over which I presided. I think about three such cases will serve to illustrate my points, especially the competent and alert police work.

The first case that comes to mind was a burglary of a home on Roxbury Drive. The house was a very fine and expensively furnished one owned by an elderly woman. At the time of the burglary the woman was in the hospital which may or may not have been known by the burglars. She employed a "house boy," an elderly Oriental, who seemed unable to decide on his ancestry. He was Chinese or Korean or Southeast Asian. At any rate, he was not a young man.

Apparently he had been asleep in an upstairs bedroom when he heard noises in the house. Shortly afterward, he saw a man or men go past the door of his bedroom. He had a telephone by his bed and quietly got in touch with the Beverly Hills police reporting the presence of burglars in the house. He assured the police that they were still there and that he actually had seen them. So, the desk radioed a prowl car nearest to the location which included a woman officer and her male partner. Arriving quietly at the scene, they observed that someone was indeed moving around in an upstairs bedroom. They radioed for more officers and began checking around the house. They noticed that a ground floor window, obscured by some bushes or hedge against the house, was open. They assumed that entry had been made there. The doors were of the old-fashioned kind which had stops at top and bottom. Feeling safe in the assumption that the window had indeed been the means of entry, and with other officers coming to watch the rest of the exterior of the house, the woman officer and her partner crouched down on each side of the window and waited. They heard the reinforcements arrive, and soon out through the window came two men loaded down with loot. Much to their surprise as they reached the ground, they were confronted by the two officers waiting with guns drawn. As the British say, a fair cop!

The first man out through the window was wearing a full-length woman's red fox fur coat which had recently been appraised for insurance purposes at $15,000. They were apparently successful in opening the safe and had taken around ten thousand dollars in cash. Additionally, they found a good deal of jewelry and were carrying it in boxes. Being easily caught, they were relieved of all these burdens and taken to the station where they were brought before me for a preliminary hearing. Since it was quite evident that a crime had been committed and highly likely that the two men caught leaving by a window with the loot were the culprits, I held them to answer on several counts.

The second case I have in mind is that of a burglary in another Beverly Hills home. The occupants were a husband, his wife and an eleven-year-old son, blonde, pink complexion, wearing heavy glasses. The father worked in some studio in the entertainment industry. He left fairly early in the morning for work, and soon thereafter his wife left for work in another place.

This left the boy and a Mexican-American maid alone in the house; it was school vacation time. Shortly after the wife left, two men appeared, both Mexican-American, though I recall one of them had an Anglo name. Both were very strong and "tough" looking men. They forced their way past the maid, holding guns on her, and captured the boy. They tied up the maid and left her in one room; they took the boy to another room and tied him up. It was the den to which they took the boy. Both were not only tied, but gagged, and I believe the boy at least was also blindfolded. There was a phone in the den, but the robbers evidently felt that the boy was too well tied and gagged to be able to make use of it. They went about their business, first trying to get the combination to the safe from the boy. He insisted that he did not know it, which was probably true. They must have finally believed him because they did not succeed in getting into the safe. They did not get much money or much jewelry.

They spent a long time going through the house at one point even helping the bound boy to go to the bathroom. They took the family silver and such other loot as they could find gathering it into boxes. They were so long, in fact, that the wife came home from work to find them there. They seized her, trussed her up and put her in still another room. Whether they made any effort to get the safe combination from her is not clear, but if they did try, they were unsuccessful. So, eventually, they gathered up their loot and carried it out.

The boy, although still bound, succeeded in getting to the telephone and getting hold of the police. I don't recall how he did it, or how he communicated with a gag, but the police figured that something was wrong and immediately got busy. The burglars had parked their car some distance from the house, and officers arrived in time to see them loading things into the car including a gun of some sort. They were apprehended and brought to the court where I again found both that a crime had been committed and that these were the likely perpetrators. They were held to answer.

Another case which demonstrated both good police work and good security precautions on the part of a bank might be of interest. A young man who worked in the office of a local recording studio, went out to lunch one day leaving his credit cards, checks and some other valuables in the top drawer of his desk. Either when he returned or before going home, he discovered that they were missing. He reported the loss not only to his employer but also to the bank.

A couple of weeks went by, and no recovery had been made. The bank had closed the account immediately upon notification of the loss of the bank card and checkbook. A young man appeared at the bank one morning and asked to cash a check. He showed his cards and other identification to the girl at the window and she, as they generally do, pressed the button for confirmation of the identifying cards. Back came the report that this account had been closed. She excused herself and went back and told her supervisor who remembered the situation and quickly called the Beverly Hills police.

This took a little time, and the young man began to get nervous. The girl told him it would be only a few moments, but he, as our British friends say, "had the wind up," and went out the door. By this time the police desk had alerted by radio a motorcycle officer who was directing traffic. The officer, who had a billy club, started for the bank as the young man left it. Seeing the officer, he started to run; the officer went in pursuit. They ran along Wilshire Boulevard for some distance; the young fellow turned up a street to the west of Beverly Wilshire Hotel, and then through the private loading drive that runs between the front of the hotel and the annex. By this time there were a number of people chasing him, so it began to look like a Keystone Kops chase. The culprit made it past the hotel area to El Camino and then turned down to Charleville Boulevard.

In the meantime, the police started a patrol car from the station, turned the corner, went down Beverly Drive and turned into Charleville. The young man, who had slowed down a bit by this time, ran head on into the patrol car. Having his description, they grabbed him, and he was brought before me for a preliminary hearing.

His story was that he had not stolen the cards and other things; they had, according to him, been stolen by a man he knew only as "Duke." He knew neither Duke's last name nor his real first name. Duke had given him the checkbook and cards and told him to go into the bank and cash a check for $195.00, presumably the balance or close to the balance of the account. However, once in the bank his nerve weakened a bit, so he made the check for only $125.00. He claimed he knew nothing about "Duke" other than what he told us; he didn't know where he lived or where he came from. I held him to answer for the attempted forgery, but not for the burglary.

I recall another little story about the same young policewoman I mentioned in connection with the burglary involving the red fox coat. She was on night duty; she and her partner were driving along Wilshire Boulevard in the direction of the beach. It was about three in the morning when they saw a car with one headlight coming toward them at a high rate of speed. The headlight had on its high beam, which is illegal on city streets. As the car sped past them, they saw that it was quite banged up and that the license plate was obscured or unilluminated. They counted four to six passengers. The officers turned around and gave chase using the siren. They were gaining rapidly when the fleeing car suddenly stopped and the occupants jumped out and ran. Apparently the young policewoman had done some pretty good driving; they had also radioed for reinforcements. The two officers ran into the alley taken by the fugitives and down into the underground garage of an apartment house. There they captured one of them very quickly, and later another male suspect in another basement garage. The others, girls I understand, made good their escape. The men were brought before me, and I held them to answer.

Their story was that they had gone to a party at which there had been a lot of people. There was a lot of drinking. This group, having done perhaps more than their share of drinking, saw a car outside and took it; no, they didn't know whose it was. They drove down to the beach, and somehow managed to roll the car over. They claimed it was a wreck when they took it. Whether or not this was so, it was certainly a wreck soon after. But, they succeeded in righting it and were headed home. So, the episode was really one of "liquor and looniness", however, a crime had been committed and had to be answered for.

You will gather from these little anecdotes that the police were still maintaining the policy of two officers to a car. I am entirely in favor of this practice, not merely for the safety of the officers. I think in most cases it results in better police work. It may even well be that it saves tax money in the long run. Better police work frequently means a saving of court time which I have pointed out is very expensive. It is a weakness of all political systems, including our own, that sometimes gains or "savings" which make one department look very good may be adopted without sufficient thought to the costs they might give rise to in another department. Again, to quote our British brethren, "What you gain on the swings, you give up on the roundabouts."

As a finale to this Beverly Hills court reminiscence, I must relate a rather interesting action brought by a Beverly Hills woman. She, her husband and sister-in-law apparently enjoyed going to Las Vegas to play Pam. I believe the original name of the game was Pamguinne, though few people call it anything but Pam. Some claim it is a game of skill, as distinguished from a game of chance, but it can be a gambling game. It is played with several decks of cards.

Apparently, the Union Plaza Hotel in Las Vegas puts on a Pam or Pamguinne tournament about twice a year, or they did at that time. They set up a special room for Pam playing during the three days of the tournament right across from the casino. I gather it was pretty well attended.

The Union Plaza is about 19 stories and has the reputation of being a good decent hotel with a good casino, though it hasn't the luxuriousness of some of the other hotels. This woman and her party went, as they had for two or three years, to play Pam. Apparently they were good players and had made money on former tournaments.

On the second night she played Pam for some time and made around a thousand dollars, she said. She then went into the casino across the hall, played awhile and won some more. She said she had about $1800 when she left. Now she could have gotten a receipt from the casino for the money, but she did not do so. She put part of it in her glasses case and the rest elsewhere in her purse and started back to her room. It was about half past ten at night, she related, and she walked from the casino area past the gift shops and the two entrances of the hotel. She walked past the desk, and again did not choose to put her money into the hotel safe. She did not ask a security guard to accompany her to her room although she could have done that. She said she did not see any security guards as she walked to the elevators. But she was not afraid and saw nothing to worry her. There are four elevators in the hotel all self-service at least at night. As she got in and pushed the button for the eleventh floor, a man and a woman got into the elevator with her. Again, she saw nothing to make her apprehensive; the man was not large, perhaps five feet eight inches in height. He was middle-aged and quite well dressed. As for the woman, there was nothing about her to attract attention, and in any case, she pushed the button for the fourth floor.

As soon as the elevator doors closed behind the couple, the man produced a gun, stuck it into the complainant's stomach, and told her to give him her money. Instead of doing so, as the police and the newspapers daily advise us all, she started to struggle with him. At the eleventh floor the doors opened, she got out still struggling with the man. At this point he struck her on the head with his gun cutting her scalp and jerked the purse away from her. By this time she also had some bruises on her arms. She began screaming and ran down the hall toward her room. The man fled dropping the purse, but he had gotten about half of her money. He missed the money in the glasses case. She lost about eight hundred dollars.

She ran to her room where her husband and sister-in-law tried to calm her and phoned for security. They came without delay, but the man was never found. Meanwhile, the paramedics had been called. Arriving, they wanted to take her to a hospital, but she refused, so they gave her some first-aid treatment. She stayed in the hotel for two or three days longer, told her story to the police and the hotel security, but refused to go either to the hospital or the police station.

When she returned to Los Angeles, she said, she began to feel dizzy and had double vision. She went first to her doctor and then to psychologists. She brought an action against the hotel and had a jury trial. Her lawyer was a bearded young fellow who impressed me as being very good at his work. The defense lawyer was from one of the downtown groups which handle chiefly negligence work. I didn't think he was nearly as capable as he might have been.

The only expert testimony for the defense was by the security officer who had been on duty that night. The only other testimony I recall was that some five years earlier some woman had claimed that she had been mugged in one of those same elevators but had successfully escaped and reported it to security. She was suing the hotel, but the case had never been brought to trial. Well, that was seven years or more, and the only occurrence of that sort. There was testimony that the police and security men of all the Las Vegas hotels met once a month. There were, they said, four security men on duty that night, one in the headquarters room, one in the parking lot, and two in the casino watching the delivery and taking away of money to the safe room downstairs. They claimed that there was one walking the halls. That would make five, wouldn't it? The woman said that she saw no security men on her way to the elevators, and she had not asked for help or the safekeeping of her money.

So, I thought it over and decided to grant a new trial, which I did. Counsel wanted a statement of reasons to which they have a right. I told them they should have had testimony as to what safeguards other hotels of the vicinity used and perhaps hotels elsewhere. Further, I said, there was no showing that officers had been on the scene. It was easy to think that perhaps someone in the casino area had signalled to this man or that he had been there and followed her to the elevators for this purpose. There was a considerable absence of testimony. Also, there was no claim of contributory negligence, and perhaps there should have been in connection with her struggling with the man and getting hit over the head. They wanted a further hearing on this motion, but it was put "off calendar."

# Chapter 20
# Thoughts On
# Retiring

*I* could have retired in the year 1966, but the age of retirement was pushed along a year or so by the law, as it then existed, so I officially retired at the age of 71, in 1967. But I went back on several assignments, so that I did my last consecutive stint in 1978; I was called back by request of the presiding judge to the chief justice of our Supreme Court, so I served until then except for about a year and a half during which I took off. For part of this time I did some private practice, and part of the time I was ill. Actually, I went back again for about five months in 1982.

Judgeship is a frustrating activity a good part of the time. There are departments which do not take a heavy toll, but most do; it's a common saying that, while some get ulcers, judges get ulcers on ulcers. I myself had an ulcer at, or near the time, I was presiding judge, but it has healed now, and I never had ulcers on ulcers. A common cause of ulcer-producing frustration is impatience with counsel. We say to ourselves, "Why must this fellow go so far around the block? Why doesn't he come to the point and stop wasting the court's time? Why doesn't he come to the point? Should I intervene and raise the point? Is he trying to badger the witness? Is he trying to get away with something?" At times we do speak up though I tried hard never to do so until the examination of a witness, including cross-examination, was complete. Then I would take a look at the notes I'd made and put in my words in an effort to get the facts out in an impartial manner thus helping the jury. I didn't always succeed, but this was my general practice and the general rule of most judges.

I want to be quite certain not to give a wrong impression in my discussion of our court system and our dispensing of justice. The fact is that our courts compare favorably with any in the world. With reference to the particular system of courts in which I had the honor to serve, the Los Angeles Superior Court was designated by a chief justice of the United States Supreme Court as the finest in the country.

I took great pride in serving on and in presiding over that court. The deep satisfaction of having been a part of it will be with me all of my days. Before I go on, let me make two points: First, our courts are as good as they are because good and conscientious men, not all of them judges by any means, strove and are striving to make them ever better and more suited to the needs of our times. I have described the efforts and accomplishments of a number of such persons, but there are many more. Secondly, no court system exists or works in a vacuum; they are part of and must work within the socio-political frame of the time—the "system." Many of the problems which hamper the court in its work are neither of its making nor within its control. It follows that there can be little benefit in any plan for "improving" our courts which does not address the underlying social, political and economic factors which bear upon and to a great extent dictate the working of the courts.

I "nibbled around the edges" for quite a number of years and may even have done a little lasting good. I like to hope so. The difficulty, I think, with most people working on these things is simply that they are not bold enough. They start out boldly, but are soon mired down in the problems they encounter from any number of directions. The mud is very sticky, and only a concerted effort is likely to meet with any success. But, there are many areas that should be addressed.

One of these is the revamping of class action proceedings. In the past we have failed to recognize that consumers in civil matters, and injured parties in criminal matters have not received justice. Many of them are entitled to not merely restitution of their bread but also a slice of cake. Now, increasingly, society and the courts are coming to recognize the rights of injured parties, and the class action proceeding is one of the remedies developed to provide relief, particularly in cases of economic damage. It is a good idea as far as it goes, and in a number of cases has forced offending companies or enterprises to disgorge at least a portion of improperly acquired gains. Unfortunately, as now structured, the proceeding does not provide proper means for the court to protect the injured parties. As now structured, the class action can, and often does, become a happy hunting ground for unscrupulous lawyers. When this happens, the injured parties who brought the action can wind up with little or no compensation for their loss while the lawyer pockets huge fees. I may say here that in recent years some of our courts have succeeded in establishing limited curbs on the rapacity of rascally lawyers. Much remains to be done in this connection, but the ground has been broken. Here in California, a limit has been set on the amount of "general damages" which may be awarded in a case of medical malpractice, formerly a wide-open field in which tremendous sums were fairly common. Moreover, a sliding scale of fee percentages has been established for these cases with severe penalties for violations. "Negligence lawyers" fought tooth and nail against the establishment of these limits; many of them refused to comply, claiming the law was not constitutionally valid. However, a test case was taken to the Supreme Court; the court declared the act constitutional and therefore binding. Much more remains to be done, and the courts must some day be given far more regulatory power than they now enjoy in these areas.

One of the most vexing problems faced by our courts in their attempt to deliver evenhanded justice is, I'm afraid, the popular media particularly television news. Let all be assured that I say this without rancor and with a complete understanding of why the problem exists. Unfortunately, understanding why a problem exists is rarely much help in finding a solution. In fact, as long as the current system prevails, I think it doubtful that any solution is possible.

It is necessary to understand the real world of mass news media as distinct from the myth. The picture held up before us, especially in the case of television news, is that of a far-flung staff of talented and dedicated experts backed by an equally talented technical staff and vast financial resources. The entire purpose of all this vast array of money and talent is the gathering and dissemination of truth. To a considerable degree, the picture is a true one. There is a great deal of talent there, and there are indeed great sums of money expended. But the brute fact is that all this effort, talent and resources are not expended in the search for truth, but in a high-stakes and highly competitive search for profit. To all media profit accrues only to the degree that the station, network or newspaper attracts people—viewers or readers. Only thus can they attract advertisers who are the sole source of their income.

Thus, the competition for viewers or readers becomes a matter of survival. With this in mind, it is understandable that the overriding consideration quickly becomes not what is nearest the truth or best for those concerned, but what sells. As we all know, facts are a poor attention-getter while sensation attracts us all. Inevitably, the news business, in order to compete, gives way to "show business"; the content of news programs and the efforts of reporters are oriented more and more toward attracting viewers and less toward what is true, important or even current.

This gives rise to such meaningless appellations as "investigative reporting" or the ridiculously self-contradicting "adversary journalism." These, and the sensation-seeking which generates them, give rise to the sensational premise which is assumed beforehand; and the "investigation" becomes an attempt to justify the premise rather than a search for truth.

One aspect of this sensation-seeking which is most troublesome to the courts is the seizing and trumpeting of all possible publicity with regard to those accused of crime in advance of investigation and trial. This practice can, and often does, make proper investigation difficult or impossible. It can and does hamper the court in its duty to provide a fair trial. In fact it occasionally makes a fair trial impossible in a given city or venue, and has been known to upset verdicts even after trial. Moreover, it can damage or even destroy the lives or reputations of innocent people—all in the name of reporting the news.

My description of Baxter Ward's "investigation" of our court operation is an example. As originally conducted by this newsman and his crew, this was a clear-cut illustration of sensation-seeking as opposed to real investigation. Coming secretly into the court building, he found an empty courtroom. It was midafternoon; why was no judge on the bench and no trial in progress? With absolutely no attempt whatsoever to determine the facts, this newsman assumed the most scandalous of possible reasons—that the judge was "goofing off," and proceeded to set up his cameras and "document" his "conclusion." Here was a really sensational scandal, brought to public attention by fearless and indefatigable "investigative reporting!" Here, also, was a real ratings-booster for his program. As I related, I was able to turn this particular incident to some use. After my talk with him, Baxter Ward did agree to do an honest and evenhanded program on the court which in the long run may have been of some value.

We Americans greatly admire the virtues of integrity and honesty. We loudly demand responsibility on the part of our political and business functionaries, and we make it an article of faith that "fair play" will prevail in all the games we play. Yet, virtually every one of us is confronted daily with compromises between our aspirations and the hard demands of the marketplace. We find it very difficult to condemn anything that makes a lot of money. And every single one of us would rather be entertained than informed—any time.

The British system has a great deal of merit, though it is hard to see how it could be imposed upon our free-swinging society. Their custom, in which their news media by and large acquiesce, is to keep the facts and names of a murder trial or a scandal of some sort in the dark until the alleged culprits are brought and witnesses' versions heard in court. This is certainly fairer than our no-holds-barred method. It may also result in better justice.

Another practice has proliferated in recent years that I find of considerable concern. This is the so-called "sting" operation, as exemplified by the FBI in their ABSCAM campaign. A variant has been the setting up of "fence" operations by various cities. In these undercover police act as receivers of stolen goods by paying for them with city funds. When enough thieves have been identified and entrapped by selling their booty, all are arrested. Is using patently unlawful methods to catch crooks a proper system?

On the face of it most people would say yes; anything that gets crooks off our streets is justified. But I wonder whether these short-run results do not cost us more in the long run than we care to pay.

We have a machinery for law enforcement which has served us well for a long time, and it does not countenance the breaking of the law by the very people sworn to uphold it. Are we wise to abandon that machinery and the principals upon which it rests for a short-term result?

Is our primary aim the catching of criminals or the preservation of a law-abiding society? If the latter, can we do that by permitting, even directing, some individual or organizations to break the law? What happens to those individuals and their organizations? Is it not inevitable that they become cynical, even contemptuous of the law they are told to disregard? What happens to the attitude of a society which comes to accept that law can be upheld only by breaking it? How long do we remain a nation of laws once we believe that only men outside the law can preserve us?

Our system directs that enforcement officers from the FBI to the corner policeman prevent crime where possible or expose and apprehend those who are accused of crime. Determination of guilt and prosecution for crime are not, and should not be, police functions. Nor is enticement or incitement to crime.

Determination of crime, assessment of guilt and imposition of punishment are functions of the grand jury, district attorney and court. These functions should not be hampered by undue publicity, especially before a trial is convened. Such matters should properly be looked into by a dispassionate district attorney or equivalent. If a trial is convened, then the public can and should know the facts. Admittedly, this would not sell as many newspapers or gain as many ratings points for television news programs.

Above, I referred to a dispassionate district attorney. And here we encounter another problem faced by the court in its endeavor to dispense evenhanded justice to all. District attorneys, being human, are rarely dispassionate. My observation has been that a gratifying number of them make every effort to be fair, but there are many who see the office as a steppingstone to higher office. Even among these, many are fair-minded. Others, unfortunately, see the cases before them in terms of their own potential advantage. This is not confined to district attorneys. I can name at present off the top of my head six young people who are each trying with all their might to find or manufacture newsworthy things that would help them become top officials. It is most laudable to aspire to be governor or even district attorney. One can do many good things in these and other offices. Undoubtedly, publicity is a great help in getting there, but it is well to examine closely the motives that underlie an undue search for that publicity.

Like the "code" of journalism, the code under which lawyers practice is a very noble and high-flown one. Both are often honored more in the breach than the observance. Considering the fact that the law is the only thing enabling us to live as civilized humans rather than as animals, it seems reasonable to me to expect those who endorse it as a profession to adhere to certain standards.

As a judge, I will always remember a portion of the Magna Charta which many judges, myself included, habitually keep on their desks: "To none will we deny or delay right or justice."

I suspect that in my discussion of the problems facing the court, and the socio-political system within which it strives to do justice, I may appear something of a doomsayer. I trust I am reasonably optimistic, but I do believe that humanity has no free ticket to glory. Our problems are many and growing, and their solutions cannot forever be delayed. I sometimes feel that "this civilization will destroy itself, as others have done before." But hope springs eternal.

I kept a great deal of data with respect to the history of the Los Angeles Superior Court. I could go back a good many years to the days before 1922 when I was studying law. One of the judges, Harold Huis, told me when he retired that he intended to write the history of the court, so I turned all the papers over to him. As fate would have it, Harold suffered a stroke and never wrote the history of the Los Angeles courts. I talked later with his wife, but she knew nothing about the notes. So I have no idea where my notes and data are. My connection with the courts went back to 1919 dealing first with the picking up of Southern California Auto Club cards left as bail with the police.

# Chapter 21
# Rememb'ring

*A*s with everyone else, it sometime happens that something I read or hear on the air or elsewhere starts a train of thought which I later feel should be "put down." Such a train of thought brought me one evening to the realization that we have been given or have acquired the power to manipulate time. I mean as it applies to ourselves and our planet. We can overcome or outspeed evolution, both as to ourselves and to living things around us. We are able to bring about in a short time many things that once would have required generations, even eons. On the other side of the coin, we have acquired the power by nuclear war, planned or unplanned, to even bring about the end of time insofar as we and our planet are concerned. Can we use this power wisely? On the record of our past it does not seem too likely. Still we must hope.

Another such musing along a line suggested by some overheard idea or event leads to an examination of the need for human beings both to act and interact. Each is necessary, yet each is a danger. Failure to consult with others and recognize the wisdom of what they say can often end the careers of prospective leaders. On the other hand leaning too much on the suggestions of others often results in trying to go in too many directions at once—ending in doubt and confusion.

As I look through my notes, I am struck with the feeling that this memoir just grew. When I was discouraged with reading newspapers, magazines and junk mail or listening to radio and television, I would jot down my thoughts and memories. Of course each of us tends to feel that he could do better. As one Arab proverb has it, "Each man thinks his own fleas are gazelles."

I fear that I do not share the feeling I note around me—especially among my younger acquaintances—that the public knows much more today than it used to know. I tend to think the opposite is true. As an illustration, I believe that in the early days of our country we had in the persons of Ben Franklin and his contemporaries much greater minds as leaders. They were not bombarded with "information" to the extent that we are today, and admittedly their problems involved fewer "loose ends." Nevertheless, these great minds not only brought about a new country but also gave it a direction and philosophy which has held up remarkably well for over two centuries. Today's leaders for the most part appear uncertain as to where they want us to go, let alone how to plan for getting there.

As I had been active for so long in politics, I thought I would put down my thoughts in some of these matters. I have done so, but times have changed. The nonimportant has become important, and the more important has become less so. Or has it, really? What has been overlooked is "the fundamental hunger of the human heart." This is my own phrase, at least so far as I know, and I have used it many times, because I consider it to be the single most important element of politics. Do we understand the fundamental hunger of the human heart? What people feel in their hearts is as important in politics as in religion.

"Walk!" said the internist. "Walk, or I will put you in a wheelchair. Do it before breakfast!"

Today, the maid jumped the gun. She rang the doorbell and entered immediately while I was showering. It was only 7:45. I am always up and dressed by 8:00, so I told her, "Never before eight!" Yes, I felt sorry for myself. But, I would do as I was told. I went out the east entrance of "The Oaks" and turned south on El Nido.

On the sidewalk down El Nido I wished that the grade were uphill so I would be able to walk downhill on the return trip. That would be easier. Yes, I use a cane and lean on it too heavily. As I walk, I look; and as I look, I think.

The ivy on the adjacent wall is rapidly covering the vacant spaces. Its leaves grow larger and the parkway looks a darker green. How fast in nature everything strives for maturity. The ferns in these areas, planned by the landscape artist, will soon reach their annual height. The planner had vision. The street trees and trees behind the wall are now more than green arbors under which I walk. I recall January's stark sticks, and now there is heavy shade. I think they had better watch out, or some gardener thinking of windstorms will trim them.

Little birds, sparrows and linnets in trees and on the power wires are discussing plans for the day. "What shall we eat, and what shall we drink, and where?" But not "wherewith shall we be clothed?" I cross the street that has but one sidewalk.

Friendly people, young and old, are walking happy dogs. Some of the dogs are even panting. A laughing couple ride north on their bicycles; their cocker spaniel, a true blooded one, proudly gallops ahead but is restrained by his leash. Friendly people walk their dogs, or vice versa. All smile and speak. Two school children, seven or eight years of age and probably brothers, run out from the house, but turn to wave to mother and a younger brother and sister. The bus stops and, shifting their knapsacks of books and their lunchboxes, they climb aboard. They were just in time on their way to school.

On I go. Gardeners all say, "Good morning, Sir." They smile too. That is better than my, "Morning." The "Sir" is pleasing; am I vain? The city of Pasadena's trash trucks, a little pickup and a great carryall come along; they stop to assist the gardeners. More people than usual are walking or being walked by their dogs. Sometimes there is no leash, but one need not worry. Small autos drive or back out of drives, and the drivers wave or stop to learn my plans. All the cars are clean, and few have open mufflers. The walks and driveways are clean too. The neat houses convey that the owners are good citizens.

Having reached San Pasqual Boulevard, I look both ways, but return homeward toward the mountains shrouded in a blue mist. A mockingbird sings. It sounds as though he is in love, but the ornithologists tell us his song is a challenge. I wonder at his repertoire. There flies the bluest bluejay I have ever seen. He has a grasshopper in his beak; it is for a nestling. I wonder why God created fish, fowl, reptile, beast and man, all of whom—all species—devour each other.

Again, I am near "The Oaks," the rear street entrance. After looking at the vacant streets, I cross. A gardener smiles and says "Good morning, Sir." A neighbor waves. He is busy holding back a golden retriever. Just then I see a hawk pursuing a blue pigeon. What a breakfast it would make him, and perhaps his family, too. I am not a pigeon fancier, though I was as a boy. This time I was pulling for the pigeon. It dives into a leafy tree, and the hawk is foiled. Good!

En route to the side door, I pass the pond with its two lazy gold-fish. One follows the other on its left rear quarter, like a destroyer on maneuvers convoying a battleship. Does that signify spring?

The side door is unlocked, and I head for the dining room. The maids smile as they say, "Good morning." I hang my cap and cane on the convenient hat tree. At my table are my favorite breakfast companions. Though I should not, I have the day's breakfast special as we discuss the current world events.

Yes, Browning was right: "The year's at the spring…The morning's dew-pearl'd…God's in His heaven…All's right with the world."

# Index